AN INTRODUCTION
TO
ECCLESIASTES

T0381695

החוט המשלש לא במהרה ינתק

AN INTRODUCTION

TO

ECCLESIASTES

WITH NOTES AND APPENDICES

BY

A. H. McNEILE, B.D.

Tyrwhitt Hebrew Scholar and Crosse Scholar,
Fellow and Theological Lecturer at
Sidney Sussex College, Cambridge

CAMBRIDGE:
at the University Press
1904

CAMBRIDGE
UNIVERSITY PRESS

University Printing House, Cambridge CB2 8BS, United Kingdom

Published in the United States of America by Cambridge University Press, New York

Cambridge University Press is part of the University of Cambridge.

It furthers the University's mission by disseminating knowledge in the pursuit of education, learning and research at the highest international levels of excellence.

www.cambridge.org
Information on this title: www.cambridge.org/9781107696853

© Cambridge University Press 1904

First published 1904
First paperback edition 2014

A catalogue record for this publication is available from the British Library

ISBN 978-1-107-69685-3 Paperback

PREFACE.

THE literature on the book of Ecclesiastes is very large, as may be seen by reference to Ginsburg's commentary, and to Aug. Palm *Die Qohelet-Litteratur* (Mannheim). But of late years it has received comparatively little attention. Palm's list was compiled in 1886, and since that time the following works may be noticed: 1. The commentaries of Cox (*Expositor's Bible*), 1890, Siegfried (in Nowack's *Handkomm. z. A. T.*), 1898, Wildeboer (in Marti's *Kurz. Handkomm. z. A. T.*), 1898. 2. Other studies of the book from various points of view: Cheyne, *Job and Solomon*, 1887, Euringer, *Der Masorahtext des Kohelet*, 1890, Leimdorfer, *Kohelet im Lichte der Geschichte*, 1892, Dillon, *Sceptics of the Old Testament*, 1895, Tyler, *Ecclesiastes* (2nd edit.), 1899. 3. To these must be added articles in periodicals—mostly German—on particular points. These are referred to where use is made of them.

The difficulty of the interpretation of the book has been an unending fascination to all who have dwelt upon it. But very few students have analysed it by the critical methods which have opened up a new world of study in the Hexateuch, the historical books and the prophets. The following pages have been written with two chief aims: firstly, to disentangle the strands which go to form the " three-fold cord " of the writing; and secondly, to estimate the position which Koheleth occupied with regard to the religious and philosophical thought of his

day. On these two subjects, treated in §§ 4, 5 and 8, hang the
chief interest and value of the book which is called by his name.
But neither of these can be accurately studied unless the writing
be placed in its historical and literary perspective; and an
attempt is made to do this in the rest of the Introduction.

It was thought unnecessary to write a complete commentary
on the Hebrew text; but it is hoped that in the Notes on select
passages, and in Appendix II., all the principal points of interest
or difficulty have been discussed.

The purpose of the Appendices is to re-open the problem of
the Greek text. Even to those who may not accept the
conclusions reached, they may prove useful in supplying
textual matter for further study.

A. H. McNEILE.

CAMBRIDGE.
Ascension Day, 1904.

CONTENTS.

ḲOHELETH.

1. Introduction.

§ 1. *The Title.*

THE title קֹהֶלֶת (xii. 8 קוֹהֶלֶת) occurs seven times in the book[1]. In xii. 8 it has the article, and probably also in vii. 27 (M.T. אמרה ק"). If the emendation אמר הקהלת in the latter passage is correct, the word is definitely shewn to be masculine in all the seven passages. The author, therefore, was a man; and, writing under the guise of Solomon, adopted 'Ḳoheleth' as a *nom de plume.*

The meaning of the word is somewhat uncertain. In form it is the feminine of the Ḳal participle of קהל. But of this root no other certain instance of the Ḳal occurs, though the Niphal and the Hiphil are not uncommon, the former = be summoned [i.e. come together] as an assembly—the latter = summon an assembly, for religious or military purposes.

The versions do not afford much help. Ǥ ἐκκλησιαστής, whence Hier. and Engl. 'Ecclesiastes,' is an attempt to represent the derivation of the word from קָהָל 'an assembly,' while Aq. Pesh. Tg. merely transliterate the Hebrew.

The following are the more probable of the explanations which have been suggested:

1. 'One who summons an assembly' (Gesenius). But this would probably require the Hiphil מַקְהֶלֶת.

2. 'One who speaks in an assembly.' (Hier. *concionator.* Luther *Prediger.* A.V. R.V. 'Preacher.' Midr. Ḳoh. "because his words are spoken in a קהל.") So Driver, *Intr. O.T.* 466. König, *Einl.* 428. Plumptre 'Debater.'

---

[1] i. 1, 2, 12, vii. 27, xii. 8, 9, 10.

3. 'A convener, or collector, of sentences' (Grotius, Mendelssohn, illustrating this meaning by reference to xii. 10, 11).

Opinions also differ as to the force intended to be conveyed by the feminine form of the word.

1. The fact that it is nearly always accompanied by a verb in the masculine renders improbable the view that the feminine refers to Wisdom (חכמה), who is represented in Prov. i. 20 f., viii. 1–4, as addressing men in places of assembly (Augustine, Rashi, Ibn Ezra: so Hitzig, Kuenen and others). Moreover the contents of the book as a whole are totally unlike the teaching which is usually put into the mouth of Wisdom in the rest of the Wisdom literature.

2. The use of the masculine of the verb is also opposed to Tyler's suggestion that the name denotes "she who is an assembly"—a personification of assemblies of men.

Two other, more probable, suggestions are:

3. That the feminine has an intensive force, as in Arabic,— 'one who completely realises the idea of a קֹהֵל.' (R.V. mg. 'great orator.' W. Wright, *Arabic Grammar*, § 233, rem. c. C. H. H. Wright, *Ecclesiastes*.)

4. That the feminine indicates a title or designation of office, arising from its use to express abstract conceptions (Ges. K. § 122, 4 b). This may be illustrated by the proper names הַסֹּפֶרֶת and פֹּכֶרֶת Ezra ii. 55, 57. Aram.: כְּנָוָת 'colleagues' Ezra iv. 7. Arab.: ḫalîfa, 'allâma. Engl.: 'Excellency,' 'Highness' etc. This is adopted by the majority of modern writers (Driver, Delitzsch, Nowack, Cheyne and others)[1].

The meaning, therefore, of the title Ḳoheleth probably is 'a (recognised and official) speaker in an assembly'—the assembly, no doubt, being all men who give their hearts to wisdom, and who are metaphorically pictured as sitting at the feet of the wise man.

---

[1] In the art. 'Ecclesiastes' in *Encycl. Bibl.* the startling suggestion is made that הקהלת is a corruption of הכל הבל i. 2, and was interpolated in i. 12, vii. 27, xii. 8, and adopted by the scribe who prefixed i. 1 and by the writer of the epilogue. The writer of the article-proposes, further, to read הקהלת in Prov. xxx. 1.

Renan suggests that קהלת is a cryptogram, perhaps for שלמה, arrived at by some method analogous to 'Athbash' and 'Albam.'

§ 2. *Canonicity*.

For the three-fold division of the Jewish Bible—Torah, Neʹbiʼim, Keʹthubim—various explanations have been offered. A Rabbinic explanation, for instance, given by Moses Maimonides and David Kimchi is that the three divisions represent three grades of inspiration; the Torah was given פה אל פה (mouth to mouth), the Neʹbiʼim by the רוח הנבואה (spirit of prophecy), and the Keʹthubim by the רוח הקדש (spirit of holiness). And other suggestions are noted by Wildeboer (*A.T. Kanon* pp. 14–16). But it is now recognised that the divisions were the result of an historical process by which the books were accepted into the Canon in three groups, i.e. (i) from the end of the exile to Ezra, (ii) from Ezra to the time of the Maccabees, (iii) from the Maccabees till shortly before the time of Christ.

The third division consists of (*a*) the Psalms, Proverbs and Job—a group that was sometimes quoted by the initial letters written in the inverse order, אמ״ת; (*b*) the five Meʹgilloth or Rolls, i.e. Song of Songs, Ruth, Ḳinoth[1] (or Lamentations), Ḳoheleth and Esther; (*c*) Daniel, Ezra-Nehemiah, and 1, 2 Chronicles[2]. The only books among the Keʹthubim that were read in the public services of the Synagogue were the 'five Rolls.' The Song of Songs was read on the 8th day of the Passover, Ruth on the 2nd day of Pentecost, Ḳinoth on the 9th day of Ab[3], Ḳoheleth on the 3rd day of the Feast of Booths, and Esther on the Feast of Purim.

The date of the reception of Ḳoheleth into the Canon is far from certain. The book is not alluded to in any canonical writing of the Old Testament. But there can be no doubt that it was known, not only in its primary but in its completed form[4], to Ben Sira[5] (c. 180 B.C.), and to the author of Wisdom[5] (c. 130 B.C.). The use made of it, however, by the former writer proves only its existence—not its canonisation—prior to his date. He was well acquainted, as his work shews, with the literature of his country; but it is impossible to insist that his

---

[1] Also called 'Ēkah from its opening word.

[2] For varieties of order and grouping see Ryle, *O.T. Canon*, ch. xii. and Excursus C.

The traditional date of the destruction of the temple by the Chaldeans.

[4] See § 5.   [5] See § 7.

quotations could have been made only from such writings as were recognised as canonical. And the author of 'Wisdom,' so far from treating Ḳoheleth as a sacred writing, seems to aim at confuting the advice contained in it with regard to the enjoyment of life.

There are Talmudic stories which, if true, would prove that Ḳoheleth was quoted as authoritative scripture in the 1st century B.C. In Jer. Bᵉrakoth vii. 2 it is related: "The king [Jannaeus[1]] said to him [Simon ben Shetach the king's brother-in-law] 'Why didst thou mock me by saying that nine hundred sacrifices were required, when half would have been sufficient?' Simon answered 'I mocked thee not; thou hast paid thy share and I mine...as it is written בצל החכמה בצל הכסף '" כי בצל החכמה בצל הכסף (Ḳoh. vii. 12 a).

In Baba Bathra 4 a there is an account of Herod after he had put to death the members of the Sanhedrin, and deprived Baba ben Buṭa of his sight. It relates that he visited the latter *incognito*, and tried to extort from him some unguarded complaint against his own tyranny. But Baba b. Buṭa steadily refused to speak a word against the king. In his answers to Herod he quoted, with the formula "it is written," a passage from the Torah (Ex. xxii. 27), and one from the Nᵉbi'im (Is. ii. 2); and with the same formula he quoted, from the Kᵉthubim, Prov. vi. 23 and the three parts of Ḳoh. x. 20[2].

A third narrative from Shabbath 30 b is given at length by Wright[3], in which Gamaliel (flor. 44 A.D.) argues on the subject of the Messianic age with a disciple[4]. That disciple (אותו תלמיד) three times opposed the great teacher's arguments with the words אין כל חדש תחת השמש (Ḳoh. i. 9), each time with 'as it is written.'

If these stories could be accepted as they stand, Simon b. Shetach would afford a fixed *terminus ad quem* for the canonicity of Ḳoheleth. But since it is impossible to determine what is history in the Talmud, and what legend, the only certain deduction is that the Talmudic compilers accepted as genuine the tradition that Ḳoheleth had been quoted as Scripture in the century before Christ.

---

[1] Jannaeus reigned 105–79 B.C.
[2] See Wright, *Ecclesiastes* pp. 19 f.   [3] pp. 23 f.
[4] Bloch maintains that this is none other than S. Paul.

Little, in fact, can be gathered from verbal quotations[1].

Nor can much help be obtained from pre-Christian evidence other than that of direct quotation.

1. In the often quoted prologue to Ecclesiasticus, B. Sira's grandson clearly recognised a third division of Hebrew writings after the Law and the Prophets. But it is impossible to say with certainty that he included Ḳoheleth in this third division, or (if he did) to what extent he considered it as strictly canonical.

2. The 'Septuagint' translation adds no evidence at all. The prologue to Ecclesiasticus shews that some books in the group of the Kᵉthubim had been translated before 132 B.C. But the translation of a book proves nothing as to the date of its canonisation. Indeed, if the theory maintained below[2] is correct—that the extant Greek version of Ḳoheleth is (so far as the true text is attainable) from the pen of Aquila—it is uncertain whether there was a Greek version of it before his time.

3. Philo's evidence is only *e silentio*, and is precarious. He makes no reference to Ezekiel, Daniel, Song of Songs, Ruth, Lamentations and Ḳoheleth. If Ezekiel were not in this list, it might be argued with probability that Philo did not quote from the Kᵉthubim because he did not recognise them as canonical[3]. But seeing that Ezekiel was canonical more than a century and a half before his time, his lack of reference to it invalidates any argument drawn from his non-use of the Kᵉthubim.

---

[1] There are no verbal quotations from Ḳoh. in the N.T., though it is not impossible that S. Paul shews reminiscences of its language.

Compare i. 2 etc. with Rom. viii. 20 ; xii. 14 with Rom. ii. 16, 2 Cor. v. 10 ; xii. 3, 5 with 2 Cor. v. 1. See Taylor, *Sayings of the Jewish Fathers*, Add. notes pp. 159 f.

But no stress can be laid on the silence of the N.T. Ezra and Nehemiah are not quoted, but they were probably coupled with Chronicles which is. Obadiah and Nahum shew no influence on N.T. writers, because they were short and dealt with special circumstances of the moment ; and Esther, Song of Songs and Ḳoheleth were scarcely of such a nature as to supply matter for quotation. (In Eph. v. 27 S. Paul may have been thinking of Song of Songs iv. 7 : ὅλη καλὴ εἶ πλησίον μου, καὶ μῶμος οὐκ ἔστιν ἐν σοί.)

[2] Appendix I.

[3] The passage in the *De Vita contemplativa* § 3, which clearly speaks of the three divisions of the Hebrew books, is of very doubtful genuineness.

Although there are no quotations from Ḳoheleth in the New Testament, yet it is here that evidence is first forthcoming which is probably trustworthy. The passages which suggest that the tripartite division of the Hebrew books was recognised, afford, it is true, no clearer evidence as to the contents of the Canon than does the prologue to Ecclesiasticus[1]. But a stronger argument can be drawn from the phrases and titles used in reference to the Old Testament, which convey a strong feeling that the Canon was thought of as a complete whole; e.g. ἡ γραφή occurs in John x. 35, xix. 36, xx. 9, 2 Pet. i. 20. In the first of these, reference is made to a passage in the Psalms which, in the preceding words, is also spoken of as ἐν τῷ νόμῳ ὑμῶν and ὁ λόγος τοῦ θεοῦ. The second passage is, perhaps, not to the point, since the following verse shews that γραφή may have the meaning of 'a passage in writing,' cf. 1 Pet. ii. 6. In the third, the word implies Old Testament prophecies in general. And in the last, the writer distinctly speaks of a well-defined body of "prophecies which stand in writing" (πᾶσα προφητεία γραφῆς) for which he claims divine inspiration. And other phrases such as αἱ γραφαὶ Mat. xxii. 29, Acts xviii. 24, γραφαὶ ἅγιαι Rom. i. 2[2], ἱερὰ γράμματα 2 Tim. iii. 15 (cf. v. 16 πᾶσα γραφὴ θεόπνευστος), all convey the same impression, that 'Scripture' meant to the Apostolic writers the same body of Old Testament writings that it means to us.

Two further references in the New Testament call for notice. Daniel, the latest book in the Jewish Canon, is expressly quoted by Jesus as an apparently authoritative writing (Mat. xxiv. 15). And His allusion to the death of Zacharias (Mat. xxiii. 35, Luke xi. 51) is usually understood to imply that the book of Chronicles was the last in order in the complete canonical collection. Wildeboer's objection to this is not conclusive. He points out that very few persons, or even synagogues, were rich enough to possess the whole collection, and that in any case the books would be written on separate rolls. And he says that even if Jesus, as the later Jews, held Chronicles to stand last in the order of Old Testament books, Mat. xxiii. 35 affords no evidence as to which books were included at that

[1] See especially Luke xxiv. 44; also Mat. xxii. 40, John vi. 45, Acts vii. 42, xiii. 40, xxvi. 22, xxviii. 23.
[2] See Sanday and Headlam in loc.

time in the third division of which Chronicles formed the close. But the fact that among a number of separate rolls Chronicles was universally reckoned as the last in order, surely goes to shew that the number of the rolls had become a fixed quantity. Wildeboer adds that it is much more probable that the Lord was thinking of the historical books in a narrower sense which excluded Jeremiah. But how could the hearers of Jesus be expected to understand that he was thinking of the 'historical books' which were never reckoned as a distinct group, when the martyrdom of Urijah (Jer. xxvi. 23), which was chronologically later than that of Zacharias, would be well known to all[1]?

It seems highly probable, therefore, that all the K^{e}thubim had obtained some sort of recognition by the beginning of the 1st century B.C., and that the three divisions of the Hebrew books were looked upon as one complete body of sacred writings by the beginning of the Christian era. Indeed, as Ryle points out (pp. 174 ff.), it is scarcely conceivable that any new book could have been introduced into the canon during the century in which the nation was divided into the opposite factions of the Pharisees and Sadducees, or during the period in which the great Rabbinic schools of Hillel and Shammai took their rise. "The Doctors whose glory it was 'to make a fence round the law' were not likely to advocate the introduction of fresh writings within the limits of the Canon; nor, if one were bold enough to advise such a step, would he have escaped vehement attacks from rival teachers."

If this conclusion be correct, and Ķoheleth had won its acceptance as canonical by c. 100 B.C., it is unnecessary to dwell on the evidence that is available at the close of the 1st century A.D.[2] 4 Esdras (c. 90 A.D.) and Josephus (c. 100 A.D.) both shew conclusively that Ķoheleth had been accepted as canonical before their date. The former (according to the

[1] Wildeboer's statement (p. 47) that "a number of reminiscences and citations from apocryphal writings prove that the N.T. writers acknowledged no canon of the O.T. which corresponds with ours" is tantamount to saying that no N.T. writers were capable of quoting anything but their Bible! They did not use extra-canonical works for the purpose of establishing doctrines; but there is no reason why they should not have used them for purposes of illustration. (See Ryle pp. 153 f.)

[2] See Ryle (pp. 156–166), and Wildeboer (pp. 37–43).

most probable reading) reckons the sacred books as 24, which
is the number borne out by the Talmudic title "the four-and-
twenty holy writings" (Jer. Sanh. x. 1). The latter reckons
them as 22, Ruth and Lamentations being combined with
Judges and Jeremiah respectively. This numbering is also
found in Melito's canon (Eus. *H.E.* iv. 26), and in that of
Origen (Eus. *H.E.* vi. 25).

The official Jewish pronouncement with regard to the Canon
was made at, or about the time of, the Synod of Jamnia (Jabne)
c. 100 A.D. Some discussion preceded the final agreement, of
which the clearest account for English readers is given in
Wright's *Ecclesiastes*, Excursus II. The discussion turned on
the question whether Ķoheleth did, or did not, "defile the
hands." This expression is explained in Shabbath 14 a. Copies
of the Scriptures had been kept in the same place as the heave-
offerings, and some had been thereby injured. As a precaution
against this danger in future, the Scriptures were pronounced
'unclean,' i.e. unfit to be included among the offerings to the
priests. The principal Talmudic passages which refer to the
discussion are *Yadaim* iii. 5, *Eduyoth* v. 3, *Megillah* 7 a[1]. The
synod was apparently convinced by R. Simon ben 'Azzai, who
stated that he had "received by tradition from the mouth of
the seventy-two elders in the day when they inducted R.
Eliezer b. 'Azariah into the seat of patriarch, that the Song
of Songs and Ķoheleth defile the hands." The books under
dispute were Ķoheleth, Song of Songs and Esther. And a
final decision was arrived at—not that these books were hence-
forth to be included among the canonical books, but—that
those who had for many years received them as canonical had
been right in so doing.

§ 3. *The circumstances of the writer.*

A writer in the *Spectator*[2] has aptly styled the book of
Ķoheleth "A Hebrew *Journal intime.*" The fascination of it
arises from the fact that it advances no theories; it is not a
thesis or a study, it is not a sermon or a collection of moral
aphorisms. It is the outpouring of the mind of a rich Jew, who

[1] See S. Schiffer, *Das Buch Kohelet, nach der Auffassung der Weisen des
Talmud und Midrasch*, Theil I. pp. 1–10.
[2] Feb. 28, 1903.

has seen much of the sad side of life, and who is intensely in
earnest. But while he reveals his mind and character, he tells
little of his personal circumstances[1]. He states that he was
wealthy, and able to provide for himself every possible luxury
(ii. 4–10). He seems to have lived in or near Jerusalem[2], for
he clearly implies that he was an eyewitness of facts which
occurred at the "holy place" (viii. 10). He must have been
an old man at the time of writing; not only because his
language seems to have lost the buoyancy of youth (for that
is a point on which different students of his book might think,
and have thought, differently), but because his feverish attempts
(i. 12–ii. 11) to find the *summum bonum* of life in pleasure,
and in wisdom, cannot have been abandoned in a few years,
while they were now far enough in the past to be looked at as
by-gone memories. He had had experience not only of youth
but also of manhood's prime, שַׁחֲרוּת[3] (xi. 10). And apparently
he had lived long enough to find himself alone in the world,
without son or brother (iv. 8: the following words seem to
shew that he is referring to himself). Lastly, he had had
private sorrows and disappointments. Here and there—"one
of a thousand"—he might find "a man," but he had never
found a woman who was worthy of her name;—which probably
means (to translate his bitter generalisation into facts) that his
life had been saddened by a woman, who had been "more
bitter than death," whose heart had been "snares and nets,
and her hands fetters" (vii. 26–28).

This is all that can be gathered with any certainty. But it
is not unreasonable to suppose that his great wealth might place
him in some official position in the country. Winckler[4] suggests

[1] Plumptre, *Eccles.* pp. 35–52, draws an elaborate, but purely fanciful,
biography, which is severely criticised by Bois, *Origines de la Philosophie
Judéo-Alexandrine* pp. 83–108.

[2] The reference to the corn trade (xi. 1), as an illustration of a busy and
energetic path of life, does not necessarily point to Alexandria as the place of
writing. The mention of the temple and the priesthood (iv. 17, v. 5, E.V.
v. 1, 6) appears to be the work of another writer, who also lived at Jerusalem.
See § 5.

[3] i.e. the age of black hairs, as opposed to שֵׂיבָה the age of grey hairs.

[4] *Altorientalische Forschungen*, 2nd series, pp. 143–159. The expression in
i. 12 "king over Israel in Jerusalem" cannot indicate this official position, for
the guise of Solomon is not dropped till ii. 12. See, however, note on i. 16—
"all that were before me over Jerusalem."

that he was either king or high-priest, for his writing was so
unorthodox that nothing but his high station could have enabled him to disregard public opinion. It is very improbable
that he was in any sense a king, in view of the scathing
criticisms which he passes on the government. But if he was
a member of a high-priestly family, and perhaps himself a
religious official, it is easier to account for the zealous care
with which his work was annotated, and made more acceptable
in religious circles[1]. And it is just possible that the feminine
form of the pseudonym *Koheleth* points in the same direction[2].

But if Koheleth does not reveal much of his personal
surroundings, he paints a lurid picture of the state of his
country. Wickedness usurped the place of judgment and
righteousness (iii. 16); and, in consequence, the powerful classes
who had the law in their hands crushed the common people
with an oppression from which there was no escape (iv. 1).
And this perversion of justice was due to the irresponsible
officialism under which the country groaned; an inferior official
was under the thumb of a higher one, and he under a higher
still; none of them could make any move in the cause of
justice, for the highest of them was a creature of the tyrannous
king (v. 7). The king raised slaves and common people, at his
caprice, to high positions, while the rich and noble might be
degraded (x. 5–7); he was despotic (viii. 2 a, 4), and when he
was in an angry mood the only prudent course was to pacify
him by yielding to his wishes (x. 4). The reason for this
tyranny lay in the fact that the king was "a child"—far too
young for his responsible position—and his courtiers spent their
days in drunken revelry (x. 16). Koheleth sadly contrasts the
unhappy state of his country with the prosperity that it might
enjoy under a good ruler (x. 17). With a young and tyrannous
king and corrupt officials, espionage was rife; a word spoken
secretly in the bedchamber, nay even a thought, would reach
the king's ears through unknown channels (x. 20).

In addition to this general description of the state of the
country, two passages must be noticed which appear to contain
allusions to contemporary history—(a) iv. 13–16, (b) ix. 13–15[3].

---

[1] See § 5.　　　　　　　　　　[2] See § 1.

[3] viii. 10 has also been usually understood to refer to an historical event.
But this is improbable. See note *in loc.*

(a)   iv. 13–16.   This passage has been variously translated, and the interpretations of it are numerous (see notes), but the following is the simplest rendering and explanation that the words will bear:

v. 13.   "Better is a poor and wise youth than an old and foolish king who knew not how to be admonished any more." The perfect יָדַע shews that Ḳoheleth is thinking of a king who lived before the time of which he writes, and who, in his old age, would no longer listen to advice.

In v. 14 he substantiates the truth of the two adjectives 'poor' and 'wise.' The youth shewed himself wise—that is clever—"because from the house of prisoners he emerged to be king"; and his previous poverty was well known—"because even in his kingdom [i.e. in the very kingdom that was afterwards his] he was born poor [or perhaps 'became poor']."

In v. 15 Ḳoheleth, by means of the imperfect יַעֲמֹד, places himself in memory at the moment when another youth was joined by multitudes and was about to oust the 'poor and wise youth' from his throne.   "I saw all the living who walked under the sun with *the second youth* who was to rise up in his place."

v. 16.   But the emptiness of this world's strivings was illustrated by the fact that even this second youth did not long retain his popularity.   "There was no end to all the people—to all before whom he was [i.e. at whose head he had placed himself]: moreover those who come after would not rejoice (יִשְׂמְחוּ) in him; surely this also is vanity and a striving after wind."

Attempts have been made to use this historical reference as an evidence for the date of the writing.   The alternation of tenses certainly shews that the events were contemporary with Ḳoheleth.   But unfortunately there is no historical period which can be selected to suit all the facts.   Delitzsch confidently refers the poor and wise youth to Cyrus, who dispossessed the old Median king Astyages, and who had been in confinement in Persia.   But his explanation forces him to treat the passage as though it spoke of one youth only, and thereby to give an unnatural meaning to הַיֶּלֶד הַשֵּׁנִי.   Hitzig prefers the period of the Ptolemies[1], and sees in the old and foolish king the High

---

[1] Nowack, in his revised edition of Hitzig, is inclined to revert to the Persian period.

Priest Onias under Ptolemy Euergetes, and in the poor and
wise youth Joseph the son of Tobias who usurped Onias'
position in the state. But the same objection applies to this
explanation as to the former, that it treats of only one youth
instead of two. Moreover it is very doubtful if a High Priest
could have been called King at that early date; Aristobulus I.
was the first who is known to have assumed the title.

Winckler, again, refers to events in Maccabean times. The
old and foolish king is Antiochus IV. Epiphanes; and the
expression " who no longer knows how to be admonished " is
explained by his obstinate and wayward policy against Judaism.
At the time of his death in his Parthian expedition his son
Antiochus V. was a minor and Lysias usurped the guardian-
ship. But a youth Demetrius, a son of Seleucus (the brother
and predecessor of Antiochus Epiphanes), who was at Rome
as a hostage, contrived to escape. He had frequently sought
permission from the senate to return home and claim his rights;
but though there was no further reason for retaining him as
a hostage when his uncle had taken the government, they had
refused to release him. He landed at Tripolis, and soon afterwards Lysias and the boy Antiochus fell into his hands
(B.C. 162). He thus " came out of prison to become king."
His rule, however, lasted scarcely ten years, when " the second
youth," Alexander Balas, " rose up in his place," and was
courted by nearly everyone.

This is ingenious, and rightly takes account of two youths.
But firstly, one detained as a hostage at Rome could hardly be
described as being in a 'prison-house'; secondly, there is nothing
to shew that Demetrius, the son of a former king, had been
'born poor'; thirdly, Ḳoheleth is alluded to by B. Sira, which
makes it impossible to bring down his date below 152, as
Winckler's theory requires[1].

(b) ix. 13–15. A different rendering of the words is here
offered to that which has usually been given. Commentators
have generally treated the passage on the supposition that the
poor wise man delivered the little city. But is it not a contradiction to say " he delivered the city by his wisdom," and

---

[1] Graetz, in the face of still more abundant evidence, places the book in the
time of Herod the Great, and finds in the career of that king illustrations of this
and other passages.

then "wisdom is better than strength, but the poor man's wisdom is despised, and his words *are not heard*"? Granted that the latter statement is a generalising complaint, it is still a deduction from the particular event. And if the poor man really delivered the city by his wisdom, his wisdom was not despised and his words were heard. It is better to render ומלט "and he would have delivered"—an apodosis of a conditional sentence with the protasis suppressed[1]. The poor wise man was in the city, and he suggested wise means of defence, but he was disregarded and his wisdom despised[2]. The passage thus refers, not to the raising of a siege, but to the capture of a small town because the few men in it would not listen to the advice of a poor wise man. If this is so, it is useless to try to determine the particular event, though the circumstances may have been well known to Ḳoheleth's readers.

It is, of course, very probable that if a more detailed knowledge were possible of the circumstances of his time, a large number of Ḳoheleth's statements and complaints would receive illustration—such, for instance, as v. 7, 8, vi. 3, x. 5–7. But as it is, they can be regarded only as side-lights on his troublous life.

§ 4. *An outline of Ḳoheleth's thoughts.*

If this *Journal intime* follows, in their true sequence, the successive phases of thought through which the writer travelled, he is shewn to be very similar to a large number of the thinkers of to-day. For, whatever his early life may have been, it was Nature that first made him think. He was sobered and saddened by the riddle of Nature without her key—the unceasing monotony of change which has no apparent aim or result. With what object does generation succeed generation, and the sun rise and set—only to rise again, and the wind go "circling circling," and the rivers run into the sea which is never full? There is nothing satisfying for the eye to see or the ear to hear; there is nothing new under the sun; the generations that come and go are, each in turn, forgotten by the generations which follow in the endless chain (i. 3–11).

[1] Cf. Ex. ix. 15, 1 Sam. xiii. 13.

[2] זכר occurs in v. 19 with somewhat the same force—'take notice of,' 'have regard to.' See also Nah. ii. 6, יזכר אדיריו.

And this trouble of heart made him ponder over the two great questions—What is life? and What does life lead to? Being a man of means and leisure he had ample opportunities for any investigations, and he used them to the full. He set himself by wisdom to gather as wide an experience as possible of men and things. And he found that there were unalterable wrongs in the world, crooked things which could not be made straight—defects which could not be supplied. The more he learnt, the more wrongs he discovered. In much wisdom was much grief, and increase of knowledge meant increase of sorrow (i. 12–18).

So he adopted a different course. He surrounded himself with all the luxury and elegance of which the times were capable; whatever his eyes desired he kept not from them; he withheld not his heart from any joy (ii. 1–10). And before long he was prepared with an answer to the first question—an answer which sounds through his book at intervals like the clang of a knell—"An empty vapour, a striving after wind" (ii. 11). But it is important to observe what this means to him. It does not mean that the refinements and interests which wealth afforded gave him no pleasure; he distinctly states (ii. 10) that his heart rejoiced in all his labour. He describes his attitude to these things very clearly in ii. 3, 9. He gave himself up to luxury and frivolity (v. 3), and magnificence (v. 9), not for the purpose of mere enjoyment but by way of a careful experiment—"my heart still acting with its customary wisdom¹"—"also my wisdom stood firmly by me." The experiment was for the purpose of finding something that could prove a permanent satisfaction and profit for mankind "throughout the number of the days of his life." He does not for a moment deny that, intrinsically, wisdom excels folly as light excels darkness (ii. 13); but—and here he approaches the answer to the second question—one event, one chance or mischance, happens to the wise man and the fool alike (ii. 15, 16). On these two answers he rings the changes throughout the book: Life is a profitless vapour; Life ends, for every living creature, in a return to dust.

Before following his detailed complaints of the wrongs of life, it is well to understand his attitude towards religion. The Divine Name JHVH occurs nowhere in his pages, while

¹ See note on v. 3.

he uses the title Elohim twenty times, in sixteen of which the word has the definite article[1]. In all these he speaks of what God *does*—of His government of the world, never of what He *is*, or of man's attitude towards Him. 'The Deity' is to him 'Nature,' the sum-total of the irresistible and inscrutable forces which govern the world. But at the same time he has not quite lost his Semitic belief that God is more than Nature, for His action shews evidence of design. He not only made everything excellent in its time, but He has so arranged that no man can understand or discover the true inwardness of His work (iii. 11, viii. 17, xi. 5). He seems to work with the purpose of shewing men that they are mere beasts (iii. 18), and of preventing them from gaining the slightest glimpse into the future (iii. 22, vi. 12 b, vii. 14). Moreover God's work—the course of Nature—appears in the form of an endless cycle. Events and phenomena are brought upon the stage of life, and banished into the past, only to be recalled and banished again (i. 4–11, iii. 15). And this, for Koheleth, paralyses all real effort; for no amount of labour and travail can produce anything new, or of real profit—no one can add to, or subtract from, the unswerving chain of facts (i. 15, iii. 1–9, 14 a, vii. 13); no one can contend with Him that is mightier than he (vi. 10).

And when Koheleth looks out upon the world he sees that this work of the Deity—this course of Nature—which cannot be fathomed or altered, involves a mass of human misery. It is not only that the righteous often suffer, while the wicked prosper (vii. 15, viii. 14). The whole race of men suffers from an evil sickness, sorrow and trouble, vain labour and disappointment. His mournful observations are not noted in any logical order; he puts them down as they occur to him. And they are mainly valuable from the picture which they give of the writer himself. He has often been called a pessimist; but that is a misnomer, because he has an intense conviction that mankind ought to be, and could be, better, if circumstances were more favourable. His sadness would not be so deep if his estimation of the potentialities of goodness in man were less high. He sees "through a mirror in a riddle," and when he imagines that "that which is crooked" (as seen in the blurred mirror)

---

[1] i. 13, ii. 24, iii. 10, 11, 13, 14 a, 15, v. 17, 18 *bis*, 19, vi. 2 *bis*, vii. 13, 14, viii. 15, 17, ix. 1, 7, xi. 5. On the other passages in which the title occurs see § 5.

"cannot be made straight," it is because the compensating thought "then face to face" was impossible for him. And he gains no relief from the expectation of Messianic peace and perfection, which animated the religious mind of the orthodox Jew. Generations had gone by since the prophets had foretold it, and every day the conception of an ideal Israel became more chimerical. There are left him only the shreds of the religious convictions of his fathers, with a species of 'natural religion' which has fatalism and altruism among its ingredients.

The section i.–ii. 11, the contents of which have been noticed above, forms a kind of exordium to the book, in which Ķoheleth writes under the guise of Solomon. Solomon had been famous for three things—his study of nature, his wisdom, and his wealthy magnificence. Each of these in turn Ķoheleth claimed for himself, shewing that he was better fitted than most men to pronounce on the two questions—What is life? and What does life lead to? But in ii. 12 he expressly threw aside his Solomonic impersonation[1], and "turned himself" to behold the wisdom and the folly displayed in the whole arena of human life. He proceeds, throughout the rest of the book, to draw a series of pictures illustrating the troubles of men, which may be briefly summarised[2]:

ii. 13–17. Although wisdom excels folly, fools and wise men die alike, "and why was I then more wise?" In the days to come all are alike forgotten.

ii. 18–21. He who gathers wealth by prudent labour must leave it to another, who has not laboured for it, and who may—for all he knows—be a fool.

ii. 22, 23. A man's labour fills his nights as well as days with harassing care.

iii. 1–9. All human action is tied by inexorable decree; so that there is no profit to a worker from his labour.

iii. 10, 11. God has given men, by the very nature with which they are endowed, a longing to understand His work, and yet He has not given them the ability to do so.

---

[1] According to the most probable interpretation of the verse: "what is the man [i.e. what can the man do] that cometh after the king? That which he [the king] hath already done." (See note *in loc.*)

[2] All the verses, or parts of verses, which are not cited in this chapter appear to be due to other writers, and are discussed in the following chapter.

iii. 14 a b, 15. God's work is eternal and unalterable, and appears as an unchanging cycle of phenomena.

iii. 16, 18–21. Wickedness and iniquity usurp the place of justice and righteousness. God allows it to shew men that they are but beasts, and will die as the beasts die. And whether there will be the slightest difference between the spirit of man and of beast who knoweth?

iv. 1–3. The weak are oppressed; but their tears avail nothing, for the oppressors have power on their side. This is such a terrible evil that the dead, and still more the unborn, are happier than the living[1].

iv. 4, 6. Successful work makes a man an object of jealousy. Peaceful poverty is better than troubled and profitless wealth.

iv. 7, 8. There is a man that works in mournful solitude, with no one to share his riches. "For whom then do I labour, and deprive my soul of good?"

iv. 13–16. The emptiness of this world's strivings is shewn by a bitter glance at contemporary history.

v. 7, 8. Marvel not at oppression and injustice, when the government is what it is. What a splendid advantage it would be to the country to have a good king!

v. 9–16. Wealth cannot satisfy its possessor, for other people "eat it." The labourer can sleep, but the pampered rich man cannot. Wealth is often kept by the owner to his own hurt; or it perishes and his son is left in poverty. Moreover the owner, when he dies, departs as destitute of his riches as a naked new-born infant, after a life spent in sorrow and trouble.

vi. 1, 2. A man has abundance of wealth, possessions and honour, but he must leave it all to a stranger.

vi. 3–5. A man who has been blessed with a large family, and a long life, and has nevertheless gained no pleasure and dies unhonoured, is in worse case than an untimely birth.

vi. 6, 8. Nay, though he has lived a thousand years twice told, yet he has seen no real good in life. Do not all go to one place? For what advantage has a wise man over a fool, or a poor man who has got on in the world by knowing how to walk prudently and successfully before his fellow-men?

---

[1] This is an outburst of pity which need not be pressed as a contradiction of such a passage as ix. 4–6, where Ḳoh. clings to life with the natural grip of one who has no certainty with regard to a future state.

vi. 10–12. Everything that exists was named [i.e. its nature and its place in the universe were fixed and determined] already; it was similarly known [i.e. determined] what man was to be; and he cannot strive against a mightier than he. Since there is a great deal of talking and arguing that only serves to multiply the emptiness of life, what advantage can man gain? For no one can tell him the two things that he wants to know— what is the *summum bonum* of this life, and what will happen to him after this life.

vii. 1 b–3. The day of death is better than the day of birth[1]; it is better to take part in a funeral than in festivities, because it reminds men that that is what they all must come to. Sorrow is better than laughter, for a sad countenance is fitting and gratifying to the miserable heart.

vii. 13, 14. God's work is unalterable, even to make crooked things straight. In the day of prosperity enjoy thyself, and in the day of adversity consider; God has given both, in order that man may draw no conclusions as to what will happen in the future.

vii. 15–18 a, 20. The righteous man often perishes in his righteousness, while the wicked man prolongs his days in wickedness. Why, then, spoil your life by being over-righteous or over-wise? At the same time do not bring destruction upon yourself by being over-wicked and foolish. Maintain the comfortable mean between the two, for no righteous man on earth is perfectly good.

vii. 21, 22. And because you cannot always be perfectly good, be judiciously deaf sometimes, lest you hear your servant curse you; for you know that you have sometimes cursed others.

vii. 23–26 a, 27, 28. When I determined to be wise, I found that wisdom was far from me, and unfathomably deep. In my general search after knowledge and the truth of things, I found one thing—the terrible snares of a wicked and designing woman. All my calculations led only to the result that one man in a thousand, and not one woman, was worthy of the name.

viii. 2 a, 3 b, 4. Obey the king, for he is a despot who does whatever pleases him.

---

[1] See § 5, p. 22, and note *in loc.*

viii. 6 b, 7, 8. The misery of man is great upon him[1], because man cannot know anything about the future. A man can no more hold back the day of death than he can hold back the wind; and there is no granting of leave to depart from the battle.

viii. 9. Sometimes a man has power over another to his hurt.

viii. 10. I have seen the wicked receiving honourable sepulture, who had lived in the holy place; and they used to be courted and flattered in the city because of their wrong-doing.

viii. 14. The wicked get what the righteous deserve, and *vice versâ*.

viii. 16, 17. When I tried to examine all the work of God upon earth—the ceaseless activity of One who sleeps not day or night—I found that no amount of labour or wisdom could discover it.

ix. 1. The righteous and the wise and their works are absolutely in God's hand; man has no idea whether God will deal with him in the future as though He loved, or hated, him. Everything in the future is an empty vapour[2];

ix. 2–6. because the righteous and the wicked, the religious and the irreligious, come to the same end—an evil which exists throughout everything under the sun. Men are full of wickedness and mad folly while they live, and then—"to the dead!" But when all is said, to be alive under any circumstances is better than to be dead; for the living have at least the mournful privilege of knowing that they will die, while the dead know nothing; they can earn no more reward by labour; they are forgotten; every kind of feeling ceases; they no longer have part or parcel in anything that is done under the sun.

ix. 11, 12. The swift, the strong, the wise, the clever, the skilful, do not get the success which they deserve; time and chance come to all alike; men are suddenly ensnared in an evil time like fish or birds.

ix. 13–16. An historical instance of a wise man who did not get the success which he deserved.

---

[1] It is exceedingly difficult to explain this passage except on the supposition that Ḳoheleth's words have been altered by the introduction of other matter. (See § 5, p. 26.)

[2] Reading הכל לפניהם הבל for הכל וג" : הכל לפניהם : הכל לפניהם. See Appendix II. p. 149.

x. 4. If a ruler is angry with you, do not leave your place in a rage.

x. 5–7. The caprice of the ruler often exalts fools and slaves to places of dignity, while the rich and noble are degraded.

[x. 14. The fool talks a great deal. Man can have no knowledge of the future[1].]

x. 16, 17. The misery of a land whose king is a child, and whose princes are drunken revellers, spending their very mornings in feasting. The happiness of a land whose king is of noble birth and bearing, and whose princes feast at the right time, without drunkenness.

x. 20. The espionage which makes a secret word, or even thought, dangerous.

Such is Ḳoheleth's survey of life. But it is impossible, in a summary, to convey his suppressed passion, the yearning for light, the pity and indignation, the bitter reaction of thought after each fresh outlook, the vain struggles against the cramping fetters by which man is tied to the present.

It remains to notice the conclusion at which he arrives. Since the work of the Deity is inscrutable from beginning to end, and no one has any idea of what the future contains, or whether after this life there is any future for man at all, and since His work is absolutely unalterable, and since, finally, His work involves or allows universal wrong and misery—man can come to no conclusion about life; he can aim at nothing, guide himself by nothing. The only course open to him is to make the most of the present. To this Ḳoheleth returns whenever he finds that the troubles or mysteries of life are beyond his power to solve: ii. 24, 25, iii. 12, 13, 22, v. 17–19, viii. 15, ix. 7–10, xi. 1–10 (exc. 9 b), xii. 1 b–7. It is not a solution of his difficulties; it is far from being a philosophy, or a theory of life. It is a mere *modus vivendi*—a contrivance allowed him by God "whereby he shall not much remember the

---

[1] This verse has been included, with much hesitation, among the words of Ḳoheleth, on account of the characteristic expressions "man knoweth not...etc." If the words are his, they may have been placed here because the first clause "the fool multiplies words" is similar in thought to the *meshalim* in *vv.* 12, 13. But the first clause is entirely unconnected with the two which follow; and the verse interrupts the series of complaints against the government with which Ḳoheleth closes his review of the troubles of life.

days of his life" (v. 19). In ix. 10, xi. 1–6 the thought of industry predominates, and in the rest of the above passages the thought of pleasure. But both are commended because life is a vapour which will soon vanish in the murky "days of darkness."

§ 5. *The integrity of the book.*

A. The picture of his own mind which Ḳoheleth unconsciously draws—his well-nigh dead faith in the God of his fathers, and blind gropings after truth, combined with his pity for suffering men, and despairing indignation at human wrongs —has fascinated thinkers in all subsequent ages.

But that which attracts also repels. Ḳoheleth's words were so entirely at variance with orthodox Jewish thought, that many were afraid of the book. They shrank from its bold expression of facts all the more timidly because the facts were only too true to experience. And they held up in opposition to it the time-worn utterances of orthodox belief. An instance of this has survived in the Book of Wisdom, in which the writer clearly combats some of Ḳoheleth's sayings; and as late as the close of the 1st century A.D., doubts were entertained in rabbinic circles as to the advisability of retaining the book in the Canon. It seems probable that it would have been thrust out of sight as altogether heretical, had it not been for the action of an unknown admirer, who 'edited' it, and commended it to the public. He emphasised the Solomonic authorship; the statement in i. 12, "I, Ḳoheleth, was king over Israel in Jerusalem," enabled him to prefix i. 1, "The words of Ḳoheleth, *the son of David*, king in Jerusalem." He then summed up the burden of the book in i. 2, xii. 8, speaking editorially of Ḳoheleth in the third person, and using the strengthened expression "Vanity of vanities," which occurs nowhere in the body of the book. Finally, he added a postscript, xii. 9, 10 (again referring to the writer in the third person), enlarging upon the value and wisdom of Ḳoheleth-Solomon's proverbial maxims and words of truth by which he taught the people.

B. Such a writing would naturally create a great stir, and be widely discussed, especially if the suggestion be correct that the writer held a high position in the state[1]. Instead of its being thrust out of sight as heretical, attempts were made to 'improve' it. The period was that in which thought was governed by 'wise men[2].' One of these appears to have been attracted by those parts of the book which wore a gnomic and philosophical dress; and, led by the ascription to Solomon, the father of the wise, and by the reference to his proverbs in xii. 9, 10, he sought to enrich the writing by the addition of *m⁰shalim*—more or less isolated apophthegms bearing on life and nature—perhaps culled from various sources. Some of these seem to be suggested by Ḳoheleth's words, and correct or enlarge upon his remarks, but many are thrown in at random with no kind of relevance. In every case their frigid didactic style is in strong contrast to the heat and sting of Ḳoheleth's complaints.

They are as follows:

iv. 5. "The fool foldeth his hands and eateth his own flesh." Ḳoheleth complains in *vv.* 4, 6 that successful work provokes jealousy; peaceful poverty is, therefore, better than troubled wealth. And the wise man inserts, as a corrective, a *mashal* on slothfulness.

iv. 9–12. On the advantages of company. This follows upon Ḳoheleth's complaint of the solitariness of his life.

vi. 7. "All the labour of man is for his mouth, and yet the appetite is not filled." Inserted, with no apparent reason, in the middle of Ḳoheleth's remarks on the unprofitableness of a long life because all men must die.

vi. 9 a. "Better is the sight of the eyes than the roaming of the appetite." Similar in thought to the last; possibly placed here owing to להלך in *v.* 8, but it has no connexion with Ḳoheleth's thought.

vii. 1 a. "A name [i.e. honour and renown] is better than ointment[3]." A fragment of a *mashal*, quite irrelevant to the context; apparently inserted here only because the form טוב..מן..

---

[1] See § 3, pp. 9, 10.

[2] See article 'Wisdom' by Siegfried in Hastings' *B.D.*, and 'Wisdom Literature' by Toy in *Encycl. Bibl.*

[3] The verse should probably be read: טוב שם משׁמן טוב יום המות מיום הולד: (see note *in loc.*).

was parallel to that of the three following aphorisms of Ķoheleth. The play on the words שֵׁם and שֶׁמֶן may be compared with הסירים and הסיר in the next insertion of the 'wise man.'

vii. 4–6. The frivolous laughter and merriment of fools contrasted, in three *mᵉshalim*, with the conduct of the wise[1]. Inserted as an enlargement upon the thought of *vv.* 1 b–3. But the spirit of these *mᵉshalim* is quite different to Ķoheleth's bitterness when he states that sorrow is more fitting than merriment to the miserable heart of man.

vii. 7. "For oppression maketh a wise man mad, and a gift destroyeth the heart." The כי has no connexion with what precedes, and shews that the *mashal* was taken from some other source.

vii. 8, 9. Two *mᵉshalim* on angry quarrelling and fretfulness.

vii. 10. *Mashal* on discontent.

vii. 11, 12. Two *mᵉshalim* on wisdom and its value. Notice that the thought of 11 b, 12 b is opposed to Ķoheleth's conclusion that wisdom can bring no real advantage to its possessors (see ii. 14–16, vi. 8).

vii. 19. *Mashal* on wisdom. This, with 18 b (see below), interrupts the connexion of *v.* 20 with *vv.* 16–18 a.

viii. 1. *Mashal* on wisdom, irrelevant to the context.

ix. 17–x. 3. Five *mᵉshalim* on wisdom and folly, evidently suggested by Ķoheleth's apologue of the poor man whose wisdom was despised.

x. 8–11. Four *mᵉshalim* which teach that men must suffer the results of their own actions or negligence. There is not the slightest traceable connexion with the preceding words of Ķoheleth.

x. 12–15. Four *mᵉshalim* on fools and their talk. [*v.* 14 may possibly be a remark of Ķoheleth. See § 4.]

x. 18. *Mashal* on slothfulness; arising out of Ķoheleth's description of nobles feasting in the morning.

x. 19. *Mashal* on the value of money compared with that of feasting.

Having inserted these scattered proverbs into the body of the book, the 'wise man' added at the end a postscript of his own (xii. 11, 12), describing the value of the words of the wise,

---

[1] וגם זה הבל a gloss. See note on the following page.

which are thrown into the form of short pithy remarks, and are like goads and nails; they are grouped into collections, but proceed ultimately from 'one shepherd,' i.e. Solomon. It is better to learn from these, than to wade through the multitude of books which are constantly being written.

C. These maxims of worldly wisdom, though thoroughly in accord with the religious thought of the time, were not, in any strict sense, religious. They helped to bear out the superscription and the postscript which Ḳoheleth's editor, or 'advertiser,' had prefixed to his work; and thus, in supporting the claim to Solomonic authorship, they were of use in preserving the book from oblivion. But far more was needed if it was to be safely used by the orthodox. It must be made to give explicit statements which should fall into line with the accepted tenets of religion. This was done by a pious Jew— one of the *Ḥᵃsidim* whose spirit afterwards appeared in the Maccabees. He moves in a calm untroubled path of religious conviction, far removed from Ḳoheleth's stormy broodings. All the additions which he makes to the book centre round two chief thoughts: (1) the paramount duty of fearing and pleasing God, and (2) the certainty of God's judgment on those who do not fear and please Him. The portions which appear to be due to him are seldom complete in themselves; they are tacked on to Ḳoheleth's remarks, sometimes separating clauses that were clearly intended to be joined. In every case but one, they are in direct opposition to Ḳoheleth's spirit, if not to his actual words.

ii. 26 a b. Ḳoheleth has just fallen back, for the first time, on the statement that there is nothing better for man than to enjoy the present. God allows it, and Ḳoheleth himself ought to know, for no one has had a better opportunity of judging than he (24 f.). But the *Ḥasid* strongly objects to this conclusion, and inserts the orthodox remark that God's gift of wisdom and knowledge and enjoyment is a reward of piety; but the sinner is allowed the labour of heaping up riches, only that he may give them to the pious[1].

---

[1] The addition גם זה הבל ורעות רוח must be a later gloss. It is meaningless in connexion with the words either of Ḳoheleth or of the *Ḥasid*. This, and the similar addition in vii. 6, appear to be the only instances of glosses introduced after the book had been completed in its triple form.

iii. 14 b. Ḳoheleth is brooding over the eternal and unalterable work of God (14 a), as it shews itself in the cycle of phenomena (15). The *Ḥasid* feels no difficulty in it. Between the two halves of Ḳoheleth's complaint he inserts the stern dictum "and God hath wrought that men may fear before Him."

iii. 17. Ḳoheleth complains that wickedness usurps the place of judgment and righteousness (16); and his conclusion is that God lets it be, for the purpose of shewing men that they are beasts (18). But the conviction of the *Ḥasid* is very different. As in *v.* 14, he anticipates Ḳoheleth's conclusion, catching up his phrase "I said in my heart," and declares that "God will judge the righteous and the wicked, for a time [i.e. of judgment] there is for every occupation and for every work[1]."

iv. 17–v. 6 [E.V. v. 1–7]. This is the only section of the *Ḥasid's* work which does not immediately correct Ḳoheleth. It inculcates sincerity in sacrificing, a reverent reticence in prayer, and the strict performance of vows, ending with the all-important command "fear thou God."

vii. 18 b. Ḳoheleth has complained that the righteous man often perishes in his righteousness, while the wicked man lives a long life in his wickedness (15). Do not, then (he advises), be over-righteous (16), but, at the same time, do not run to the opposite extreme and ruin the chances of the present by being foolishly over-wicked (17). Keep in the safe comfortable mean between the two (18 a). But here the *Ḥasid* sweeps away this worldly compromise: "for he that feareth God shall be quit [i.e. shall do the right thing] from every point of view."

vii. 26 b. Ḳoheleth is troubled by the badness of women, and their fatal fascination (26 a); and the *Ḥasid* inserts the religious remark "He that pleaseth God shall escape from her, but a sinner shall be captured by her."

vii. 29. Ḳoheleth's sweeping stricture on men and women (28) appears to the *Ḥasid* to condemn God's own handiwork. So he maintains (echoing Ḳoheleth's "I have found") that man has deliberately departed from the original purity and uprightness with which God endowed him.

viii. 2 b, 3 ab, 5, 6 a. Ḳoheleth advises submission to the despotism of the king (2 a, 3 b, 4). But the *Ḥasid*, who knows that the king's service often clashes with God's service, is

---

[1] Omitting אֵת (see note *in loc.*).

anxious to enter a proviso. "But on account of [your] oath to God be not frightened[1]; out of his (the king's) presence shalt thou go[2]; persist not in an evil thing." And again "Whoso keepeth the [Divine] command, מצוה, will countenance no evil thing." And he continues that a wise man will realise that a time and judgment are coming: for a time and judgment there will be for every occupation.

This is the only passage in which an insertion of the *Ḥasid* appears to have altered words of Ḳoheleth. The words "because the רעת of man is great upon him" may be connected equally well with the foregoing or with the following words. In the former case they belong to the *Ḥasid*, and רעת means 'wickedness': in the latter they belong to Ḳoheleth, and רעת means 'misery.' But in either case Ḳoheleth's thought in *vv.* 7, 8 has no connexion whatever with any of the preceding verses, and yet is introduced by כי. Perhaps the simplest explanation would be that Ḳoheleth originally began a new complaint with the words "the misery of man is great upon him, for he knoweth not...etc." and that the *Ḥasid* added the first כי, adapting the phrase to suit his own statement about the time and judgment.

viii. 11–13. To Ḳoheleth's complaint that the wicked are honoured after their death, and courted during their life, the *Ḥasid* adds that men are wicked because their sentence is long in coming; but however long and prosperous a sinner's life may be, yet he knows that it will be well with those who fear God, and not well with the wicked.

xi. 9 b, xii. 1 a. Ḳoheleth falls back, for the last time, on the position "Live for the present, while old age and death draw not nigh" (xi.–xii. 7). And here the *Ḥasid* throws in his last warnings: "but know that for all these God will bring thee into judgment[3]"; "but remember thy Creator in the days of thy youth."

This latter clause breaks the connexion of Ḳoheleth's thought. xi. 10 a "And remove vexation...thy flesh" is evidently in close connexion with "before the evil days come...etc.," the phrase "for youth and the prime of life are vanity" being a parenthesis.

---

[1] Making no break between *vv.* 2 and 3.

[2] Contrast Ḳoheleth's advice in x. 4.

[3] This judgment is not necessarily for condemnation. In his last fragment the *Ḥasid* foretells a judgment for good works as well as bad (xii. 14).

The *Ḥasid,* having thus borne his testimony by pious additions to the book, added (as the first editor and the 'wise man' had done) a postscript of his own (xii. 13, 14): "Fear and obey God, for He will bring into judgment every work, good and bad."

And it may be gladly admitted that, under these successive hands, Ḳoheleth's *Journal* has been not spoilt but enriched. By the annotations and criticisms of two contemporary thinkers its value has been multiplied historically and doctrinally. It became a "three-fold cord" whose drawing and attracting power has been "not quickly broken." It is in this triple form that Jews and Christians alike have counted it inspired. It is (to borrow three terms from a Christian writer) the attempt of a σοφὸς and of a γραμματεὺς to supply, as far as they were able, the defects of a συνζητητὴς τοῦ αἰῶνος τούτου[1].

The attempts which have been made to explain the difficulties in the book on the basis of a unity of authorship are innumerable. Among later writers who follow this line of treatment the most noticeable are Ginsburg (who gives a full historical sketch of the commentaries till his day), Wright, Tyler and Plumptre, in English; and Delitzsch, Nowack and Wildeboer in German. The great majority represent the book as depicting different phases of thought through which Ḳoheleth passes—that he alternates between sceptical doubt and religious faith, and that his faith at last proves triumphant.

This is drawn out most attractively by Plumptre, who compares this mental conflict with Tennyson's "Two Voices." It is as though Ḳoheleth is seen passing through a region in which dark clouds of doubt are from time to time broken by fitful gleams of sunshine; and these gleams gradually become brighter, till the clouds are at last chased away, and are succeeded by a sunny calm. But the more the book is read, the more convinced the reader feels that this is not so. It is an unnatural region, in which clouds vanish automatically, and moments of calm suddenly occur, only to give way as suddenly to the same clouds once more. These dissolving views are not pictures of a mind halting between two opinions, and slowly fighting its way towards the light of faith.

[1] See 1 Cor. i. 20–25.

Moreover the theory of the unity of authorship affords no explanation of the miscellaneous proverbs wedged into chaps. iv.-x., which breathe neither doubt nor faith. It is difficult to conceive of any state of mind which could give vent, for example, to the three successive paragraphs iv. 9–12, iv. 13–16 and iv. 17–v. 6. And, lastly, it offers no solution of the difficulties of the epilogue xii. 9–14.

The ingenious theory whereby Bickell maintains the unity of authorship[1] stands by itself. It is accepted entire by Dillon in *Sceptics of the Old Testament*. He re-arranges[2] the book as follows (the subdivisions of his analysis being omitted):

The Worth of Existence.

A. *The vanity of its supposed unconditioned good.*

1. Proposition. i. 1–ii. 11.
2. Proof.

(i) v. 9–vi. 7, iii. 9, 12, 13. Possession and enjoyment made possible thereby.

(ii) iii. 10, 11, 14–22, iv. 1–8. Knowledge; its limited nature and discouraging results.

(iii) ii. 12–16, iii. 1–8, viii. 6–14, 16–17 b, ix. 1–3, viii. 15. Wisdom as a religious-moral sentiment.

(iv) ix. 11–18, vi. 8, 11–12. Wisdom as prudence and practical ability.

B. *Recommendation of proportional good.*

1. Wisdom.

(i) vii. 1–6, vi. 9, vii. 7–10, 13–19, 11, 12, 21, 22, 30, iv. 9–16. as Self-restraint.

(ii) iv. 17–v. 6, as the Fear of God.

(iii) v. 7, 8, x. 16–20, xi. 1–3, 6, 4, 5, as Industry.

(iv) vii. 23–29, viii. 1–4, x. 2–14 a, 15, as Discretion.

2. Pleasures of Life. x. 14 b, ix. 3–10, xi. 7–xii. 8.

---

[1] He is obliged, however, to assign some words and expressions to redactors; and he does not include the epilogue in his scheme.

[2] The first writer who suggested dislocations in the book was van der Palm, *Ecclesiastes philologice et critice illustratus*, Leyden, 1784. Haupt, *Oriental Studies*, pp. 242–278, though his re-arrangement of the book is not of such a wholesale description as that of Bickell, thinks that the original writing was disarranged deliberately, and marred by numerous glosses.

This result is arrived at by the supposition of an accident to a Hebrew manuscript, whereby sheets were placed in a wrong order, and some turned inside out. But the theory is also assisted by arbitrary transpositions of single verses and half verses. Moreover the final result does not come up to expectations, and some passages need force to fit them into the scheme; e.g. viii. 12, 13 occur in a passage which Bickell takes to shew the vanity of Wisdom as a religious-moral sentiment owing to "the want of preference accorded to the righteous in the fate of life and death"! Again, the accident to the manuscript involves the splitting asunder of only a single verse (x. 14), and that exactly at the end of a clause. That is to say that Bickell chooses to transpose 14 b and 15, and says that the present arrangement is due to an editor who re-arranged the book, and thought that "city" should be connected with "land" which occurred in the first verse of the next sheet in the accident-manuscript.

But apart from all such inherent objections, there is the improbability of the existence of a Hebrew manuscript in codex form at the early date at which the accident must have occurred. The codex form came into general use not earlier than the 4th century A.D. and certainly did not exist before the Christian era[1]. The book of Ḳoheleth was well known and minutely discussed long before the Christian era; and if it was translated into Greek (at whatever date the translation was made) according to the new 'accidental' order, it is inconceivable that no notice should have been taken of the change.

Other writers, without having recourse to theories of dislocation, have allowed that interpolations have been made in a few isolated passages. For example, Peake (Art. 'Ecclesiastes' in Hastings' *B.D.*) sums up a section on the integrity of the book by saying "It seems on the whole most probable that at least xii. 1 a, 13, 14 are later interpolations (assuming that 'thy Creator' is correctly read in xii. 1 a), and possibly also iii. 17 and xi. 9 c." Similarly A. B. Davidson (Art. 'Ecclesiastes' in *Encycl. Bibl.*) holds that xi. 9 b is probably an addition, and xii. 1 certainly; but that there is less objection to iii. 17; also that viii. 10, 12, 13 "are in some way corrupt." And he admits

---

[1] See Birt, *Das antike Buchwesen*, ch. 2 and p. 373. Blau, *Studien zum althebräischen Buchwesen*, Theil 1, ch. 2 and p. 60.

that "in a book such as Ecclesiastes,—the line of thought and (particularly) the tone of which diverge so greatly from the other O.T. writings—it was to be expected that there would be some interpolations: *qualifications* which the reader or scribe felt constrained to add to the author's somewhat strong statements."

This is the (right) principle which underlies the treatment of the book by Siegfried[1]. Other writers have condemned one or two verses and phrases; but they have left untouched the mass of contradictions and abrupt transitions of tone of which the book is full. Siegfried, on the other hand, is unnecessarily ruthless in his dissection.

His scheme is as follows:

Koheleth himself (Q^1) was a pessimistic philosopher, whose book would have disappeared, had it not been rescued by Solomon's name at the beginning.

The first interpolator (Q^2) was an Epicurean Sadducee; he recommends the pleasures of eating and drinking as the recompense for all men's troubles; life is sweet, and busy work affords real enjoyment; the extravagancies of Pharisaic religion are to be avoided. Kraetzschmar (*Th. LZ.* Sept. 1900), though he questions the rest of Siegfried's analysis, accepts the distinction between Q^1 and Q^2. But Siegfried himself helps to throw doubt on the distinction. He assigns iii. 22, viii. 15, among other passages, to Q^2, but ii. 24 a, iii. 12 to Q^1, explaining that Koheleth shews (ii. 3, 10, 17, 18, 20) that his meaning is that there is no genuine pleasure to be had at all. But is it reasonable to say that the advice "there is nothing better than to enjoy life" is from Q^1 in two passages, and from Q^2 in two others? It has been shewn in the last chapter that this conclusion with regard to the enjoyment of life is an integral portion of his complaints.

The second interpolator (Q^3) was a Ḥakam, or 'wise man,' who puts a high value upon wisdom, in opposition to Koheleth.

The interpolations of a 'wise man' have been noted above, pp. 22, 23; but that enumeration agrees with Siegfried's only in respect to iv. 5, vi. 9 a, vii. 11, 12, 19, viii. 1, x. 1-3, 12-15. Some of the passages which Siegfried assigns to him (ii. 13, 14 a, vi. 8, ix. 13-18) are altogether in the style of Koheleth;

---

[1] In *Handkommentar zum AT.*

they introduce the personal element, the disappointment at the lack of advantage and appreciation accorded to the wise; they form part of Ḳoheleth's picture of the wrongs of the world.

The third interpolator (Q⁴) is a *Ḥasid*—a pious Jew, who was strongly opposed to Ḳoheleth's statements about the Divine government of the world[1]. This is accepted in substance above, pp. 24–26.

Under the designation Q⁵ Siegfried includes several other interpolators, who inculcate general moral maxims of proverbial wisdom. But in this multiplying of interpolators few will follow him. If the *Ḥakam* could contrast wise men and fools in such proverbs as ii. 14 a, ix. 17, x. 2, 12, why should vii. 5, 6 a be denied him? If he could describe the action of the fool in iv. 5, x. 3, why not in vii. 9? There is nothing improbable in supposing that all the isolated proverbs which do not form part of Ḳoheleth's complaints are added by one hand, though the *Ḥakam* may, of course, have collected them from various sources, as, indeed, his postscript implies that he did.

Siegfried adds that the whole writing i. 2–xii. 7 was edited by a redactor, with a heading i. 1, and a closing formula xii. 8; and that xii. 9, 10, xii. 11, 12 and xii. 13, 14 are three further additions. He does not suggest the source of the two former of these couplets; but he makes the strange statement that "xii. 13, 14 betray a Pharisee who believes in a judgment hereafter, which Q⁴ the *Ḥasid* (iii. 17, xi. 9 b) knows not of." It is difficult to see how the verses bear out this distinction.

Kraetzschmar, in reviewing Siegfried's work, says "it is questionable whether Siegfried will find many followers in his extreme interpolation theory. It is a right idea overstrained in the endeavour to explain all the difficulties in the book.... But the unravelling is done with energy, and will incite to further investigation from this point of view." The analysis given above, in this and the preceding chapter, is an attempt at further investigation, incited by Siegfried's interesting commentary.

<hr/>

[1] Lauer (*Das Buch Koh. und die Interpolationshypothese Siegfried's*, Wittenberg, 1900) agrees with all Siegfried's passages except viii. 2–4, xi. 5, which he thinks are from an independent writing. Bickell assigns some passages to R¹, a zealot hostile to the book.

§ 6. *The style and vocabulary.*

The book of Ḳoheleth is unlike any other Hebrew writing
in its style and subject-matter. It has, indeed, some affinities
of thought with the book of Proverbs[1] (there are many
in the additions of the 'wise man' and of the *Ḥasid*); and
some of the problems which troubled Ḳoheleth, troubled the
writers of Job and a few of the Psalms such as xxxvii., xlix.
and lxxiii. But under the stress of keen disappointment, and
indignation at the wrongs of the world, his style has a stinging
sarcasm, a tendency to epigram, a *moan* in it, which is unique
in Hebrew literature. At the same time he is capable of real
poetic feeling, as the opening[2] and the close of his writing shew,
i. 2–11, xii. 1 b–7. This intense originality raised him far above
the literary level of his day. The fact that two contemporary
writers, totally unlike him in style and tone, were anxious to
perpetuate his work, is a proof of the high regard in which it
was held. If it is compared with the almost contemporary
writing of Ben Sira (which was highly thought of, and may
be taken as representative of the literature of the last two
centuries B.C.), the strong originality of Ḳoheleth's work stands
out in high relief. Schechter[3] points out the artificial or Paitanic
tendency betrayed by Ben Sira's quotations and adaptations
from canonical writings. "His success in producing a work
'the predominant character' of which 'is classical,' is...to be
ascribed to the author's knowledge of the Bible, the language
and style of which he was constantly copying, whilst his most
admired 'boldness and freedom' in employing Biblical phrases
is in most cases nothing more than a mere Paitanic artificiality
so common in post-Biblical Hebrew poetry. In fact B. S. should
rather be described as the first of the Paitanim than as one
of the last of the canonical writers." Now although Ḳoheleth
cannot have been prior to B. Sira by much more than a
quarter of a century, he has not a trace of this Paitanic style;
there is scarcely a single passage in his own portions of the

---

[1] Compare vii. 26 with the warnings against women in Prov. vi. 26 b, vii. 6–27;
ix. 9 with Prov. v. 18; x. 4 with Prov. xvi. 14; x. 7 with Prov. xix. 10 b.

[2] For a metrical analysis of ch. i. see H. Grimme, 'Abriss der Biblisch-
hebräischen Metrik,' *ZDMG.* 1897, 689 f.

[3] In his edition of the Genizah fragments, Introd. pp. 12–38.

book which can be called a quotation, or even adaptation, from the Bible[1]. The contrast, therefore, between his nervous intensity and independence of thought, and the artificiality of the "many books" which were being composed around him, must have been very pronounced.

But it is not only in regard to quotations that Koheleth forms a contrast with B. Sira. Schechter goes on to point out that though B. Sira tried hard to imitate the Scriptures, he failed in the end. "In unguarded moments such phrases, idioms, particles and peculiar constructions escaped him as to furnish us with a sufficiently strong number of criteria, betraying the real character of the language of his time." Koheleth, who is no imitator, and who writes the language of his time out of the fulness of his heart, does not make the slightest pretensions to classical Hebrew. The Hebrew language, which had been pure enough for some time after the return from Babylon, began to decay from the time of Nehemiah. The memoirs of Ezra and Nehemiah, and (in a less degree) the writing of Malachi, shew signs of the change, "which is still more palpable in the Chronicles (end of the 4th cent. B.C.), Esther, and Ecclesiastes....The three books named do not, however, exhibit these peculiarities in equal proportions; Ecclesiastes has the most striking *Mishnic* idioms[2]." For the Aramaic and Mishnic peculiarities to be found in Koheleth, reference should be made to the glossary in Delitzsch's commentary, or to Wright's *Ecclesiastes*, pp. 488 ff. See also Siegfried's commentary, pp. 13–23.

The linguistic peculiarities of Koheleth are one of the safest criterions for fixing a date after which the book must have been written. It must be later (probably much later) than Esther, which is usually dated c. 300 B.C. And it will be seen in the next chapter that a *terminus ad quem* is supplied by the use made of the book by Ben Sira.

---

[1] iii. 20 is a reference to Gen. iii. 19; and v. 14 is possibly a reminiscence of Job i. 21.

[2] Driver, *Intr. O.T.* pp. 473 f. See also pp. 444 ff.

§ 7. *The relation of Ḳoheleth to B. Sira and the Book of Wisdom.*

1. To former commentators on Ḳoheleth only the versions of B. Sira's work were available, together with a few small fragments of the original preserved by Rabbinic writers. But since the discovery of large portions of the Hebrew text, a more trustworthy comparison between the two books has been made possible. There can be no room for doubt that B. Sira knew not only Ḳoheleth's original writing, but also the later additions made to it. According to his custom he does not quote *verbatim*; but he adapts several phrases, altering them to suit his context. In many cases it is quite evident that it is he who is borrowing from Ḳoheleth, and not *vice versâ*. The following list of passages will shew the extent and nature of his indebtedness[1]:

Ḳoheleth.		B. Sira.	
iii. 1	לכל זמן ועת	iv. 20	בני עת ²וזמן שמר
iii. 11	את הכל עשה יפה בעתו	xxxix. 16	מעשי אל כלם טובים
			³לכל צורך בעתו יספיק
		xxxix. 33	מעשה אל כלם טובים
			לכל צורך בעתו [ים]פוק
iii. 15	⁴והאלהים יבקש את נרדף	v. 3	כי י״י מבקש נרדפים
iii. 20, 21	⁵הכל היה מן העפר	xl. 11	כל מארץ אל ארץ ישוב
	והכל שב אל העפר :		
	מי יודע רוח בני אדם		ואשר ⁶ממרום אל מרום :
	העולה היא למעלה		
	ורוח הבהמה		
	הירדת היא למטה לארץ :		

---

[1] The references to B. Sira are numbered according to Swete's edition of the LXX.

[2] Schechter's probable conjecture for המון, which, however, Peters retains.

[3] וכל ?.

[4] 𝕲 καὶ ὁ θεὸς ζητήσει τὸν διωκόμενον, following B. Sira's thought of the avenging of the persecuted, cf. B. Sir. 𝕲 ὁ γὰρ κύριος ἐκδικῶν ἐκδικήσει σε.

[5] Cf. xii. 7.

[6] 𝕲 ἀπὸ ὑδάτων εἰς θάλασσαν = ממים אל ים, cf. Ḳoh. i. 7.

Ķoheleth.		B. Sira.	
vii. 12	כי בצל החכמה בצל הכסף	xiv. 27	¹וחסה בצלה מחרב
vii. 16	ואל תתחכם יותר	xxxv. 4	²ובל עת מה תתחכם
vii. 28	אדם אחד מאלף מצאתי	vi. 6	[אנשי שלומך יהיו רבים]
			ובעל סודך ³אחד מאלף :
viii. 1	חכמת אדם תאיר פניו	xiii. 25	לב אנוש ⁴ישנא פניו
	ועו פניו ישנא :		
xii. 14	אם טוב ואם רע		אם לטוב ואם לרע :
			? ?
viii. 5	שומר מצוה לא ידע דבר רע	xxxvii. 12	אך עם איש מפחד תמיד
			אשר תדע שומר מצוה
ix. 10	כל אשר תמצא ידך לעשות	xiv. 11, 12	ואם יש לך היטיב לך
	בכחך עשה		ולאל ידך הדשן
	כי אין מעשה וחשבון ודעת וחכמה		זכור כי ⁵[לא בשאול תענוג
	בשאול אשר אתה הלך שמה :		ו] לא מות יתמהמה :
			וחוק לשאול לא הגד לך
xii. 13	סוף הדבר הכל נשמע	xliii. 27	⁶עוד כאלה לא נוסף
	את האלהים ירא ואת מצותיו שמור		
	כי זה כל אדם :		וקץ דבר הוא הכל :

The following may also be noted from passages in B. Sira not yet extant in Hebrew :

iii.14	עליו אין להוסיף וממנו אין לנרע	xviii. 6	οὐκ ἔστιν ἐλαττῶσαι οὐδὲ προσθεῖναι,
	where עליו refers to "all that God doeth."		καὶ οὐκ ἔστιν ἐξιχνιάσαι τὰ θαυμάσια τοῦ κυρίου.
v. 3	כאשר תדר נדר לאלהים	xviii. 22	μὴ ἐμποδισθῇς τοῦ ἀπο-
	אל תאחר לשלמו :		δοῦναι εὐχὴν εὐκαίρως.

¹ This is in connexion with *v.* 20 אשרי אנוש בחכמה יהגה.

² ? בלא. Syr. בכל.

³ It is more likely that the reference is to Ķoheleth than to Job xxxiii. 23. Seʻadyah, however, cities B. Sir. as מני אלף, as in Job. See Cowley and Neubauer p. xx.

⁴ Cf. xii. 18.

⁵ 𝔊 omits. Cf. *v.* 16 כי אין בשאול לבקש תענוג. But see Peters on the whole passage.

⁶ xlii. 25 mg. has לכל צורך הכל נשמע.

Ḳoheleth.		B. Sira.
viii. 12	כי גם יודע אני	i. 13 τῷ φοβουμένῳ τὸν κύριον εὖ
	אשר יהיה טוב ליראי האלהים	ἔσται ἐπ᾽ ἐσχάτων.
	אשר יראו מלפניו :	
x. 8	חפר גומץ בו יפול	xxvii. 26 ὁ ὀρύσσων βόθρον εἰς
		αὐτὸν ἐμπεσεῖται¹.
xii. 9	ויתר שהיה קהלת חכם	xxxvii. 23 ἀνὴρ σοφὸς τὸν ἑαυτοῦ
	עוד למד דעת את ²העם :	λαὸν παιδεύσει.

To the above instances may be appended one from the first 'Alphabet' or Acrostic of B. Sira (given in Cowley and Neubauer, pp. xxviii. f., and Dukes' *Rabbinische Blumenlese*, p. 73). Many of the aphorisms in this collection are undoubtedly spurious: but some have been shewn to be genuine by the discovery of the Hebrew fragments, and this may therefore be genuine also.

xi. 1	שלח לחמך על פני המים	זרוק לחמך על אפי מיא³
	כי ברוב הימים תמצאנו :	ואת משכח ליה בסוף יומיא :

But besides the passages in which there is a more or less close approximation in language, there are not a few in which Ben Sira has echoes of Ḳoheleth's thoughts. Several of these are noted by Wright (*Eccl.* pp. 41–46), but a few of his instances must be discarded, B. Sira's meaning having been made clearer by the Hebrew text. The following, however, deserve consideration:

Ḳoh. i. 4. B. S. xiv. 18 (Heb.). "As leaves grow upon a green tree, whereof one withereth and another springeth up—so of the generations of flesh and blood, one perisheth and another ripeneth."

Ḳoh. iii. 7. B. S. xx. 6, 7 (Heb.). "There is one that is silent because he cannot answer, and there is one that is silent

¹ Perhaps from Prov. xxvi. 27, the latter half of which appears to have suggested B. S. xxvii. 27. 𝔊 Ḳoh. is identical with B. S.

² 𝔊 τὸν ἄνθρωπον.

³ Dukes +וביבשתא. See also earlier in the Alphabet:

בר דלא בר (סבר?) שבקיה על אפי מיא וישט,

i.e. let him take to trading.

because he seeth [it is] time (עת). A wise man is silent until the time, but a fool observeth not the time."

Ḳoh. iv. 8 b. B. S. xiv. 4 (Heb.). "He that depriveth (מונע) his soul[1], gathereth for another; and in his good things (בטובתו) shall a stranger revel."

Ḳoh. v. 1 (E. V. v. 2). "Therefore let thy words be few." B. S. vii. 14 (Heb.). "And repeat not (אל תישן) a word in a prayer."

Ḳoh. v. 2, 6 (E. V. v. 3, 7) on the emptiness of dreams, cf. B. S. xxxi. 1-7 (𝔊).

Ḳoh. v. 11 b (E. V. v. 12 b). "The abundance of the rich will not suffer him to sleep." B. S. xxxiv. 1 (Heb.). "The wakefulness of the rich wasteth his flesh; his care dissipateth slumber."

Ḳoh. vii. 8 b. B. S. v. 11 (Heb.). "In patience of spirit (ארך רוח) return answer."

Ḳoh. vii. 14. B.S. xxxvi. 14, 15 (𝔊). "Over against the evil is the good, and over against death is life; so over against a pious man is a sinner. And thus look at all the works of the Most High, two and two, one over against the other." See also xlii. 24.

Ḳoh. viii. 4 b. B. S. xxxiii. 10 b (Syr. only). "For who shall say unto thee What doest thou?" But cf. Job ix. 12.

Ḳoh. ix. 16. B. S. xiii. 22 c d (Heb.). "A poor man speaketh[2], and they hoot at him[3]; though he be wise that speaketh, there is no place for him."

Ḳoh. xi. 10. B.S. xxx. 23 a b (Heb.). "Rejoice thy soul, and make thy heart joyful; and put vexation far from thee."

2. The use made of Ḳoheleth by Ben Sira is important as a landmark for arriving at Ḳoheleth's date.

The allusions to it in Wisdom are also important, but for a different reason. They afford an illustration of the light in which the book was regarded by the pious. As the *Ḥasid* annotator sometimes catches up Ḳoheleth's language in order to oppose him, so (even more strikingly) the writer of Wisdom puts his thoughts, and his very wording, into the mouth of the

---

[1] Cf. Ḳoh. ii. 10.

[2] So Syr. נמוט Heb. 𝔊.

[3] ישאו נע נע. Cf. Is. xxviii. 10.

ungodly, and raises his protest against them. In Wisdom,
unlike Ben Sira, all the allusions are placed together in a con-
tinuous passage (ii. 1–9)[1], as follows:—

Ḳoheleth.		Wisdom.
	v. 1.	For they [the ungodly i. 16] said within themselves, reasoning not rightly,
ii. 23, v. 17.		Short and sorrowful is our life,
		And there is no healing at a man's end,
viii. 8.		And none was ever known who released from Hades.
iii. 19, ix. 11.	*v.* 2.	Because by mere chance (αὐτοσχε-δίως) were we born,
		And hereafter we shall be as though we had never been;
		Because a smoke is the breath in our nostrils,
		And reason is a spark in[2] the beating of our hearts,
xi. 7.	*v.* 3.	Which being quenched, the body shall be turned into ashes,
		And the spirit shall be dispersed as thin air.
i. 11, ii. 16, ix. 5.	*v.* 4.	And our name shall be forgotten in time,
		And no one shall remember our works;
		And our life shall pass away like the track of a cloud,
הבל ii. 11 etc.		And shall be scattered as a mist Chased by the beams of the sun And by its heat overcome.
vi. 12.	*v.* 5.	For our life is the passing of a shadow,
viii. 8.		And there is no retreating of our end,

---

[1] Plumptre, pp. 71–74, cites several other passages in Wisdom which are in
no sense quotations from Ḳoheleth, or even allusions to his language, though
they are opposed to his spirit.　　　　　[2] i.e. either *during*, or *kindled by*.

Ḳoheleth.	Wisdom.
viii. 8.	*v.* 5. Because it is sealed, and none turneth it back.
ii. 24 etc.	*v.* 6. Come then, and let us enjoy the good things that exist,
xi. 9.	And let us use the created world, as youth[1] [alone] can, eagerly;
ix. 8.	*v.* 7. With costly wine and ointments let us be filled, And let no flower of spring pass us by.
	v. 8. Let us crown ourselves with rose buds ere they be withered;
	v. 9. Let none of us be without a share in our wanton revelry, Everywhere let us leave tokens of our mirth,
iii. 22, v. 18, ix. 9 b.	For this is our portion and this is our lot.

§ 8. *Greek language and thought.*

It has been urged as evidence for a late date of writing that the book has a strong Greek colouring—that is, 1st that it contains Greek idioms and expressions, and 2nd that it is saturated with Greek philosophic thought. These two theories are quite distinct and must be treated separately.

1. The presence of a large number of Graecisms in Ḳoheleth's language was first maintained by D. Zirkel[2], and he is followed more or less completely by Kleinert, Graetz, Tyler, Plumptre, Siegfried and Wildeboer[3]. But though Ḳoheleth has a few expressions which *might* have resulted from the prevailing Greek atmosphere of his time, there are none that *demand* this explanation; and several of the instances offered can be traced to the Greek language only by violence.

i. 3 al. תחת השמש. Plumptre confidently asserts this to be due to Greek influence; but Kleinert admits that it may be a favourite idiom of the author, and need not be Greek. Ḳoheleth

---

[1] καὶ χρησώμεθα τῇ κτίσει ὡς νεότητι σπουδαίως. "As in youth" or "as belongs to youth." But the text may be corrupt.

[2] The subject, however, was broached a few years earlier by van der Palm.

[3] See *Literature* at the end of the chapter.

varies it with תחת השמים i. 13, ii. 3, iii. 1 and על הארץ viii. 14, 16, xi. 2. It is interesting to note that the expression occurs in two Sidonian inscriptions of the 3rd century B.C.[1]

i. 13. תור, it is said, must be explained by σκέπτεσθαι. But it is good Hebrew for 'explore.' Cf. Num. xiii. 2, 16, 17.

id. הוא ענין רע. Zirkel says that הוא corresponds to the Homeric use of the article as a demonstrative pronoun, and renders the words ἣν ἀσχολίαν πονηράν! But this has commended itself to no other writer.

ii. 5. פרדס. This, though corresponding to παράδεισος, is not derived from it. Both[2] are derived from the Persian *pairidaêza.* פרדס occurs also in S. of S. iv. 13, Neh. ii. 8, both of which books were entirely out of the range of Greek influence.

ii. 14, iii. 19, ix. 2, 3. מקרה. van der Palm connects it with συμφορά, and it is pointed out that Solon's reminder to Croesus[3] "Man is altogether συμφορή" is a thought parallel to that of Koheleth. But מקרה in the sense of 'mischance,' 'catastrophe,' is not necessarily Greek. The word, indeed, is colourless in Ruth ii. 3, but it certainly has a bad sense in 1 Sam. vi. 9[4].

ii. 15. אז יתר. Zirkel renders ἔτι μᾶλλον. But אז cannot be equivalent to ἔτι. It means "in these circumstances," as in Jer. xxii. 15 אז טוב לו.

iii. 12. עשות טוב. Kleinert, Tyler and Siegfried take this to be a literal, and un-Hebrew, rendering of εὖ πράττειν. It is true that the ethical sense 'to lead a good life' is vetoed by the following ראה טוב, and is alien to the context. But though it means (as does εὖ πράττειν) 'to fare well,' 'to be in a prosperous state,' it is not necessary to go to the Greek idiom for an explanation[5]. The verb עשה, as frequently in the book, has the force of 'prepare,' 'acquire,' 'arrange for' (cf. ii. 3); and the expression implies 'to pursue a course of action that will bring prosperity,' as Luther has it *sich gütlich thun.* Moreover the opposite

---

[1] Inscr. of Tabnith, c. 290 B.C. Constantinople, no. 4 in G. A. Cooke's *North Semitic Inscriptions:*

אל יכן לך זרע בחים תחת שמש

Inscr. of Eshmun-'azar, c. 275 B.C., Louvre, CIS I. 3, no. 5 in Cooke:

אל יכן לם שרש למט ופר למעל ותאר בחים תחת השמש

[2] παράδεισος came into the Greek language through Xenophon.

[3] Herod. I. 32.

[4] Cf. קרה Dt. xxiii. 11.

[5] Still less to read ראות טוב with Graetz, Bickell, Nowack, Cheyne.

expression עשה רעה occurs in 2 Sam. xii. 18 with the corresponding meaning 'be in a bad way'—'vex himself.'

iv. 15. הילד השני. Zirkel's reference to the Greek phrase δεύτερος τοῦ βασιλέως is not only unnecessary, but is in conflict with the straightforward meaning of the words, which state that a second youth rose up and took the place of the first youth who had succeeded the old and foolish king. The same questionable interpretation leads Delitzsch (followed by Wright) to seek an explanation in the construction ἕτερος τῶν μαθητῶν of Mat. viii. 21[1].

v. 9. אהב כסף. This, says Zirkel, is a rendering of φιλάργυρος. It might similarly be maintained that the book of Proverbs contains Graecisms: אהב שמחה (xxi. 17) = φιλήδονος. אהב חכמה (xxix. 3) = φιλόσοφος!

v. 17. טוב אשר יפה. Graetz and Pfleiderer strive to maintain that this represents καλὸν κἀγαθόν. So Plumptre, Siegfried and Wildeboer. But it is inconceivable that a writer with this Greek expression in mind should not have written טוב ויפה or rather יפה וטוב. It is very doubtful if אשר can thus couple the adjectives with the meaning "good which is also beautiful," though it is so taken in 𝔊, Syr. and Tg.[2] It seems necessary, with Delitzsch, to depart from the Masoretic accentuation, and make אשר יפה resumptive of אשר ראיתי אני טוב—"Behold what I have seen is good—what beautiful; namely that one should eat...etc."

v. 19. כי אלהים מענה בשמחת לבו. Zirkel suggests that מענה has the force of remunerari, and has borrowed this meaning from ἀμείβεσθαι which can mean both remunerari and respondere. Various explanations of the passage are given in the notes. But a very simple one is available—"God answereth with the joy of his heart"—i.e. God answers his wishes and desires by giving him joy. Ps. lxv. 6 נוראות...תעננו illustrates the meaning of the verb; but an exact parallel occurs in 1 K. xviii. 24, האלהים אשר יענה באש.

vi. 9. הלך נפש. Zirkel compares ὁρμὴ τῆς ψυχῆς in M. Aurel. iii. 15, a very late parallel! But הלך occurs with a similar force in Job xxxi. 7, Ez. xi. 21.

---

[1] Bickell and Siegfried omit השני as a gloss.

[2] Hos. xii. 9 עון אשר חטא is quite different. "Guilt which is sin"=Guilt of such a kind as to deserve punishment.

vi. 12. ויעשם. Zirkel and Graetz refer this to ποιεῖν χρόνον as its only explanation. See notes.

vii. 14. יום טובה. Kleinert says the connexion between this and the Greek εὐημερία is 'evident'; Siegfried holds it to be 'questionable,' and Menzel condemns it as 'frivolous.' But what other expression could possibly have been chosen as a contrast to יום רעה?

vii. 18. יצא את כלם. Zirkel thinks that this can only be explained by the Greek μέσην βαδίζειν. But even if that were the meaning (which is improbable), the expression might be quite independent of Greek; and it would, in any case, be a very awkward way of rendering the Greek idiom. יצא is used in the sense, frequent in later Hebrew, of 'being quit of,' or 'discharging,' a duty. Cf. Mish. B'rak. ii. 1, Shabb. i. 3. If the view taken above (§ 5) on the composition of the book be correct, the clause כי ירא...כלם is the work of the God-fearing Jew who introduces such passages as iii. 14 b, 17, v. 6 b. He sweeps away Koheleth's bitter worldly wisdom with an earnest comment in the interests of true religion—"for he that feareth God shall be quit of them all," i.e. shall fully accomplish his duty with regard to both sides of the question. He thus anticipates his final word in xii. 13 f.: "Fear God...for this is כל האדם."

vii. 24. מה שהיה. Kleinert explains this as "the essence of the thing" = τὸ τί ἐστιν. But the meaning of the expression is clearly shewn in i. 9, iii. 15, vi. 9, where τὸ τί ἐστιν is impossible. The words must have the same force in all the passages, 'that which has come into existence,' i.e. 'that which is.'

vii. 28. אדם. This word is usually distinguished from איש as Mensch from Mann. Its use here with the latter meaning is explained by Graetz as being due to the Greek ἄνθρωπος. But in Gen. ii. 22, 23, 25, iii. 8, 12, 17, 20, 21 it is opposed to 'woman' as here; and the Greek influence is entirely imaginary.

viii. 11. פתגם. Zirkel suggests that this is derived from φθέγμα. But the resemblance is accidental. ἐπίταγμα has also been proposed as the source of the Hebrew word! Delitzsch derives it from the Persian paigam, Arm. patgam, which is derived from the ancient Persian paiti-gama—'tidings,' 'news.' It occurs in Esth. i. 20, Dan. iii. 16[1].

xii. 13. הכל. Tyler illustrates this by the Mishnic formula

---

[1] See Bevan on the latter passage.

זה הכלל—"this is the general rule" or "the universal law." He
thinks that there is here "a pretty certain trace" of the influence
of Greek philosophical terminology; and he refers to τὸ καθόλου,
or τὸ ὅλον, which is used in the same sense in Plato,—'the
Universal' deduced from the Particular. So Siegfried.

But הכל probably refers, quite simply, to the teaching which the
Ḥasid has inserted in the body of the book,—"All that I wish to
say has been said already, and it comes to this: Fear God...etc."

It is thus, to say the least, very difficult to find any Graecisms
in the *language* of the book.

2. But the question whether Ḳoheleth shews traces of the
influence of Greek *thought* must now be considered; and it is
one of the most interesting that his work affords.

The most divergent views have been held on the subject.
On the one hand Renan asserts "Everything in the book can
be completely explained by the logical development of Jewish
thought. The author is very probably later than Epicurus; he
seems, however, not to have received an Hellenic education.
His style is purely Semitic. In all his language there is not a
single Greek word, not a single characteristic of Hellenism."
On the other hand Tyler finds abundant evidence of the clearest
kind of the influence of both Stoic and Epicurean philosophy.
There is nothing, in the nature of the case, to render the
supposition of Greek influence impossible. Alexander's con-
quests brought Eastern and Western thought into close contact;
and during the last century and a half before the Christian era
Palestine was saturated with Hellenism. Josephus (*c. Ap.* 1,
§ 22) witnesses to the esteem in which Jews were held by
Greeks. The book of Wisdom is strongly coloured by Greek
thought[1], and the writings of Philo. There are allusions to
Stoicism in 4 Maccabees, "and more or less probable vestiges
of Stoicism have been found in the oldest Jewish sibyl (c. 140)
and in the Targum of Onkelos[2]." Greek thought and feeling
was thus "in the air," and had profound effects on the whole
of Asia Minor[3].

[1] See Bois, *Origines de la Philosophie Judéo-Alexandrine*, pp. 211–309.

[2] Cheyne, *Job and Solomon*, p. 264.

[3] Moreover in the 1st century A.D. Josephus could say of the sect of the
Pharisees ἣ παραπλήσιός ἐστι τῇ παρ᾽ Ἕλλησι Στωικῇ λεγομένῃ (*Vita* § 2). He
describes their attempt to combine fatalism with moral responsibility (*Ant.*
xiii. 5, § 9. *B. J.* ii. 8, § 14), and their conduct of life according to the dictates
of reason (*Ant.* xviii. 1, § 3).

But when Hellenism met Judaism the effects were not all on one side; there was action and re-action. Greek thought, like the queen of Sheba, not only brought gifts, but gained much by her presence among the Hebrews. The Stoic school, though it arose on Hellenic soil from public lectures at Athens, was not a purely Greek product. Zeno of Citium, the first founder of Stoicism, was of Phoenician descent, and his adherents and successors came from Hellenistic (as distinct from Hellenic) quarters—such as Syria, Cilicia and Pontus, Seleucia on the Tigris, Sidon, Carthage and other towns[1]. Stoicism, therefore, had its roots in the Oriental, and especially the Semitic, character. And a careful study of Ḳoheleth's thought and language tends to shew, not that he wrote under the influence of Stoicism or of any other branch of Greek philosophy, but that *as a thinking Jew he had the makings of a Greek philosopher.* For Judaism and Stoicism could not have interpenetrated had there not been a common substratum of thought to render their juncture possible. It is shewn in E. Caird's *Evolution of Religion*[2] that each of the three religions, Buddhism, Stoicism and Judaism, was the result of a development from the Objective to the Subjective. Buddhism rose from the polytheistic worship of the powers of Nature in the Vedic hymns, through the pantheism of the Upanishads, to the religion of Gautama. The Greeks first 'humanised' their ancient pantheon—the gods who had personified the powers of Nature becoming gods who personified human aspirations and virtues; and thence, through the thought of an abstract fate or law of necessity, they passed to that of Reason, to that ideal of a spiritual principle which is implied in monotheism. And similarly, but on a higher plane, the Hebrew religion passed from primitive nature-worship, through the worship of an anthropomorphic Deity, to a purely spiritual conception of God. And thus it is that affinities can be found between these three religions owing to natural development, more than to any direct influence of one upon another[3]. But the Hebrew and the Greek religions,

---

[1] See article 'Stoics' in *Encycl. Brit.*

[2] Vol. i., Lectures vii., x., xiii., xiv.

[3] Dillon, *Sceptics of the O.T.*, pp. 122–129, notes a relationship between Ḳoheleth and Buddhism, though he offers very small ground for his belief that "Ḳoheleth was acquainted, and to some extent imbued, with the doctrines of Gautama Buddha."

having advanced with an analogous development, began, in
their later phases, to converge. And thus Ḳoheleth's affinities
with Greek thought are close and significant. His book
exhibits, more clearly than any other writing in the Old
Testament, that observant philosophical side of the Semitic
mind from which Stoicism sprang.

It is possible, indeed, to go behind Stoicism, and to compare
his thoughts with a phase of Greek philosophy with which it is
extremely improbable that he had ever come in contact—the
teaching of Xenophanes[1] of Colophon, the reputed founder of
the Eleatic school. In the article 'Xenophanes'[2] in *Encycl.
Brit.* the position is summed up as follows: "The wisdom of
Xenophanes, like the wisdom of the Hebrew Preacher, showed
itself, not in a theory of the universe, but in a sorrowful
recognition of the nothingness of things and the futility of
endeavour. His theism was a declaration not so much of the
greatness of God as rather of the littleness of man. His
cosmology was an assertion not so much of the immutability
of the One as rather of the mutability of the Many." Of the
few utterances of Xenophanes which survive, the following
invite comparison with Ḳoheleth: "From earth all things are,
and to earth all things return." This recalls not only Ḳoh. iii.
20, but also his manifold complaints as to the nothingness of
things, the empty vapour of human life, the uselessness of
striving after wisdom, wealth, or true happiness, for "all things
go to one place." Again, Xenophanes has no expectation that
any man can arrive at certain knowledge of anything. "No
man hath certainly known, nor shall certainly know, aught of
that which I say about the gods and about all things: for be
that which he saith ever so perfect, yet doth he not know it....
The gods did not reveal all things to mortals in the beginning:
long is the search ere man findeth that which is better." This
is a faithful mirror of Ḳoheleth's despair of arriving at wisdom
with all his searching (vii. 23 f. and viii. 17); and of the
scepticism of his reiterated questions Who knoweth? Who
can bring a man to see? Who can tell a man? (iii. 21 and
vi. 12). With regard to God, Xenophanes appears to be a
theologian rather than a philosopher, a monotheist rather than

---

[1] *flor.* c. 520 B.C.
[2] By Dr H. Jackson.

a pantheist—that is if the surviving fragments of his own
words are to be trusted, and not the statements made about
him by later writers. He maintains the unity of God by
opposing polytheism: but this need not imply the pantheistic
unity of Being afterwards taught by his successor Parmenides.
And it is exactly on this somewhat colourless monotheism that
Ḳoheleth takes his stand. He has lost the vitality of belief in
a personal God, which inspired the earlier prophets. He never
uses the personal Name JHVH, but always the descriptive
title 'Elohim' or 'the Elohim'[1]—the Deity who manifests
Himself in the cosmic forces of Nature. At the same time he
never commits himself to any definitely pantheistic statements,
though some of his utterances shew that if he had come into
immediate contact with any of the later Greek schools he
would probably have moved in that direction[2]. Ḳoheleth thus
occupies (what may be called) debateable ground between
Semitic and Greek thought. And it is possible that if more
of Xenophanes' writings were extant they might afford the
closest parallel to that of the Hebrew thinker. But as it is,
a more fruitful comparison can be drawn with the teaching of
the *Stoics*, of whom a fairly extensive knowledge is available.

At the outset it should be noticed that Ḳoheleth does not
shew the slightest trace of any borrowing from the Stoic
terminology[3]. It is true that for some expressions it would
be difficult to find Hebrew equivalents. But had he come
into immediate contact with Stoicism, he could not have
failed to shew some linguistic traces of its influence. But this
does not affect the possibility of his Hebrew mind containing
germs of Stoic ideas.

In iii. 10 f. he says that though man cannot discover God's
work from beginning to end, yet העולם has been placed in his
heart; he is endued with an innate longing to gaze into
eternity; he has in him something of the Infinite. This
thought, if carefully guarded, would not transgress the monotheism of the Jew. The writer of the 8th Psalm could rejoice
that man has been made to lack but little of Divinity—
ותחסרהו מעט מאלהים. And yet there is but a step from this to

---

[1] See p. 15.   [2] See below.

[3] Cheyne mentions εἱμαρμένη, πρόνοια, φαντασία, φύσις, φρόνησις, ἀρετή,—to
which might be added τὸ ὑποκείμενον, ὕλη, ἀξίωμα, τὸ ἡγεμονικόν, κρᾶσις, δύναμις,
λόγος (*ratio*), αἰτία, and others.

Stoic monism. God or Zeus is for the Stoic the world-soul, the all-pervading principle, the fiery and ethereal Pneuma, which is identical with the Universe; so that man is a limb, a part, of the Universal Being. The Infinite has been placed within him. Thus the Jewish philosopher Koheleth who had "eternity in his heart" foreshadowed the Jewish philosopher Spinoza who viewed things *sub specie aeternitatis*.

A direct corollary of Pantheism is Determinism. Since everything is derived from—since everything *is*—universal law and reason, every event, action, or phenomenon, is an inevitable result in the changeless causal connexion which governs the universe. There is no room for the free responsible action of any individual. And Koheleth, though he beats against the bars, feels that escape is impossible from the prison house of Fate. His book is full of this complaint. In iii. 1–9 he shews that every action, lying between the moment of a man's birth and the moment of his death, must occur at a fixed time—fixed not by himself but by the Universal Cause of all things, which is God; man, therefore, can hope for no solid result dependent on himself—"what profit can accrue to a worker from his labours?" This Universal Cause is infinitely stronger than man, so that it is useless to contend with it (vi. 10). "A crooked thing cannot be set right, and a defect cannot be numbered" (i. 15, vii. 13). "Everything which God doeth shall be for ever; to it nothing can be added, and from it nothing can be subtracted" (iii. 14). And as with the smallest events in life, so with the iron necessity of death. No one can restrain the wind, nor can anyone "have power over the day of death, and there is no discharge in the war" (viii. 8). "No man knoweth his time; as fish that are caught in an evil net, and as birds that are caught in a snare—like them are the sons of men entrapped at an evil time when it falleth upon them suddenly" (ix. 12).

But not only are *men* subject to an unalterable destiny. The whole creation groaneth and travaileth together in the same bondage. In the Stoic system this thought grew into an elaborate cosmology, partly derived from the earlier teaching of Heraclitus of Ephesus[1]. The infinite Pneuma exists in

---

[1] E. Pfleiderer, *Die Philosophie des Heraklit von Ephesus*, tries to shew that Koheleth borrows not only his teaching but many details of language from Heraclitus. This is ridiculed by Bois, pp. 109–128.

varying degrees of tension; by this variety of tension it brings into being—not outside but within itself—all the countless individual things which make up the universe. But this differentiation will not be for ever. All things will again be resolved into the primary substance; all things will ultimately be re-absorbed into God. Then, in due order, the last cycle of development will be reproduced in its minutest details, and so on for ever. If Ḳoheleth shewed any trace of this cycle doctrine in its Stoic form, it would be an indisputable proof that he had come under the immediate influence of the school. But though he shews no trace of the doctrine, he has in germ the underlying thought which contributed towards the formation of it. He is burdened with "the flux of all things"; it is the cry of i. 4–11—the unceasing changes in Nature which produce nothing new; in iii. 15 he says "That which is, hath already been: and that which is to be, already is; and God seeketh out that which is driven away,"—i.e. brings again and again on the scene of the present that which has been driven into the past by the lapse of time; in vi. 12 a man's life is said to be spent "like a shadow," as in Ps. cxliv. 4[1]; and, finally, the lament for the lost strength of youth in xii. 1–6 ends with an assertion (*v.* 7) which is not far removed from Stoic teaching. Some writers have thought that the latter half of xii. 7—"and the spirit shall return unto God who gave it"—is an orthodox interpolation, and is opposed to iii. 21. But so far from being an interpolation, the words are valuable as shewing how near Hebrew thought could approach to the Stoic tenet of the re-absorption of all beings into the Infinite Being. The meaning may be made clearer by reference to Ps. civ. 29, 30. The Psalmist has been speaking, not of men, but of birds, beasts and fish: and he says "Thou takest away (תוסף lit. Thou *gatherest* to Thyself) their breath: they die, and to their dust they return. Thou sendest forth Thy breath: they are created, and Thou renewest the face of the earth." And what is said in the Psalm of birds, beasts and fish Ḳoheleth here implies of men; and in iii. 21 he doubts if it is possible to assume that there will, in this respect, be the slightest difference between men and beasts.

---

[1] Note the difference of thought in viii. 13, where the *Ḥasid* assigns to the wicked alone short-lived days like a shadow.

As long as the Stoic system confined itself to natural science
it was possible for its supporters to maintain their theories.
But confronted with the *moral* aspect of life, they were thrust
between the horns of a dilemma. Either moral evil is the
direct result of natural causes, in which case it is unavoidable,
and therefore not really evil—or it is the result of a free-will
which makes man's soul in some sense independent of the law
of causation. Chrysippus, and at a later time Seneca, strove
hard to reconcile the two. The least unsuccessful of their
answers to the problem was that Providence, or Causation, or
God, works towards the general development and advantage of
the Universe as a *whole*; individual men or animals or things
are cared for only in that they are parts of the whole, and
conditioned by it. So that that which appears to men evil—
that which society must condemn and punish—is only part of
the universal Providence, leading to a good result for the
whole. Evil is not evil *per se*, but only in respect to individuals.

And Ḳoheleth, confronted, as he shews all through the
book, with the same problem of evil, is not satisfied with the
solution which had sufficed for many of his forefathers, and
which was offered by his orthodox annotator in ii. 26, iii. 17,
viii. 12, 13, xii. 14—the solution of Psalms i., xxxvii., lxxiii. and
many others—that the wicked are bound to suffer for their wrong-
doing, and the righteous to be saved and rewarded for their
righteousness. He inclines to the Stoic solution. Exactly the
same end comes to wise men and fools (ii. 14 b–16), righteous
and unrighteous (ix. 2, 3); there is no advantage in being swift
or strong, wise or clever or skilful (ix. 11, 12); nay the
very beasts are not distinguishable from man, for all have one
breath and go to one place (iii. 18–21). All created things are
infinitesimal fractions of the Universe. If, therefore, judgment
and righteousness are dethroned from their place by wickedness (iii. 16), if the righteous often suffer while the wicked
prosper (vii. 15, viii. 14), it is only that men, as individuals,
may realise their true insignificance in the eternal order of
things.

There is yet another point to which the lines of Hebrew and
Greek thought converge—the opposition of wisdom to folly.
The Stoics taught that the wise man is he who is governed by

reason: the foolish man is irrational, i.e. mad. There can be no mean between them. πᾶς ἄφρων μαίνεται. Those who have rational common-sense (ἐπιστήμη), and those who have it not, make up the whole of mankind. This division of the world between the wise and the foolish obtains throughout the whole of the Hebrew *Ḥokmah* Literature. 'Wisdom' sometimes approached very closely to Piety: "the fear of the Lord is wisdom, and to depart from evil is understanding" (Job xxviii. 28, cf. Prov. i. 7, Ps. cxi. 10). But the tendency was towards the philosophical conception of Wisdom as the personification of the Divine Providence which created the world and which governs and preserves it. Thus from one point of view the 'fool' was a sinner. But the nearer the idea of Wisdom approached that of the Greek *Logos*, the more was folly regarded as the senseless rashness of the man who acted contrary to reason and his own interests and destroyed himself—i.e. madness. And it is this aspect that is prominent in Ḳoheleth. Folly and madness (הוללות) are closely associated in i. 17, ii. 12, vii. 25, ix. 3; and in vii. 17 to be over-wicked is to be foolish and to bring premature destruction upon oneself.

Thus Ḳoheleth contains many of the 'seed-thoughts' from which Stoicism sprang. Some of them are found in earlier writings—Job, Proverbs and a few of the Psalms; but Ḳoheleth, as one of the latest of the Old Testament writers, has made the furthest advance along the line of philosophical development.

But the truth of the position maintained in this chapter, that he had not come under the immediate influence of Stoicism, has no stronger proof than the *scepticism* which he displays. The Stoic was in the highest degree dogmatic: he left, as he fondly hoped, nothing unexplained. But Ḳoheleth's earnestness, the real pain that he feels when he sees wickedness in the place of righteousness, his keen desire for the welfare of his fellow men, all combine to make him dissatisfied with a philosophical dogmatism. Man and beast are equally insignificant and go to the dust together; but have either of them a future? What of the 'hereafter' for which some were beginning to hope? He longs to discover God's work from beginning to end. But he cannot; and he gives expression to doubts which are really more religious than Stoic certainty. His despair of knowledge has been compared above with the temper of Xenophanes. But it may also be compared with that of Pyrrho and the later sceptics. Zeller sums up the teaching of Pyrrho under three heads: (1) the impossibility of knowledge, (2) the withholding of judgment, (3) imperturbability. Of these the first two find a close counterpart in Ḳoheleth.

(1) Although he feels that there is a wide gulf fixed between wisdom and folly, yet he discovers that his wisdom leads to nothing. His great experience of wisdom and knowledge proved to be a striving after wind (i. 17). The increase of wisdom and knowledge brings no advantage, but rather sorrow and grief (i. 18). Although wisdom intrinsically excels folly as light excels darkness, yet wise men and fools meet the same end. Why then did he take the trouble to be superlatively wise? It was all mere vapour (ii. 13–15). Nay, God has so arranged the nature of man (iii. 11), and of things in general (vii. 14), that it is impossible for man to discover what he really wants to know. In spite of failures Ḳoheleth does not give up the attempt. He says to himself *I will make myself wise.* But it is all of no use; wisdom is far removed from him; the knowledge of what exists is far off, and unfathomably deep (vii. 23, 24). The sole miserable result of his searchings and enquiries and calculations is the discovery that nearly all men, and all women, are unworthy of the name (vii. 25–28). The work of the Deity is as unknowable as the way of the wind, or the growth of the embryo in the mother's womb (xi. 5).

(2) This being so, the only attitude that he can adopt is one of scepticism (viii. 17). Six times he asks " Who knoweth ? " or similar questions (i. 19, iii. 21, 22 b, vi. 12, viii. 7, x. 14), not with the gleam of hope with which David asked[1] " Who knoweth whether God will shew me pity, that the child may live ?", but with a hopelessness implying that knowledge is impossible; man must give up the attempt to reach it.

(3) But of Pyrrhonic *imperturbability* Ḳoheleth has none. Had his question ' Who knoweth what is good for man in life ?' (vi. 12), been put to the Greek philosophers, their answers—though arrived at in different ways—would have been very similar.

The *Stoic* would say—It is to obtain peace and happiness by living in conformity to Nature. Man's attitude towards fate

[1] 2 Sam. xii. 22.

must be that of Cleanthes[1]. The wise course is to act voluntarily, not to be forced to act involuntarily, according to the dictates of Fate.

The *Epicurean* would reply—The obvious duty laid upon you by Nature is to seek happiness—i.e. pleasure. A certain amount even of self-denial and pain may be advisable, if the result of it is likely to be the prevention of greater suffering or trouble. The *summum bonum* is a serene freedom from physical, and more especially from mental, ills—in a word ἀταραξία.

The *Sceptic's* answer would be—The impossibility of knowledge makes it foolish to strive after it. By completely withholding his judgment (ἀφασία—ἐποχή—ἀκαταληψία) man can arrive at an absolute calmness, unruffled by passion or desire.

The contrast between these answers and Ḳoheleth's state of mind is evident. He flings himself against fate in despair. Every fresh wrong or injustice or inequality which he meets in the world causes a new pang. He "hates life" (ii. 17), and he "hates all his labour" that he has wrought (*v.* 18), and he "makes his heart despair of all his labour" (*v.* 20). And each time that his heart is driven back wounded and sore, he cries "there is no good in life except present enjoyment!" It is not the *summum bonum*; that is quite unattainable; he had made every possible attempt to reach it, and had failed (i. 12– ii. 11). It is simply a *minimum malum*, fortunately allowed to man by God, whereby "he shall not much remember the days of his life." (See ii. 24 f., iii. 12 f., 22, v. 18, 19, viii. 15, ix. 7–10, xi. 9 a, 10.)

To sum up. In the mind of Ḳoheleth were germinating thoughts which find striking parallels in the fragments of Xenophanes, in the teaching of the earlier Stoics, and in that of the Sceptics represented by Pyrrho. And this is but a concrete example of the state of mind which must have been wide-spread in the Hebrew race during the last two centuries before Christ. It shews—not that Ḳoheleth came under the immediate influence of any one Greek school, but—that the natural development of the two religions, Hebrew and Greek,

---

[1] ἄγου δέ μ' ὦ Ζεῦ καὶ σύ γ' ἡ Πεπρωμένη
ὅποι ποθ' ὑμῖν εἰμι διατεταγμένος·
ὡς ἕψομαί γ' ἄοκνος· ἢν δὲ μὴ θέλω
κακὸς γενόμενος οὐδὲν ἧττον ἕψομαι.

proceeded (broadly speaking) on the same lines, and produced certain affinities between them. Before Christ came, and proved in His own Person that the Divine Being was not only Infinite but also Personal, it was inevitable that all religious thought which was unrestrained by orthodoxy and ancient tradition should tend towards Pantheism—and its necessary corollary Fatalism. Before Christ rose from the dead, and proved in His own Person the certainty of a 'hereafter,' it was inevitable that, the key to life's problems not yet being found, all knowledge should be only a 'perhaps,' and human judgment should be perforce withheld.

But while the problems were the same to the Greeks and to Koheleth, his Semitic earnestness and his bitter disappointments at the wrongs of the world prevented him from acquiescing in the complacent ἀταραξία which the Greek schools accepted as their final aim.

It is unfortunate that Tyler, who points out some of the affinities with Stoicism, has tried to go further, and to shew that Koheleth was not only well acquainted with Stoicism, but that he was no less acquainted with Epicureanism, and that he set the teaching of the two schools over against each other to dissuade his readers from following either[1]!

It is exceedingly difficult to find the slightest trace of Epicureanism in the book.

As in the case of Stoicism, Koheleth makes no use of the scholastic terminology[2].

But the passages on which Tyler, and the writers who follow him, lay great stress are those in which present enjoyment is stated to be the only good thing for man. Siegfried goes so far as to assign all these passages to a Sadducean interpolator with Epicurean tendencies[3]. It has been shewn above that Koheleth's thought is totally distinct from that of Epicurus. Tyler represents Koheleth as teaching that "there

[1] Jerome, *Comm. on Eccl.*, says on ix. 7–9 that the author appears to reproduce the ideas of some Greek philosophers, in order to refute them. Bar Hebraeus († 1286) thinks that Solomon wished to defend in this book the opinions of Empedocles the Pythagorean.

[2] e.g. τὸ κανονικόν, πρόληψις, εἴδωλον, σύμπτωμα.

[3] See § 5, p. 30.

is no special divine care manifested on man's behalf. *If he is wise*[1], therefore, he will derive the utmost possible enjoyment from the world, during the continuance of his fleeting life." But he misconstrues his meaning. The expression is very different from Ḳoheleth's repeated complaint—"*There is nothing good* for a man except to eat and drink and enjoy himself."

In iii. 19–21 Tyler sees the Epicurean denial of the Stoic belief that man is distinguished from the beasts by a rational soul; and he thinks that *v.* 20 is not inconsistent with the Epicurean theory that the soul is composed of fine ethereal atoms, which are scattered into the ether at the moment of death. If it is not inconsistent with the theory, it is only because it has nothing to do with it. Ḳoheleth's meaning is perfectly clear: The bodies of men and beasts both return to dust; and what will happen to the spirit of each, no man can possibly say.

In v. 19 Tyler finds another trace of Epicurean doctrine. Since all the universe is composed of atoms, the Gods must also be of the same nature. They are composed of very fine atoms; they live in the empty spaces between the worlds; they have dwellings and nourishment; and they enjoy the pleasures of conversation—in the Greek language, or something like it. They are, in fact, men in an ideally perfect state, immortal and free from pain or want. They may, therefore, be conceived as enjoying life in a manner analogous to that of men. In v. 19 the influence of his religion causes Ḳoheleth to retain the name האלהים as a singular noun, but otherwise the phrase is strictly Epicurean. God has a joy answering to—antiphonal with—the joy of man.

A startling theory is thus built upon a very narrow foundation. Two or three suggestions have been made for the rendering of מענה בשמחת לבו (see notes). The simplest is that of Ewald and Nowack noticed above, p. 41; "God answers with—by means of—the joy of his heart." This use of the preposition finds an exact parallel in 1 K. xviii. 24: האלהים אשר יענה באש—"the God who shall answer by fire," i.e. by granting the fire for which we pray.

---

[1] The italics are mine.

LITERATURE. The following are among the principal writings which bear upon the question of Greek influence, either in language, or in philosophic thought.

a. Those who are more or less fully in favour of it:

Zirkel, *Untersuchungen über den Prediger*, Würzburg 1792. Hitzig, *Comm.* 1st Ed. 1847. Kleinert, *Der Prediger Salomo*, Berlin 1864, see *St. Kr.* 1883, 761–782. Graetz, *Comm.* 1871. Tyler, *Comm.* 1st Ed. 1874, 2nd Ed. 1899, see *Modern Review* 1882, 225–251, 614–617. Plumptre, *Comm.* 1881. Aug. Palm, *Q. über die nacharistotel. Philosophie*, Mannheim 1885. Kuenen, *Einl. A. T.* § 105. 9. Cornill, *Einl. A. T.* § 45. 4. E. Pfleiderer, *Die Philosophie des Heraklit von Eph., nebst einem Anhang über heraklitische Einflüsse im alttestamentlichen Koheleth und besonders im Buch der Weisheit*, 1886, see *JprTh.* 1887, 177–180. C. Siegfried, *Prediger u. Hoheslied* (in *Handkomm. z. A. T.*) 1898, see *ZwTh.* 1875, 284–291, 465–489. Wildeboer (in Marti's *Kurz. Handkomm. z. A. T.*) 1898.

b. Those who are opposed to it:

Fr. Delitzsch, *Bibl. Komm.* Vol. 4, 1875, p. 319. Renan, *l'Ecclésiaste*, 1882, p. 63. Nowack, in *Kurzgef. Exeget. Handbuch z. A. T.* (2nd Ed. of Hitzig), 1883, pp. 194 f. Cheyne, *Job and Solomon*, 1887, pp. 260–272. Menzel, *Der griechische Einfluss auf Prediger u. Weisheit Salomos*, Halle 1889, pp. 8–38. Bois, *Origines de la Philosophie Judéo-Alexandrine*, Paris, 1890, pp. 53–128. Article 'Ecclesiastes' in Hastings' *B.D.* by Peake; do. in *Encycl. Bibl.* by A. B. Davidson. Volz, *Th.LZ.* Feb. 3, 1900, review of Tyler's 2nd Ed.

2. Notes on Select Passages.

Chap. I.

Ch. i. *v.* 4. לעולם 'in perpetuity,' 'continuously,' i.e. as contrasted with the changing generations of men. The expression does not imply the *eternity* of the material world, and is not opposed to the writer's feeling of the 'flux of all things,' which, had he been under the immediate influence of the Stoics, might have led him to their cycle doctrine. See p. 48.

v. 7. שהנחלים. The relative שׁ cannot mean 'whence,' as Σ Vg. Luth. A. V., but 'whither'—cf. Num. xiii. 27, 1 K. xii. 2; and שם means 'thither'—cf. 1 S. ix. 6, Jer. xxiii. 3. Hier. and Tg. explain the method of circulation—that the waters run back from the sea by hidden channels (*venae*) to their sources. Ibn Ezra prefers evaporation. For both cf. Lucret. v. 261–272.

v. 8. יגעים not 'wearisome,' Σ κοπώδεις, but 'wearied,' as in Dt. xxv. 18, 2 S. xvii. 2, the only other passages in which the word occurs. All creation shares with man the weariness caused by unceasing, but aimless, change.

לדבר 'No man can utter it'—the weariness.

v. 10. יש דבר שיאמר, see App. ii. p. 138. שיאמר. Elliptical for שׁ ע"ליו. Cf. xii. 1, Ex. xxii. 8.

זה חדש הוא. זה is not governed by ראה. The expression approaches the Mishnic זֶהוּ in a predicative sentence. Cf. *Kelim* v. 10, *B^ekoroth* vii. 5. It occurs i. 17, ii. 23, iv. 8, v. 18, vi. 2.

כבר 'already.' NH and Aram. In BH only Koh. ii. 12, 16, iii. 15, iv. 2, vi. 10, ix. 6, 7. In Syr. and Tg. sometimes 'perhaps.'

היה. Sing. after the collective עולמים, as in ii. 7 a. Cf. Ges. K. § 145 *u*.

v. 14. רעות רוח. The expression occurs seven times in Ḳoh. The derivation of רעות from רעע 'break' may be discarded at once, though it was the favourite derivation in early times. Tg. תבירות. Rashi שבר. Vg. *Afflictio.* A. V. Vexation.

Derived from רעה 'feed,' it may have one of two meanings:

1. Lit. 'feeding on wind'; so Aq. Σ Θ. In his Comm. on Ḳoh. Jerome says "Rooth Aquila et Theodotion νομὴν, Symmachus βόσκησιν, transtulerunt."

2. From the sense of 'feed on' comes that of 'delight in[1],'
and so 'be eager for,' 'strive after'—which is probably Ḳoh.'s
meaning. Cf. Prov. xv. 14 ∥ בקש, and especially Hos. xii. 2
רדף קדים ∥ רעה רוח. The cognate רעיון occurs with the same
meaning: i. 17, iv. 16 רוח "ר; ii. 22 לבו "ר.

v. 15. Perhaps, as Renan suggests, an aphorism well known
at the time.

לתקן. Dan. iv. 33 and frequently in Syr. Tg. In BH only
vii. 13, xii. 9 (both Piel). Siegfried may be right in emending to
לְהִתָּקֵן?, parallel with להמנות, as ᴳ ἐπικοσμηθῆναι with ἀριθμηθῆναι.

v. 16. הגדלתי והוספתי. Coordination to express 'I greatly
multiplied'; as in iv. 1, 7. Cf. Ges. K. § 120, *d* and *e*.

על ירושלם. Ḳoheleth finds it difficult to wear consistently
his Solomonic disguise—which, indeed, he deliberately throws
off in ii. 12. The expressions (here and in ii. 7, 9) "*all* that
were before me over J."—"in J."—are unsuitable as referring
to David and Saul, and make it probable that he himself really
held some high official position in the city. See pp. 9, 10.

v. 17. ואתנה. *Waw* consecutive. iv. 1, 7 are the only other
instances in the book. In NH it is unknown.

ודעת. According to the Masoretes it is an infinitive = ולדעת,
"to know wisdom, and to know madness and folly." But the
balance of the verse is better maintained if (with ᴳ Pesh. Tg.) it
is treated as a substantive, and pointed וָדַעַת. Ḳoheleth determined to know 'wisdom' and 'knowledge' on the one hand,
and their opposites 'madness' and 'folly' on the other.

הוללות, ii. 12, vii. 25. The sing. הוללה nowhere occurs. In
this passage ᴳ renders by a plur., but in the other two by a
sing. In all three, however, the word should probably be
pointed הוֹללוּת, as in x. 13. In each case the form in וּת– may
have been due to סכלות which stands in close connexion with
it. See on x. 13.

שכלות for סכלות, here only. Hier. *stultitiam*. But ᴳ Pesh.
Tg. Venet. all render 'understanding.' Cf. משׂמרות xii. 11.

ודעת···ואתנה. On the clause see App. II. p. 156.

v. 18. ויוסיף. For the construction cf. Prov. xii. 17,
xviii. 22.

---

[1] Gesenius compares Cicero, *Pis.* 20, "his ego rebus pascor, his delector, his
perfruor."

CHAP. II.

Ch. ii. *v.* 3. לִמְשׁוֹךְ. Hitzig endeavours to explain this, in connexion with the following נהג; as a metaphor from a beast of burden drawing a cart. But משך is evidently used in the NH meaning 'refresh.' Delitzsch refers to *Ḥagigah* 14 a: בעלי אגדה מושכין לבו של אדם כמים—"the Haggadists refresh the heart of men like water."

ולבי נהג בחכמה. A circumstantial clause, forming a parenthesis, so that ולאחז is a second infinitive dependent on תרתי. נהג (in BH 'drive') is here used, like משך, with a force peculiar to NH. In the Mishna it has two shades of meaning—1. 'act' or 'behave,' cf. *Abod. Zar.* iii. 4: 2. 'be accustomed,' cf. *Pᵉsaḥ.* iv. 1. These meanings pass into each other; so that the expression here may be rendered 'my heart *behaving as usual* with wisdom.'

v. 5. פרדסים. See § 8, p. 40. Cant. iv. 13, Neh. ii. 8 only (both in sing.). In the Mishna the plur. is פרדסות.

v. 6. ברכות. In Neh. ii. 14 the 'king's pool' is mentioned, which appears as 'Solomon's pool' in Jos. *B. J.* v. 4. 2.

מהם masc. after ברכות, as Gen. xxxii. 16, Job i. 14 *al.* Cf. Ges. K. § 145 *u.*

עצים. An accusative qualifying, or particularising, an intrans. verb. Cf. Is. v. 6, Prov. xxiv. 31.

v. 7. מקנה. See Baer *Qu. Vol.* p. 61.

v. 8. שדה ושדות. For this collocation of numbers to express a large or indefinite quantity cf. Jud. v. 30 רחם רחמתים (and Moore's note).

Of the numerous explanations of the ἅπαξ λεγ. שדה the following may be noticed[1]:

(1) 'Cup-bearers.' 𝔊 ⊙ οἰνοχόον καὶ οἰνοχόας. Hier. Comm. *Ministros vini et ministras*, apparently reading the words as שָׁדֶה וְשָׁדוֹת, and connecting them with √ שרא 'pour.' Hier. transliterates SADDA and SADDOTH.

(2) 'Cups.' Aq. κυλίκον καὶ κυλίκια. Σ (Hier.) *Mensarum species et appositiones.* Hier. *Scyphos et urceos in ministerio ad vina fundenda.* Tg. "pipes which pour tepid water and pipes which pour hot water" (!).

[1] For others see Delitzsch's commentary *in loc.*

(3) 'Musical instruments.' Kimchi כלי זמר. Luther *allerlei saitenspiel.*

(4) 'Chariot' or 'Litter.' Rashi on *Erub.* 30 b.

(5) 'Lady' or 'concubine.' This meaning is arrived at in various ways: (a) from the meaning 'chariot.' Parallels are suggested in Arab. *z'ynat*, a woman's carriage, and so the woman herself; Turk. *odaliske*, a woman's chamber, and so 'woman.' (b) שׁדּה = שׁידה from √ שׁוד 'be violent' (cf. Ps. xci. 6), and so 'be strong or lordly.' Arab. *sayyid* (cf. Span. *cid*) 'a lord,' fem. *sayyidat* 'a lady'; whence the vulgar Arab. *sidi* 'my lord,' *sitti* 'my lady.' Siegfried notes that in the Spanish Arabic of Petro de Alcala *sitt* denotes 'concubine.'

Whether any of these derivations be correct or not, the meaning 'concubine' seems clearly required by the context; for, firstly, the words appear to be explanatory of תענגות בני האדם, and secondly, an enumeration of the luxuries of a Solomon would be incomplete without a reference to his harem[1].

v. 9. והוספתי. Siegfried emends הגדלתי וה״ מעשׂי in accordance with i. 16, ii. 4; but this is unnecessary. The object of the verb is the idea contained in גדלתי—'I grew great and continually greater.' Cf. Ges. K. § 120 d.

v. 11. ופניתי אני בכל. For the pregnant construction 'turn to and fix the attention upon' cf. Job vi. 28 פנו בי.

שעמלתי לעשׂות. Cf. Gen. ii. 3, Joel ii. 20 f. On the gerund, see Ges. K. § 114 o.

v. 12. הוללות. See on i. 17, x. 13.

Siegfried transposes the two halves of the verse—'there was no profit under the sun (*v.* 11), for what can men (do) that come after the king? That which they have already done.' This, he says, supplies the reason for *v.* 11, the reason being 'that Solomon, who is here introduced as speaking, has no certainty that his work, on which he has bestowed such labour, will abide.' But it is difficult to see how this meaning can be derived from the words.

Euringer would read עֲשׂוֹהוּ (cf. Ex. xviii. 18), which he takes to be the reading which gave rise to עָשׂוּהוּ MT, and עָשׂהוּ Hier. Pesh.,—'that which was long ago his doing.'

But the versions point to a simpler explanation:

[1] Euringer (*Der Masorahtext des Koheleth*) suggests the emendation שָׂרָה וְשָׂרוֹת, which is simple and attractive, but without support.

𝕲 ὅτι τίς ἄνθρωπος ὃς ἐπελεύσεται ὀπίσω τῆς βουλῆς; τὰ ὅσα ἐποίησεν αὐτήν. [βουλή here and in Σ is a rendering of the Aram. מְלַךְ, cf. Dan. iv. 24.]

Θ...ὃς ἐλεύσεται ὀπίσω τοῦ βασιλεως, σὺν τὰ ὅσα ἐποίησαν αὐτήν.

Hier. C....qui possit ire post regem atque factorem suum.

Pesh...."after the king in judgment, still more with his Maker."

B'resh. Rab. ‎אֶת אֲשֶׁר כְּבָר עָשָׂהוּ.

Tg. is a loose paraphrase, but apparently followed the MT.

Two points require notice: (1) that ‎עָשׂוּהוּ is variously read ‎עָשׂוּהוּ (or ‎עָשָׂהוּ) Θ, ‎עָשָׂהוּ Pesh. Hier., ‎עָשָׂהוּ 𝕲; (2) that ‎כבר is omitted in all except Tg. and *B'resh. Rabb.* It seems therefore that the reading ‎עָשָׂהוּ explains the others; and the passage will run "What is man [i.e. what can man do] that cometh after the king? That which he [the king] hath done" [or with ‎כבר "hath already done"].

Delitzsch's rendering "him whom they made so long ago" involves an awkwardness in the use of ‎עָשָׂה; and as a description of Solomon the phrase is somewhat pointless; moreover it necessitates the retention of the doubtful ‎כבר.

For the redundant ‎אֵת אֲשֶׁר עָשׂוּהוּ cf. Zech. xii. 10; but see Ges. K. § 138 *e*, footnote 1.

v. 15. ‎כְּמִקְרֶה. So Baer; but ‎מִקְרֶה in the Mantua edition. Cf. *v.* 7, iii. 19.

‎גַּם אָנִי. Cf. Gen. xxiv. 27. Ges. K. § 135 *e*.

‎אָז. Cf. Jer. xxii. 15.

v. 16. ‎בְּשֶׁכְּבָר הַיָּמִים הַבָּאִים. Ḳoh. takes his stand at a point in the future, and looks back into the past.

‎בְּשֶׁכְּבָר. Cf. ‎בְּשֶׁל אֲשֶׁר viii. 17, ‎מִשֶּׁתְּדוּר *v.* 4.

‎הַיָּמִים. *Accus. temporis.* Ges. K. § 118 *i*.

‎וְאֵיךְ. Winckler's emendation ‎וְאַךְ is quite unnecessary. Ḳoh. uses the style of the taunting Ḳinah. Cf. Is. xiv. 4, Ez. xxvi. 17.

v. 20. ‎לְיַאֵשׁ. See Baer. In BH elsewhere only in Niphal. Pael occurs in Aram. and Hithp. in NH.

v. 22. ‎הֹוֶה. The participle occurs in BH Neh. vi. 6 only.

‎שֶׁהוּא. See Baer. Cf. ‎שֶׁהֵם iii. 18.

v. 24. ‎שֶׁיֹּאכַל. Evidently to be emended ‎מִשֶּׁיֹּאכַל; it arose either from the dropping of the ‎מ after ‎בָּאָדָם, or under the influence of iii. 13.

‎וְשָׁתָה וְהֶרְאָה. The best MSS of 𝕲, and Pesh., point to a reading ושישתה וישראה (see App. II. p. 153). If this was the original reading, the similarity of the first two syllables וישיש may have caused one of them to be dropped, forming ושתה, and then והראה would arise to assimilate the constructions; or, as before, the corruption may have been due to iii. 13.

v. 25. יחוש. In NH and Aram. חוש, שא, means 'feel pain'; Tg. here חששא. Hence it may denote any kind of feeling; here it is one of enjoyment. On 𝔊 see App. II. p. 153.

חוץ ממני 'apart from—without—me' is meaningless, and the rendering 'more than I' is impossible. There is strong evidence (𝔊, Pesh., S. H., Hier. C., Copt.) for the emendation ח" ממנו 'apart from Him,' i.e. God. The expression is unique in BH, corresponding to Aram. בר מן, هﻰ لبد.

v. 26. נם זה הבל ורעות רוח must be a gloss. It is meaningless in connexion with the words either of Ḳoheleth or the *Ḥasid.* This, and the similar addition in vii. 6, appear to be the only instances of glosses introduced after the book had been completed in its triple form.

CHAP. III.

Ch. iii. *vv.* 2–8. It has been suggested that the 14 couplets were not originally in their present haphazard order. The simplest re-arrangement would be to transpose 2 b and 3 a, and to make 5 a precede 4 a. The couplets then fall into groups:— a pair of contrasts whose subject is human life and death (birth and death, killing and healing) are followed by four sets of three: (1) the treatment of landed property, (2) emotions of joy and sorrow, (3) the preservation and loss of property in general, (4) emotions of friendship and enmity. But such artificial arrangements are alien to the temper of Ḳoheleth.

v. 5. להשליך אבנים implies the marring of good soil.

כנוס אבנים. Cf. Is. v. 2.

The three hostile actions in 2 b, 3 b, 5 a are found in 2 Kin. iii. 19, 25.

v. 11. יפה. In classical Heb. 'beautiful'; but in NH it has the more general force which belongs to καλὸς—good, proper, fitting. Cf. v. 17.

את העלם. This passage is discussed by Hitzig (*Th. St. Kr.* 1839, p. 513), Umbreit (do. 1846, p. 417), and W. Grimm (*ZwTh.*

1880, p. 274). The various methods of treating the words are
of three kinds:

(1) Emendations. Hitzig invents a word עֶלֶם, to correspond
to the Arab. *'ilam* 'knowledge.' Bickell proposes הַעֲלֻם 'that
which is hidden.' Cheyne, הָעִנְיָן 'the task.'

(2) The second class of explanations follow 𝔊 τὸν αἰῶνα,
giving עלם the late meaning 'world' which it bears in Pesh.
Tg. Mishn.

Gesenius and others understand it of 'worldliness' (cf.
1 John ii. 16) or of worldly duties considered as good things
(Luther): but these are impossible. A favourite explanation
has been that God has placed the world in man's heart, so that
his heart is "a Microcosm in which the great world is mirrored."
So Ewald, and formerly Cheyne. The latter (*Job and Solomon*,
p. 210) quotes Bacon's *Advancement of Learning*—"God has
framed the mind like a glass, capable of the image of the
universe, and desirous to receive it as the eye to receive light."

But not only does עלם[1] occur nowhere else in BH with the
NH sense of 'world,' while it is found in six other passages in
Ḳoh. with a temporal force—but it is, in this passage, in evident
contrast with the word עת 'time,' which occurs 30 times in the
preceding verses of the chapter.

(3) 'Eternity.' Zöckler understands it of man's inborn
intuition of God's eternal Being and government. Cf. Rom.
i. 19.

Delitzsch gives *desiderium aeternitatis*; man knows that
everything has its appointed עת, but there is planted within
him an impulse towards that which is beyond time.

But the best explanation is that of Grimm, who is followed
by Nowack and Wildeboer. He suggests *notio aeternitatis*.
The popular conception of 'eternity' is that of unlimited time—
innumerable עתות stretching into the past and future[2]. Man
can see that God has made everything excellent in its own
proper time—he can understand, that is, individual עתות in
which God's working is revealed to him; but God has also
placed in his heart (i.e. mind) a conception of the sum-total of
the עתות; "but in such a way that" (מבלי אשר) he cannot

---

[1] See Dalman, *The Words of Jesus*, Engl. transl. pp. 162–166.

[2] Cf. Cicero, *De juvent.* i. 26, "Tempus est pars aeternitatis."

"discover"—understand the true inwardness of—"the work which God doeth from beginning to end."

סוף. Late Heb. for קץ, vii. 2, xii. 13; Joel ii. 20; 2 Chr. xx. 16 only.

v. 12. ולעשות טוב. Some have thought that this is a Graecism, representing εὖ πράττειν. But see § 8, p. 40.

v. 15. ואשר להיות. Cf. Ges. K. § 114 h, i.

יבקש את נרדף. God seeks out, and brings again on to the scene of the present, that which has been driven into the past by the lapse of time.

But in early times נרדף was universally considered as masculine—𝔊 Aq. τὸν διωκόμενον, Σ ὑπὲρ τῶν ἐκδιωκομένων, and even B. Sira v. 3 כי י״י מבקש נרדפים. So Pesh. Tg. And Lucifer Calar. has et deus requiret eum qui persecutionem patitur.

v. 16. הרשע and הצדק. 𝔊 reads them as הָרֶשַׁע and הַצַּדִּק; so Lucifer, vidi sub sole locum judicii, illic impius, et locum justi, illic impius[1]. The following verse was evidently the cause.

v. 17. שם. (1) This has been explained as referring to a future time; Hier. in tempore judicii, in futurum judicium. Tg. ביום דינא רבא.

(2) Some writers understand שם to mean 'with God'; but only one, equally doubtful, expression is adduced to support it—Gen. xlix. 24 משם רעה אבן ישראל.

(3) Del. Now. Wildeb. and others read שָׂם 'he hath appointed,' cf. Ex. xxi. 13. This makes good sense; but a strong objection to it is the distance at which the word stands from its object עת. Ḳoheleth, though his style is not classical, is never awkward or unrhythmical. A verb, especially a monosyllable, in such a position is as unlikely in Hebrew as it would be in English.

(4) 𝔊ᴮ omits it (see App. II. p. 141); and it is not impossible that שם was a mere corruption, arising from the accidental doubling either of the last syllable of the foregoing מעשה or the first of the following אמרתי.

v. 18. על דברת with an ellipse of 'it is' or 'it happens,' referring to the state of things described in v. 16. Siegfr. unnecessarily inserts שָׂם, having omitted it at the end of v. 17. על דברת occurs vii. 14, viii. 2 only. Classical Heb. על דבר or על דברי.

[1] Reading εὐσεβής as ἀσεβής.

לברם Inf. Kal, √ ברר, cf. לְרֹד Is. xlv. 1, כִּשֵּׁד Jer. v. 26.

The root meaning is 'purify'; Venet. καθαιρεῖν αὐτούς, cf. Ass. *barâru* 'be shining.' 𝕲 διακρινεῖ, Hier. C. *separat*, adopt the secondary meaning 'choose,' 'select,' found in 1 Chr. vii. 40, ix. 22, xvi. 41, Neh. v. 18 only (always partcp.). BDB (with R.V.) "that God may prove them," as Vg. *ut probaret eos*, and Tg. "that there may come upon them plagues and evil diseases to try them and prove them."

But this is without parallel in BH; and (if the gist of the passage has been rightly explained in § 4, pp. 15, 17) it is not Ḳoheleth's meaning at all.

In NH the word frequently denotes 'make clear,' 'bring to light,' cf. *Shabb.* 74 a, 138 a; the adj. ברור *Sanh.* 7 b; and the Rabbinic על בוריו *perspicue*. And this gives the required sense here. The rendering of A.V. is perfectly adequate, "that God might manifest them," i.e. shew them in their true light—as beasts.

ולראות. Tg. למחזי: "that He [God] might see whether they would turn in repentance." But all the other versions express 'to shew,' i.e. וְלִרְאֹות (= ולהראות), which should probably be read.

שֶׁהַם, cf. שֶׁהוּא ii. 22. Baer accentuates as follows: שֶׁהֵם בְּהֵמָה הֵמָּה לָהֶם, "that they are beasts—they for their part," the last two words being ironical; "even men who vaunt their superiority over the beasts!" (Ewald *höchstselbst*.) If the text is to stand this is the best explanation of it.

Delitzsch: "they in and of themselves,"—viewed as mere men—reads too much into the words.

But it is probable that the text is corrupt. In 𝕲 the following verse begins with καί γε αὐτοῖς οὐ [ὡς S, om. AC, ? ὅτι] συνάντημα... which suggests that גם להם is the true reading at the end of *v.* 18, the corruption המה having been due to the same syllables in the preceding word. גם להם "even to themselves" will mean "even in their own estimation."

v. 19. כי 1°. It is not improbable that οὐ in 𝕲ᴮ may be an intentional corruption of ὅτι for the sake of orthodoxy. Some alterations in 𝕲 are undoubtedly of this nature, cf. xi. 9. But since the unorthodox conclusion συνάντημα ἐν αὐτοῖς is left untampered with, it is possible that the error was accidental.

כי מקרה וג׳. It is clear that מקרה must have the same

meaning throughout the verse; and the words, therefore, cannot be rendered "for a chance are the sons of men and a chance are the beasts, and one chance is unto them." מקרה is in each case the 'mischance,' the 'catastrophe' of death. All the versions treat the first and second מקרה as in the construct state. A proverbial sentence is thus formed, after the manner of Prov. xxv. 20, 25, xxvi. 9, 14, 21 etc., which must be rendered "as the mischance of the sons of men, so is the mischance of the beasts." According to Baer this may be spelt מִקְרֶה, cf. ii. 15.

ומותר. The word is unique in Ḳoh. It occurs only in Prov. xiv. 23, xxi. 5, in both of which it assumes this hiphilic form in opposition to another hiphilic form מַחְסוֹר. Ḳoh. elsewhere uses יתרון and יותר; and since in this passage 𝔊, Σ and Θ all render the clause as an interrogation, מותר should be emended to מה יותר (cf. vi. 8, 11): "what superiority hath the man over the beast? None!"

v. 21. העלה...הירדת. That the ה in these words should be the article (A.V.) is rendered impossible both by the sense of the passage, and by the presence of the pronoun היא. Following the versions the words must be pointed interrogatively, הֲירדת and הַעלה: "who knoweth with regard to the spirit of the sons of men (casus pend. as in v. 13) whether it goeth upwards, and the spirit of the beast whether it goeth downwards to the earth?"

On the connexion of thought between this and xii. 7 see § 8, p. 48.

CHAP. IV.

Ch. iv. v. 1. העשׁקים. Cf. Am. iii. 9, Job xxxv. 9. The pointing here is evidently intentional, to distinguish the abstract subst. 'oppressions' from the pass. particp. in v. 2.

ומיד עשקיהם כח. It is possible to supply אין from the preceding clause: "and from the hand of their oppressors (there was no) power (of deliverance)." But this is awkward. A.V., R.V. "and on the side of their oppressors was power," making מיד equivalent to על יד; but there is no other instance to support this. The same sense, however, can be reached in another way: "and from the hand of their oppressors (went forth) power." Gins., Del., Now., Siegfr. give כח the meaning 'violence' (Vg.

violentiae), which it nowhere else bears. Ḳoh. simply means that as the oppressed had no helper, for the oppressors might was right. Pesh. omits the *waw* of ומיד.

v. 2. ושבח. See Ges. K. § 113 *gg*. Emendations משבח (Siegfr.), ומשבח (Euringer), are unnecessary.

עד הן (*v.* 3) = עד הנה. Cf. ערן. עד הנה = עדנה. Mishn. עֲדַיִן.

v. 3. את אשר ערן וג׳. The verb is mentally supplied from the foregoing שבח.

v. 4. כשרון. 'Skill,' 'ability' as in ii. 21. In v. 10 it rather means the success or profit which ability earns. Cf. verb Ḳal xi. 6, Hiph. x. 10.

היא. The nearest English equivalent for this predicative construction is: "I saw all the labour and all the skilful work that *it meant* the jealousy etc."—it was both incited by it and resulted in it.

קנאת איש מרעהו. This might mean 'the jealousy felt by a man because of his neighbour' (i.e. because of his neighbour's successes). But since קנא is usually followed by ב or את with the object of jealousy, it is better to take איש as an objective acc.: "the jealousy felt for a man by [proceeding from the heart of] his neighbour."

v. 6. נחת acc. of the thing measured, cf. מלא כף קמח 1 Kin. xvii. 12.

v. 10. יפלו. Strictly speaking, they do not both fall. The plur. denotes an indefinite singular. Ges. K. § 124 *o*.

אי לו = ואילו, Alas for him! cf. x. 16. For the pleonastic dat. ethic. see Ges. K. § 119 *s*.

v. 12. יתקפו האחד. The noun is in apposition to, and further defines, the pron. suffix, cf. Ex. xxxv. 5, Ges. K. § 131 *m*.

The suffix in נגדו refers to the unexpressed subj. of יתקפו: "if (someone) overpower the solitary man, (yet) two can withstand him" (i.e. the aggressor).

יעמדו נגדו. Cf. Dan. x. 13.

v. 13. מסכן, "poor" ix. 15, 16 only. מִסְכֵּנֻת Dt. viii. 9. See BDB s.v.

v. 14. Having described the youth as 'poor and wise,' Ḳoheleth cites two facts, each introduced by כי, to justify the two adjectives. He was wise—*for* he managed to escape from prison to be king; he was poor—*for* even in his kingdom (i.e. in the kingdom that he afterwards gained) he was born poor.

This is simpler than (with Del., Now., Siegfr.) to take כי גם as meaning 'although,' and the suffix in מלכותו as referring to the old king:—The youth gained the throne, although in his (i.e. the old king's) reign he (the youth) had been born poor. For this use of כי גם, viii. 12 is cited.

Σ and Tg.[1] cause still further confusion by referring the יצא clause to the youth, and the נולד clause to the old king.

הסורים is for האסורים 'the prisoners,' cf. הרמים 2 Chr. xxii. 5, מסורת Ez. xx. 37 (but text doubtful).

נולד may possibly have the Mishnic meaning 'became.' Tg. אתעביד, Vg. inopia consumatur. So Rashi, Ginsb., A.V.

v. 15. הילד השני must mean "the second youth." Now., Del. take השני as 'the second one' in apposition to הילד who succeeded the old king who was the first. The only parallels which Del. offers are from N. T. Greek: Mat. viii. 21 ἕτερος τῶν μαθητῶν, Lk. xxiii. 32 ἕτεροι κακοῦργοι δύο. Even more improbable is Ewald's suggestion that השני has the sense of המשנה in Gen. xli. 43. Bickell and Siegfr. omit the word as a gloss, the former suggesting that it is a reminiscence of the foregoing proverbs!

The imperfs. יעמד, and ישמחו in v. 16, are explained in § 3, p. 11, where the historical reference is discussed.

v. 16. לפניהם. Ewald strives to give this a temporal sense— "all the people who were before them." Bickell, with the same object, supplements the verse with a long insertion from his own pen.

But it is simpler to render "there was no end to all the people before whom [at whose head] he was," referring to the second youth. Cf. 1 S. xviii. 16. So Tg. דהוה מדבר קדמיהון.

כי might mean 'surely'; but Ķoh. never uses the particle thus. It rather expresses the thought that the historical facts just mentioned are only another illustration of the vanity of human strivings—"for this [popularity and success] also is a vapour."

---

[1] In Tg. the 'old king' is Nimrod, and the 'youth' Abraham; "for Abraham went forth from the race of idol-worshippers and reigned over the land of the Canaanites; for even in the days of Abraham's reign Nimrod became poor in the world."

CHAP. IV. 17, V.

Ch. iv. 17. וקרוב לשמע "and to draw near to hear is better than..." For the absol. inf. cf. היטיב Jer. x. 5, המשל Job xxv. 2; and for the ellipse of טוב cf. ix. 17. Aq. Pesh. Vg. Tg. take קרוב with an imperatival force, a new sentence beginning with מתת.

מתת הכסילים זבח. The only grammatical rendering of these words is "than that fools should give a sacrifice."

Pesh. transposes the substantives: "than the gift of the sacrifice of fools"; and Siegfr. would make this emendation.

The versions are divided between מִמַּתַּת (𝔊 ὑπὲρ δόμα. Pesh. ܡܢ ܡܘܗܒܬܐ) and מַתַּת (Aq. Θ δόμα, Hier. *donum*). The latter is impossible, as the writer cannot have said that "sacrifice is the gift of fools"; but 𝔊, which also has θυσία σου, represents a reading וק׳ ל׳ ממתת הכ׳ זבחך—"and draw near to hear; better than the gift of fools is thy sacrifice," i.e. if thou draw near to hear, thy sacrifice is better than the gift of fools. This was perhaps the original reading.

אינם יודעים לעשות רע evidently cannot be rendered on the analogy of v. 13. "They are ignorant, so that they do evil" (Del.) is impossible. Now., Wright follow Renan in adding כי אם before לעשות. But the simplest emendation is מלעשות (Siegfr.); the מ would easily drop out after יודעים[1].

Ch. v. 5. לחטיא "to cause thy flesh to incur the penalty of sin," Dt. xxiv. 4, Is. xxix. 21. Tg. "to cause the judgment of Gehenna upon thy flesh." Physical punishment was the usual conception of Divine retribution.

המלאך, i.e. the priest. The use of the word may have been suggested by Mal. ii. 7, but the coincidence cannot be taken as indicating the date of Ḳoh. Compare the use of ἄγγελος for 'bishop' in the N. T. Apoc.

But 𝔊 πρὸ προσώπου τοῦ Θεοῦ and Pesh. ܩܕܡ ܐܠܗܐ point to an early reading לפני האלהים. This would still mean 'in the presence of the priest,' as God's representative, just as in Ex. xxi. 6, xxii. 7, 8, 27 judges or rulers are called Elohim. The alteration to המלאך may have been made from fear of irreverence.

---

[1] 𝔊ᵃ Pesh. boldly cut the knot by rendering רע as καλόν, ܛܒ.

שגנה, x. 5. Frequent in the priestly laws in Leviticus and
Numbers, for an unintentional misdemeanour for the expiation
of which special offerings were commanded. In the present
case a man who has failed to pay a vow might be tempted to
offer the excuse כי שגגה היא because the offering enjoined for
such a case was smaller than that which he had vowed.

v. 6. כי את האלהים ירא is meaningless in its present position,
and כי should follow a negative. It is evidently the conclusion
of *v.* 5.

The intervening proverb seems to be corrupt. R.V. renders
"for *thus it cometh to pass* through the multitude...etc.," cf.
the construction in iii. 18. It is also possible to render "for
in the multitude of dreams there are also vanities and many
words" (Ewald; so apparently Σ, reading הבלים without *waw*).
But the proverb appears to be a doublet of that in *v.* 2; and it
seems probable that a slightly varying form of *v.* 2 was written
in the margin, and found its way into the text. In *v.* 2 החלום is
a *result* and not a cause; and the emendation suggests itself
here : כי ברב [ענין] חלומות והבלים [ב]דברים הרבה[^1].

v. 7. שמר. Each official 'is watching,' i.e. is jealously on
the look out for any action of a subordinate that may hurt his
interests.

גבהים may be either a plural *majestatis*, referring to the
king, or it may simply describe the numerous grades of officials
rising one above another.

Siegfried assigns the passage to the Ḥasid. Emending שמר
to נִשְׁמָר, he explains it as follows: each official "is on his guard
against the other"—each is afraid of opposing a higher one in
the interests of the poor; but this state of things will not last,
for the 'Highest,' i.e. God, is over all. But as explained above,
the passage is entirely consonant with Ḳoheleth's spirit; and
the words which follow, whatever their exact meaning may be,
shew that it is the action of the king that fills his thoughts.

v. 8. Two points in this verse stand out clearly—that ארץ
and שדה must be translated differently, and cannot refer to the
same thing—and that נעבד agrees with שדה, not with מלך. The
latter is in accordance with the Mas. punctuation מֶלֶךְ לְשָׂדֶה נֶעֱבָד
(see Baer[^2]).

[^1]: Siegfr. reconstructs the words : כי ברב הבלים חלמות ובדברים הרבה שגגה.
Pesh. adds ﺣﺴﻮﻝﻫ﹐ 'of error' after 'many words.'
[^2]: Other editions, however, מֶלֶךְ לְשָׂדֶה נ".

Two or three renderings that have been suggested may thus be put out of account at once, such as: "a king made for (i.e. set over) a land" (Ewald); "a king who is served by the land (i.e. his subjects)" (Gesen., Knob., al.); "a king who is subject to (i.e. depends for his sustenance upon) the land" (Tg., Rashi, Ibn Ezr.); "a king given to the arable land"—"agro addictus" (Del., Rosenm.).

Siegfr. thinks the passage corrupt, and does not attempt a translation. It is possible that a word agreeing with מלך has dropped out; but as it stands it may be rendered: "but an advantage to a country in all respects is—a king for [i.e. interested in, devoted to] cultivated land." Ḳoheleth wistfully pictures the good government of a king who (like Uzziah 2 Chr. xxvi. 10) loves husbandry.

For בכל cf. Gen. xxiv. 1. 𝔊 ἐπὶ παντί ἐστι..."over all is a king..." refers to the grades of officials in v. 7, and adopts the Ḳᵉri הוא.

The Niphal of עבד occurs only in Dt. xxi. 4, Ezek. xxxvi. 9, 34, in each case with the meaning 'tilled.' And this rendering is borne out by 𝔊 ⊙ ⵣ Pesh., and is adopted by Nowack.

v. 9. מי אהב. Not a question—"who has joy in wealth which bringeth in no increase?" (Hitz.), which contradicts the thought of the preceding verse. Render "he who loveth wealth (shall have) no profit (from it)." It is not necessary (with Zöckl., Siegfr.) to supply ישבע before תבואה.

אהב ב is not found elsewhere; but it is analogous with חפץ ב and חשק ב. On the reading לו תבואה see App. II. pp. 143, 159.

v. 12. לבעליו either 'kept by its owner' (Ew., Now., Del. and Hier.C. a domine) or 'kept for its owner,' i.e., as Ḳoh. would say, by 'time and chance.'

v. 14. שילך בידו "that he can take with him." For the form cf. יַגִּיר x. 20.

But 𝔊 ⵣ Pesh. Hier.C. Tg. read שֶׁיֵּלֵךְ, referring to מאומה— "and nothing shall he carry away by his labour, which can go with him"—which is simpler.

v. 15. כל-עמת. Parchon and Kimchi in their lexicons (s.v. עמת) support the division into two words; cf. Aram. כל-קבל.

But it is probable that כל is only a combination of כ and ל used as prepositions. (See Lambert, Reṿ. d'Études Juives, xxxi.

47–51. Rahlfs *Th.LZ.* 1896, p. 587.) לקבל without ב occurs in
a causative sense Ezr. iv. 16, vi. 13, and in a locative sense
Dan. ii. 31, iii. 3, while קבל occurs nowhere alone; thus בְּלָקֳבֵל
arises by metathesis for בְּקָלְבֵל. And the case of כלעמת is
similar. לעמת occurs frequently (esp. in Ezek.), and מלעמת
1 K. vii. 20, but never עמת alone.

The word should therefore be pointed בְּלְעֻמַּת, the ב having
its counterpart in כן ילך. ᴳ Pesh. Hier. read כי לעמת.

v. 16. יאכל. It is possible that this is a figurative expression,
like 'sit' or 'walk in darkness.' Del. takes it literally: the rich
man is miserly, and "does not allow himself table comforts
in a well lighted room"! Midr. Ḳoh. reads יֻלֵ; so several codd.
of Kenn. and De Rossi; adopted by Kraetzschmar. Houbigant
יֵאָכֵל. Böttch. וְאָפֵל.

But it is simpler to follow ᴳ καὶ ἐν πένθει, and read וְאָבֵל
(Siegfr.).

In the latter half of the verse, the M.T. וְכָעַם and וְחָלְיוֹ are
untranslateable. It is true that כעם is used intransitively in
vii. 9; but in the present passage a substantive is clearly
required; all the versions read וְכַעַם 'and vexation'; and for
וחליו they read וחלי; M.T. evidently arose from the accidental
doubling of the following *waw*.

These emendations give a series of substantives, all governed
by the preposition in בחשך: "moreover all his days (are spent)
in darkness and mourning, and great vexation, and sickness
and wrath."

v. 17. טוב אשר יפה. See § 8, p. 41.

v. 19. מענה בשמחת לבו. This participle may be derived
from (1) ענה 'to be occupied,' (2) ענה 'to answer.'

(1) ᴳ ὅτι ὁ θεὸς περισπᾷ αὐτὸν ἐν εὐφροσύνῃ καρδίας αὐτοῦ. Hier.
C. *quia Deus occupat in laetitia cor eius.* This explanation
is adopted by Siegfr., Wildeb., al.: "because God keeps him
engrossed in the joy of his heart." It makes good sense, but
there are two objections to it:—1st, either the object to מענה
must be supplied, or (with Hier.) בשמחה must be read; 2nd, this
meaning of ענה is confined to i. 13, iii. 10, in both of which it is
Ḳal. inf. followed by the cognate word ענין.

(2) Ibn Ezr., Kimchi, "God causes (all things) to respond
with the joy of his heart." Hitz. compares Hos. ii. 23 f. But
even if that could be used to illustrate the Hiphil, the omission

of the object is very awkward. Del. al. assume that the Hiphil
has the same meaning as the Ḳal:—"God answers to—assents,
corresponds to—the joy of his heart." But this use of ב is
without parallel. On Tyler's use of this explanation, see
§ 8, p. 54.

Ewald and Nowack have given the simplest solution: "God
answers with, by means of, the joy of his heart," i.e. He grants
the joy which man desires. Ps. lxv. 6 is scarcely a complete
parallel, because the verb is followed not by ב but by a second
acc. But no commentator that the present writer has seen
refers to 1 K. xviii. 24 "the God that answers with, by means
of, fire." Lastly, it is possible that the true reading should be
אלהים ענה, the מ which causes the difficulty having been due to
dittography.

CHAP. VI.

Ch. vi. *v.* 3. יוליד מאה. Cf. 1 Sam. ii. 5 ילדה שבעה.

ורב וג׳ lit. "and it is many that the days of his years are."
This looks like a gloss, but it may have been added by Ḳoh. to
the preceding clause for the sake of emphasis.

Tg. tries to avoid the tautology—"and he is in power and
authority (רבנותא) during the days of the years which he hath."

v. 5. נחת. Del. refers to the Mishnic sense of נוח 'better
than.' And this seems to underlie Σ διαφορᾶς, Tg. ולא ידע בין
טב לביש, and Vg. *distantiam boni et mali*; all of which take
נחת as governed by ידע. But נחת must have the meaning which
it bears in iv. 6, ix. 17; and the verb נוח is used in the same
connexion in Job iii. 11–13.

v. 6. אלו "if"; frequent in Mishna. BH Est. vii. 4 only.

v. 8. Bernstein[1] and Ginsburg supply מ before יודע: "what
(advantage) hath the poor man *over* him who knoweth...,"
over a leader or magnate in society. But the passage yields
good sense without so harsh an ellipse; יודע וג׳ must be a
description of the poor man. Del., Now., Siegfr., al., explain it
"who understands the right rule of life—how to maintain his
proper social position, keeping his desires under control." But
the explanation adopted above, § 4, p. 17, is simpler: "[what

---

[1] *Quaestiones nonnullae Koheletanae*, Breslau, 1854.

advantage has] a poor man who has got on in the world by knowing how to walk prudently and successfully before his fellow men?" In ix. 13–16 an instance is given of a poor wise man who gained no profit from his prudent wisdom.

v. 10. נקרא שמו. Its place in the order of the world was fixed—"like the stars, Ps. cxlvii. 4, Is. xl. 26" (Siegfr.).

ונודע וג׳. אשר is not ὅτι, but (as most modern commentators) ὅ τι—"and it was known [predetermined] what man was" or "was to be." 𝔊 καὶ ἐγνώσθη ὅ ἐστιν ἄνθρωπος.

שהתקיף. Kᵉri omits the article, cf. x. 3, 20. The alteration here may have arisen to prevent the word being pronounced as a Hiphil (Euringer). The Hiphil, though not found in BH, is common in Talmudic writings, and the Aphel in Targ. The adj. תקיף is a ἅπ. λεγ. in BH. Cf. יתקפו iv. 12.

v. 12. ויעשם "seeing that he spends them"; an extension of the construction of a circumstantial clause. עשה in this sense is not found elsewhere in M.T. But in Prov. xiii. 23, 𝔊 seems to point to a reading which contained it or a similar word. It is possible, however, to make כצל complete the thought of the verb—"seeing that he makes them like a shadow"; i.e. he dies so soon that his days are made as evanescent as a shadow. The expression need not be considered a Graecism.

CHAP. VII.

Ch. vii. 1 (2). *v.* 1 a has no kind of relevancy to the context. The *Mashal* editor appears to have inserted it because it was cast in the same form as the following aphorisms of Ḳoheleth. If it is an independent proverb, *v.* 1 b is incomplete as it stands. Bickell emends טוב שם משמן יקר טובה חכמה מכבוד, extracting יקר and the last two words from x. 1, which, in his arrangement of the book, stands immediately before vi. 8. In *v.* 1 b he goes so far as to create half a distich: טוב לא היות אדם מהיותו, thus supplying a subject for the suffix in הולדו. Some change in the text seems necessary; and the simplest which suggests itself is: טוב שם משמן טוב יום המות מיום הלדו.

הולדו is followed by 𝔊ᴬᶜ S.H. Aq. Hier. The suffix is difficult, and is omitted in 𝔊ᴮˢ Pesh. Delitzsch compares iv. 12, v. 17; but in both these passages the suffix (in יתקפו and נגדו

and in עֲמָלוֹ) refers quite naturally to the subjects treated of in the context, while here the suffix can be referred to nothing. Either הַגֹּלֶל or perhaps (with Bickell) הַלֶּדֶת, should be read.

v. 2 (3). מִשְׁתֶּה may be used of birthday festivities, thus connecting *v.* 2 closely with *v.* 1 b.

v. 5 (6). מְאִישׁ שֹׁמֵעַ for מִשֹּׁמֵעַ, the change of construction expressing that the two actions of hearing are performed by different people.

v. 6 (7). For the paronomasia סִירִים...סִיר cf. the Latin proverb *ipsa hollera olla legit* (Catull. 94. 2). 'Nettles' and 'kettle' have been suggested.

Σ (ap. Hier.), *per vocem enim imperitorum vinculis quispiam colligatur*, seems to confuse סִירִים with כְּסִילִים and סִיר with אִסּוּר.

וְגַם זֶה הָבֶל, probably a gloss. See § 5, p. 24, footnote.

v. 7 (8). Ingenuity has been taxed to the utmost to find a connexion of thought suggested by כִּי. For some of the suggestions which have been made see Delitzsch *in loc.* But the clause is evidently the second half of a *Mashal* taken from some unknown source. The lost half may have resembled Prov. xvi. 8 (Del.).

הָעֹשֶׁק וג". The judge instead of being 'a wise man' is rendered 'mad' in his responsible position by the 'extortion' which forces a man to bribe him in order that he may win his case. Ewald's emendation עֹשֶׁר for עֹשֶׁק is unnecessary.

אֶת לֵב. Cf. Prov. xiii. 21, Is. l. 4 (Ges. K. § 117 c).

מַתָּנָה. For the versions see App. II. p. 161. Midr. Ḳoh. reads מַתּוֹנָה "rebellion." Hier. compares the thought of Dt. xvi. 19.

v. 8 (9). אֶרֶךְ. Elsewhere always with אַפַּיִם (אַפֵּךְ Jer. xv. 15) exc. Ez. xvii. 3 אֶרֶךְ הָאֵבֶר.

v. 10 (11). *Mashal* on discontent, the spirit of the old man:

> *difficilis querulus laudator temporis acti*
> *se puero.*

v. 11 (12). There is no reason for departing from the simple meaning of the words — "Wisdom is good with an inheritance." This need not at all imply that it is not good without an inheritance.

Wright compares

> μακάριος ὅστις οὐσίαν καὶ νοῦν ἔχει·
> χρῆται γὰρ οὗτος εἰς ἃ δεῖ ταύτῃ καλῶς. (Menander)

And see Pirḳe Aboth ii. 2: ‏יפה תלמוד תורה עם דרך ארץ‎, and
1 Tim. vi. 6.

Some have rendered "W. is as good as an inheritance."
But there is no support for ‏טוב עם‎ in this sense. Such passages
as Job ix. 26, xxxvii. 18, Ps. xxviii. 1 scarcely bear it out.

Pesh. rend. "Wisdom is better than weapons of war,"
apparently connecting ‏נחלה‎ with ‏חיל‎.

‏בל חזו שמש‎, lviii. 9 ‏לא יראו אור‎, Cf. Ps. xlix. 20 ‏לראי השמש‎.

v. 12 (13). ‏בצל...בצל‎. If the text is to stand the clause
may be rendered "in the shadow of wisdom *it is as* in the
shadow of money"; or the preposition may be the ' ‏ב‎ *essentiae*'
—"as a shadow [protection] is wisdom, as a shadow is money,"
cf. Ps. liv. 6 (Ges. K. § 119 *i*). But it is probable that the true
reading is ‏כצל...כצל‎, as in Gen. xviii. 25, Hos. iv. 9. See App. II.
pp. 145 f. For ‏צל‎ cf. Num. xiv. 9.

v. 14 (15). On the meaning of this verse see § 4, p. 18; and
cf. ix. 1.

v. 15 (16). ‏מאריך‎. Sc. ‏ימים‎. Prov. xxviii. 2.

v. 18 (19). ‏בזה‎, i.e. ‏צדק‎ and ‏חכמה‎ from *v.* 16. ‏מזה‎, i.e. ‏רשע‎
and ‏סכלות‎ from *v.* 17. ‏יצא את כלם‎, see § 8, p. 42. Pesh. ‏نصب‎
"adhering, following close, to" must be a slip for ‏نصب‎.

v. 25 (26). ‏ולבי‎. So the versions, exc. Tg. But this is
impossible. Siegfr. reads ‏ואתנה לבי‎ from i. 17; but ‏בלבי‎ is
simpler, with Tg. and several codd. of Kenn. and De R.

‏חשבון‎, "reckoning." A NH and Aram. word; in BH only
v. 27, ix. 10.

Here and in *v.* 27 it means 'the *rationale* of things'—a law
by which the perplexing phenomena of life can be explained.
Vg. *rationem*[1].

‏רשע...הוללות‎. As the text stands ‏כסל‎ and ‏הוללות‎ are predi-
cates—"to know that wickedness is folly, and foolishness is
madness." But there is evidence for the transposition ‏כסל רשע‎
and the reading ‏והללות‎ "to know the folly of wickedness, and
foolishness and madness." (See App. II. p. 146.) ‏כסל‎ with this
meaning occurs in Ps. xlix. 14 only, in the form ‏כְּסֶל‎[2]. It usually
means 'confidence.' But ‏כסיל‎ 'a fool' is common. On ‏הוללות‎
see on i. 17, x. 13.

---

[1] Hier. "Esebon....et numerum possumus, et summam, et rationem, et
cogitationem dicere."

[2] Printed ‏כֵּסֶל‎ in some editions.

v. 26 (27). מוצא. "With reference to this passage and Prov. xviii. 22 it was common in Palestine when someone was married to ask מצא או מוצא = happy or unhappy? Jeb. 63 b." (Delitzsch.)

אשר היא מ" "the woman who is nets," cf. ואני תפלה Ps. cix. 4.

v. 28 (29). עוד "again and again," Gen. xlvi. 29, Ruth i. 14.

v. 29 (30). חשבנות "contrivances," 2 Chr. xxvi. 15 only. The *Ḥasid* speaks of civilization with the evils that are apt to follow in its train.

CHAP. VIII.

Ch. viii. 1. פשר. Here only in BH. A loan word from Aram. פשרא, cf. פתר, פתרון only in Gen. xl., xli.

עז. All the versions read the adj. עז, which should probably be adopted. The subst. nowhere has the bad sense here implied, but with the adj. it is not uncommon. Dt. xxviii. 50, Is. lvi. 11, Dan. viii. 23.

Render "he that is bold (impudent, coarse) of countenance."

ישנא Kᵉthib. ישנה Kᵉri. For שנא = שנה cf. 2 K. xxv. 29, Lam. iv. 1.

The א is supported by 𝕲 Pesh. Hier. (all of which read יִשָּׂנֵא 'is hated'), and by Taanith 7 b: "every man who has עזות פ" one may hate, as the Scripture saith וְעֹז פָּנָיו יְשֻׁנֶּא"—a note being added that יְשֻׁנֶּא is not to be read. If עז is adopted, it is natural to read יִשָּׂנֵא; but the pointing ישנא can be illustrated by מוֹצָא vii. 26.

In § 7, p. 35, B.S. xiii. 25, xii. 18 are referred to.

vv. 2–6. Ḳoheleth's complaints on the tyranny of the king, interspersed with comments of the *Ḥasid*. See § 4, pp. 18 f., and § 5, pp. 25 f.

v. 2. אני should probably be omitted. See App. II. p. 155.

Del., Siegfr. al. supply אמרתי in accordance with ii. 1, iii. 17 f. But in all the nine passages in which 'I said' occurs, Ḳoh. states the conclusions which he drew from his ponderings on the problems of life: they form no parallel to the present passage[1].

In the explanation of *vv.* 2–6 given in § 5 the following points should be noticed. אל תבהל is (with 𝕲, Σ) taken with *v.* 2. מצוה is a Divine command, as nearly always; see BDB s.v.

---

[1] Jer. Sanh. 21 β, אשמר...מ" פי אני.

לא ידע 'will not countenance,' cf. Ps. ci. 4 רע לא אדע. The second ידע, with a different force, finds a parallel in ix. 12. רעת (v. 6 b) means 'trouble' if it is from the pen of Ḳoheleth, and 'wickedness' if from that of the Ḥasid.

For other explanations of the passage see Delitzsch *in loc.*, and Kraetzschmar *Th.LZ.* Sept. 15, 1900.

v. 9. ונתון. The inf. absol. is a continuation of a preceding finite verb, cf. ix. 11, Gen. xli. 43 (Ges. K. § 113 *z*).

v. 10. As it stands the M.T. must refer to two sets of people, the description of the second beginning at וממקום: " And then I saw wicked men buried and they came. And from the holy place they who have done rightly[1] must depart and be forgotten in the city."

But ובאו is impossibly abrupt[2]; there is no other instance of the Piel הלך being used in the sense of the Ḳal, 'depart'; the reading וישתכחו is very doubtful; and כן seems as though it should have some connexion with בכן.

Two very slight emendations make the passage much clearer: omit ו before ממקום (it would easily arise by the doubling of the preceding ו), and read וישתבחו. Perhaps also read ויהלכו. The MS. authority for these readings is given in App. II. pp. 147, 155. The passage then refers solely to the wicked, whom Ḳoheleth watched when they received honourable burial in Jerusalem, and thought of the insolent success of their past life:

" And then [in the face of this glaring wrong] I saw wicked men buried, and they came from a holy place [where they ought never to have been tolerated]; and they used to go about, and be praised in the city because they had so done [i.e. because they had ruled over others to their hurt]."

בכן. " Then," BH Est. iv. 16 only, where it has rather a temporal force.

ממקום קדוש lit. " From the place of a holy one." Cf. Mat. xxiv. 15 ἐν τόπῳ ἁγίῳ ‖ Mk ὅπου οὐ δεῖ.

יהלכו. For the meaning of the Piel cf. iv. 15, xi. 9, Job xxiv. 10 al.

For שבח cf. iv. 2, viii. 15. The Hithp. may have a reflexive force, like נפשו יברך Ps. xlix. 19.

v. 11. פתגם. On the derivation see § 8, p. 42. It is here

---

[1] Σ ὡς δίκαια πράξαντες.
[2] R.V. is obliged to supply ' to the grave.'

treated as feminine, since נעשה must be a participle; and it is a construct depending on מעשה, as the latter is on הרעה.

הרעה obj. acc. "the doing of evil."

v. 12. אשר "forasmuch as," as in *vv.* 10, 11 (BDB s.v. 8 c). The clause is resumptive of *v.* 11 a, and practically repeats its thought.

כי גם "surely also." Some render אשר 'although,' and take כי גם in an adversative sense 'yet—nevertheless.' But both these meanings are very doubtful.

מְאַת should perhaps be read מֵאָת (see BDB s.v.). The omission of פעם or פעמים is harsh; מאה vi. 3 is not parallel, but אחת 'once' is not infrequent. Cf. 2 K. vi. 10, Job xl. 5 al.

The word completely puzzled the early translators, which is strange if מאת were the original reading. It should perhaps be omitted, or read מאד. See App. II. p. 148.

ומאריך לו. Σ ⦿ Hier. supply אפו (cf. Is. xlviii. 9, Prov. xix. 11). So Siegfr. But the introduction of an unconnected participle, whose subject is God, is very abrupt. It is much simpler to supply ימים (cf. *v.* 13, vii. 15): "and prolongeth unto himself [days]."

v. 13. כצל need not be taken as a predicate with the following words (Hitzig, al.). Siegfried thinks that the words mean that the wicked shall not prolong his days as a shadow lengthens in the evening! But צל, when used to describe man's life, always denotes transitoriness, vi. 12, Job *ter*, Pss. *ter*. The expression is cast into a negative form to make it parallel to טוב לא יהיה; but it is equivalent to "he shall shorten his days like a shadow." Cf. ויעשם כצל as explained above, vi. 12.

v. 16. כי גם...ראה is a parenthesis. Cf. xi. 10.

v. 17. בשל אשר = Talm. בדיל ד. Cf. Jon. i. 7, 12 with 8.

CHAP. IX.

Ch. ix. 1. לבור. An unique form, perhaps cognate to ברר. Possibly it should be read לבוֹר, inf. Ḳal of that verb (cf. iii. 18). Some would read לתור, cf. i. 13, ii. 3, vii. 25. But 𝔊 reads ולבי ראה, see App. II. p. 148.

גם אהבה...האדם. For the meaning see § 4, p. 19.

v. 2. הכל. There is strong evidence for reading הבל, and including it in the preceding verse—"all that is before them is

vanity." See App. II. p. 149. If this is done, כאשר means
'inasmuch as.'

v. 2. הנשבע evidently implies false or wrongful swearing,
cf. Zech. v. 3.

v. 3. הוללות. See on i. 17, x. 13.

ואחריו. Either 'after him,' i.e. when he is dead, cf. ii. 12, 18,
iii. 22, vi. 12, vii. 14, or 'afterwards,' Hier. *post haec.* The
former is the simpler explanation. Siegfried is led by Σ τὰ δὲ
τελευταῖα αὐτῶν εἰς νεκρούς to read ואחריתו. ᶀ reads ואחריהם.

אל המתים. Cf. the exclamation לתורה ולתעודה Is. viii. 20.

v. 4. מי אשר וג׳. As the text stands the Masoretes appear
to have intended the first clause to end with יבחר. "Who is he
that chooseth—or is chosen?" But both the punctuation and
the consonants of the Kᵉthib are impossible. The Zaḳeph Ḳaṭon
must be placed (with Del.) on החיים, and the Kᵉri יחבר must be
read: "Whosoever is joined unto all the living, there is hope
(for him)." See § 4, p. 19.

לכלב חי "as regards a live dog." The ל either introduces
the subst., making it equivalent to a *nom. pend.*, or it may
perhaps be an emphasizing particle corresponding to the Arab.
lă, Ass. *lû*—'surely,' cf. 1 Chr. vii. 1, 2 Chr. vii. 21. (See
Ges. K. § 143 *e*. Budde on Is. viii. 1, ZATW ix. 156.)

v. 7. כי כבר וג׳. "For already God hath consented to thy
works," i.e. God determined in the past that man should be
allowed to have industry and pleasure to fall back upon as
a means of forgetting the sadness and shortness of his life.
The thought is parallel to that in v. 19. See § 4, p. 20. For
רצה cf. Ps. xl. 14.

v. 9. כל ימי הבלך. There is good evidence for the omission
of these words in the early text (App. II. p. 150), and they have
the appearance of being an accidental repetition from the prec.
clause.

v. 10. בשאול here only in the book. But that is not enough
to shew that the writer of the passage must be other than the
writer of such passages as iii. 20, vi. 6 (Siegfr.). In Ps. xxx.
the same writer who speaks of Sheol in *v.* 4 describes, in *v.* 10,
those who are in Sheol as "the dust" which cannot praise God.

vv. 11, 12. A poetical exposition of the thought of iii. 1-9.

v. 11. וראה. See on viii. 9.

פגע. 1 K. v. 18 only. Here (as there) it implies 'mischance,'
as is shewn by the following verse.

v. 14. וסבב "surrounded," 2 K. vi. 15, not necessarily 'walked round,' Jos. vi. 4 (Siegfr.).

מצודים must mean 'siege-works,' and is so understood in all the versions; but the word nowhere else occurs with this meaning (contrast vii. 26). מצורים must evidently be read. The ד was probably due to the proximity of מצודה in *v.* 12. מצורים occurs in two MSS. of de Rossi.

v. 15. מסכן. See iv. 13.

ומלט. This is usually rendered 'and he delivered'; but this is contradicted by *v.* 16 b: if the poor man was not heard, his wise counsel could not deliver the city. Render "and he would have delivered"—an apodosis with the protasis suppressed, cf. Ex. ix. 15, 1 Sam. xiii. 13. On the whole passage see § 3, pp. 12 f.

v. 17. נחת is the restful quiet which pervades the conversation of the wise; זעקת is the noisy undisciplined talk of fools, among whom the chiefest of them must talk louder than any, in order to be heard.

נשמעים. Bickell unnecessarily omits, and reads וזעקת.

מושל ב". One who takes the place of chief among fools—an arch-fool. It is not a Graecism; cf. 2 Sam. xxiii. 3.

CHAP. X.

Ch. x. *v.* 1. זבובי מות must = זבובים מתים (Nowack). Siegfr. says it is against the analogy of מקשי מ", חבלי מות, כלי מ"; but it is not 'deadly' flies but 'dead' flies that contaminate ointment. On 𝕲 μυῖαι θανατοῦσαι see App. II. p. 165. Winckler's emendation זבובים מת יבאישו creates greater difficulties than it solves. But the plur. יבאישו should probably be read; the omission of the final ו may have been due to the insertion of the gloss יביע. The latter word is omitted in 𝕲 Σ Pesh. Hier. Tg.

מכבוד. It is natural to emend ומכבוד, which occurs in some editions (Del.). The clause, as it stands, gives a thought *parallel* to that of *v.* a; but 𝕲 suggests an early reading יקר מעט חכמה מכבוד סכלות רב, "more valuable is a little wisdom than the great glory of folly," which is *converse* to the thought of *v.* a. See App. II. pp. 150 f. Siegfr. emends יָקָר [ה]חכמה מִ[א]גְּד סכלות מעט.

v. 2. Compare the *Mashal* ii. 14.

לימינו. Not 'at his right hand,' an anatomical statement to which the most unscientific of writers would not commit himself; but "is (directed) towards his right hand" (Del., Now.). Del. notes that השמאל in late Heb. denotes 'to turn to the wrong side'—take a wrong course. Siegfr. understands it to mean that wisdom and folly will not combine; they go in opposite directions.

v. 3. לבו חסר. His understanding is lacking, cf. ix. 8.

ואמר ונ". "And he saith concerning everyone He is a fool," Hitz. Siegfr. after Σ Hier. This gives force to גם בדרך. While he is actually travelling on the wrong course 'leftwards,' he is in such a state of infatuated folly that he says about everyone but himself that he is a fool. The explanation "he declareth (by his actions and behaviour) to everyone that he (himself) is a fool" (Del., Now.) gives an unusual meaning to אמר, and renders גם בדרך pointless. On 𝔊, which reads סָכָל for סָכָל, see App. II. pp. 151, 165.

v. 4. מקומך ונ" i.e. do not throw up your post in a rage. Contrast the injunction of the *Ḥasid*, viii. 3 (note *in loc.*).

מרפא "healing," and so soothing, pacifying; Prov. xii. 18. Σ curiously σωφροσύνη; ap. Hier. *pudicitiam.*

v. 5. כשגגה "of the nature of an error." Del., Now. describe the preposition as 'כ *veritatis*': but see Ges. K. § 119 *d*, Rem. For שגגה cf. v. 5. The מרפה spirit is shewn by Koheleth in implying that the glaring injustice of the ruler is 'an unintentional error.'

יֵצָא. A א"ל verb with the form of a ל"ה. Ges. K. § 75 *qq.*

v. 6. במרומים רבים. If this is not to be read בְּמ", the adjective must be considered as loosely added in apposition—"In the high positions [among men]—many of them." The passage is not included among analogous instances in Ges. K. § 126 *y*, *z*. Luzzatto reads נָתַן "folly hath set many in high places"; but the parallelism of *v.* b forbids this; and it is not folly but the שגגה of the ruler that is responsible.

v. 8. גומץ "a pit." An Aram. loan word, in BH here only. It occurs in Pesh. Tg. of Prov. xxvi. 27 (Heb. שחת). The *Mashal* was apparently well known in different forms, since it occurs in Prov. *loc. cit.*, and in B.S. xxvii. 26.

v. 9. יעצב. Usually 'be grieved,' Gen. xlv. 5, 1 Sam. xx. 3; only here used of physical pain.

יסכן "endangers himself." A NH word. Del. cites Berach. i. 3, and adds that in Tg. and Talm. the Ithpael אסתכן has the same meaning.

v. 10. "If the axe be blunt, and he hath not sharpened the edge, then he must strengthen his force," i.e. put more force into his strokes.

קהה, Piel in the sense of Ḳal. The latter occurs of teeth in Jer. xxxi. 29, 30, Ez. xviii. 2.

הוא is the man already mentioned as endangering himself by cutting logs.

לא. See App. II. p. 151.

פנים "edge," cf. Ez. xxi. 21 (Engl. 16).

קלקל "make smooth," i.e. not notched or rough. Cf. נחשת קלל Ez. i. 7, Dan. x. 6, i.e. smooth (and so shining) bronze.

וחילים ינבר, cf. נברו חיל Job xxi. 7, the frequent גבור חיל, and גבור חילים 1 Chr. vii. 5, 7, 11, 40.

For other interpretations see Del. *in loc.*

ויתרון וג׳ "And wisdom is advantageous for giving success." But the Hiphil occurs nowhere else, and the construction is awkward. Winckler's transposition וית׳ הכ׳ הכשיר would make it easier. But 𝔊, Pesh. Hier. suggest הכשׁר the Ḳal participle, "an advantage to the successful man is wisdom"—which is attractive. The same construct יתרון occurs in iii. 9, "advantage of (for) העושה."

v. 11. בלא לחש "without enchantment," i.e. because there is no enchantment ready.

ואין וג׳, i.e. if the charmer come too late.

v. 12. שפתות, plural for dual.

תבלענו "destroys him." The suffix refers to the fool himself, cf. *v.* 15.

v. 13. הללות. Here only in this form, though it should probably be read for הוללות in i. 17, ii. 12, vii. 25, ix. 3. It is the only instance in which the abstract termination ות is affixed to the form of the Ḳal participle. See Barth NB. pp. 414 f.

v. 14. If *v.* b is a misplaced fragment of Ḳoheleth's writing (see § 4, p. 20), the second half of the *Mashal* beginning *v.* a may have been lost; and this *Mashal* makes clearer the meaning of *v.* 15 a.

v. 15. The *Mashal* appears to mean 'The fool worries

himself about a great many matters, whereas he is as ignorant as a child about the simplest things.' So Ibn Ezr., Del.

Siegfr. explains, "The bother *caused by* the fool wearies only him who...etc.," i.e. no one but the most helplessly ignorant would suffer himself to be bothered by a fool.

עמל is elsewhere masc.

אל עיר for אל העיר. A colloquial expression like the Engl. 'to go to town.'

v. 18. בעצלתים, Dual of עַצְלָת. Ew., Hitz. follow Ibn Ezr. in explaining it of 'two idle hands.' But this is awkward and improbable. It may be עַצְלָתַיִם, Dual of עַצְלָה (Prov. xix. 15), with an intensive force; cf. רִשְׁעָתִים (Del.). An emendation seems to be required. Bickell suggests בעצלוּת, cf. Prov. xxxi. 27. Siegfr. בעצלת ידים. This is better, and would easily arise from a scribal error. בעצלה is also possible; the ים of ימך having been accidentally doubled, the apparent Dual ending would cause the ה to become ת.

ימך. Ps. cvi. 43, Job xxiv. 24 only; both metaphorical.

המקרה. Dagesh was placed in the מ to distinguish it from the participle, Ps. civ. 3. See Baer, *Qu. Vol.* here, and on xi. 5.

ידלף "drips," i.e. leaks.

v. 19. ישמח. Perhaps read לשמח. See App. ii. p. 152.

יענה את הכל "answers everything," i.e. meets all desires (cf. v. 19), Σ εὐχρηστήσει. 𝕲, Hier. make הכסף the object; "all things answer (obey) money." But there is no exact parallel to this use of ענה, except perhaps the subst. מענה Prov. xxix. 19. In 𝕲 a gloss ταπεινώσει has been added. See App. ii. p. 166.

v. 20. במדעך. The pre-formative מ may have a local force (Ges. K. § 85 *e*)—'the place of knowledge,' and so 'mind,' 'thought.' Elsewhere = 'knowledge,' 2 Chr. i. 10, 11, 12, Dan. i. 4, 17 only.

יגיר for יגד, Ex. xix. 3 (Ges. K. § 53 *n*). "The jussive serves to express facts which may happen contingently, or may be expected" (*id.* § 109 *i*).

Chap. XI.

Ch. xi. *vv.* 1–6. Ḳoheleth advises prudent industry (cf. ix. 10) combined with pleasures (7–10) as the last resort before old age and death come on (xii. 1–7).

v. 1. Several explanations have been offered, of which the favourite is that the verse inculcates a liberal charity—'Give your bread to any who chance to need it, and you will at some distant time receive a reward.'

Palm's reference to the Greek σπείρειν ὕδωρ = undertake a fruitless task, is of course negatived by *v.* b. And other equally impossible explanations are mentioned by Del. *in loc.*

There can be little doubt that the words refer to trading— to those "who do business in great waters." לחם may denote literally the corn trade, or it may be a figurative expression for any goods sent out on the sea with hopes of subsequent profit. A parallel proverb is ascribed to B.S. See § 7, p. 36.

"In the course of many days" is suitable, because trading voyages were often long and dangerous.

It is unsafe to assume (as Kleinert, *St. Kr.* 779 ff.) that this proves Alexandria to have been the place of writing. viii. 10 makes Jerusalem much more probable.

v. 2. More advice to business men. 'Do not embark your capital in one enterprise, but in seven, yea in eight.' The explanation which refers this to the giving of charity is forbidden by *v.* b.

On the collocation of numerals to express an indefinite total see Ges. K. § 135 *s.*

vv. 2–6. Ḳoheleth reverts to the thought of man's helplessness in the face of Necessity. Nature works by invincible and inscrutable laws; so that in all his industry man can only do his little best (*v.* 6) and hope for a successful result.

v. 3. ואם יפול עץ. Two explanations are possible. 1. By an unchangeable law of Nature a tree that has fallen by a tempest must lie in the direction in which it is impelled. The only objection to this is that, as an illustration of man's helplessness, it seems rather weak. Man cannot prevent the rain from falling or undo its effects, but when a tree has fallen man can alter its direction. The proverb is not concerned with the

falling, but with the subsequent direction of the עץ—and this
is so whether יהוא or הוא is read. 2. It is not impossible that
the words refer to a process of divination. If a stick is tossed
up in the air, that a man may guide his action by the direction
in which it comes to rest, he has no control over the result.
Rhabdomancy is referred to in Hos. iv. 12, but it is not
known what form it took; and belomancy in Ez. xxi. 26
(Engl. 21), where the king of Babylon shook (perhaps shuffled)
arrows. See art. 'Divination' in *Encycl. Bibl.*

יהוא. According to Ges. K. § 23 *i*, an early scribal error for
יהי = יהו (*id.* § 75 *s*). It is quite as likely to have been a scribal
error for הוא, which Bick. and Siegfr. adopt.

v. 4. It is useless to wait until outward conditions are
perfect before you pursue your industry; because they are
seldom perfect, and you cannot control them.

v. 5. כעצמים " As in the case of bones,"—resumptive of the
clause כאשר וג': and both are answered by ככה.

v. 6. לערב. Not " in the evening," but " until the evening,"
cf. Job iv. 20.

אי זה, with this meaning ii. 3 only.

v. 8. כל שבא הבל. Cf. ix. 1 as emended.

v. 10. השחרות "manhood's prime," i. e. the age of black
hairs (שחור) as distinct from שיבה the age of hoary hairs. So
Mishn. Midr., see Del. The derivation from שחר " dawn " would
imply a period of life even earlier than הילדות, which would be
inappropriate.

If the right view is taken in § 5, p. 26, that xii. 1 a is an
insertion by the *Ḥasid*, the clause כי היל׳ והש״ הבל is a parenthesis (cf. viii. 16 b), and the continuation of *v.* 10 a is xii. 1 b.

CHAP. XII.

Ch. xii. *v.* 1 a. בוראך. Graetz, followed by Bickell, reads
בורך " thy fountain," understanding it of the wife of youth;
and Cheyne inclines to it. But this, as Davidson[1] truly says,
" strikes a lower note than is heard anywhere in the book."

If the text is retained, but the words are assigned to
Koheleth, they imply, as Cheyne points out, that an old man

---

[1] Art. 'Ecclesiastes' in *Encycl. Bibl.*

is unable to "remember his Creator." But if the words are by the Ḥasid, all difficulty is removed.

vv. 1 b—6. On these verses there have been *quot homines tot sententiae*; but the interpretations are mainly five:

(1) The verses are held to describe the failing of an old man's physical powers (early Jewish writers, and many moderns).

(2) They contain a picture of a storm, representing the approach of death (Umbreit, Ginsburg, Plumptre).

(3) They represent the approach of death under the figure of the fall of night (Michaelis, Nachtigal; discussed by Taylor).

(4) They are a literal picture of the gloom and sadness in a household when the master has just died (Taylor[1]).

(5) They are to be explained by the seven "days of death," i.e. days of cold and wintry weather, immediately preceding the Palestinian springtime, which are peculiarly dangerous for the aged and weakly (C. H. H. Wright, after Wetzstein).

It is unnecessary to discuss these views in detail. All that is worth knowing about them may be learnt from Taylor, Delitzsch and Wright.

The explanation that is here offered differs from others, in that it does not assume one line of thought to be sustained throughout the verses. The verses divide themselves into distinct paragraphs[2], indicating changes of thought and metaphor.

(i) *v.* 1 b, introduced by עד אשר לא, is (as stated above) merely a continuation of xi. 9 a, 10.

(ii) In *v.* 2, introduced by עד אשר לא, the coronach on departed youth begins, with a description of the gloom and frequent sorrows with which old age is overcast.

(iii) In *vv.* 3, 4 the construction changes with ביום ש״, and seven details are poetically enumerated, figurative of the physical failure of the old man's body.

(iv) In *v.* 5 a נם[3] marks another, but slighter change, introducing four further details, describing physical incapacity of other kinds.

(v) *v.* 5 b contains the author's remark, explaining, without metaphor, that the foregoing descriptions refer to old age.

---

[1] *The Dirge of Coheleth*, London, 1874. He further suggests that the passage was taken from a recognised collection of dirges.

[2] They are not called stanzas, because they vary so greatly in length.

[3] Possibly, however, ומנבה is the true reading (App. ii. p. 152).

(vi) *vv.* 6, 7 contain an entirely fresh thought, introduced
by עַד אֲשֶׁר לֹא; the author passes from signs of decay to the
moment of death, describing it first under figures (*v.* 6) and
then literally (*v.* 7).

v. 2. A general description of gloom. The clouds returning
after the rain represent the recurrent sorrows of an old man,
as he feels his powers forsaking him, and from time to time
mourns the death of relatives and friends.

vv. 3, 4. Those who are opposed to the view that these
verses describe the failing powers of the old man's body are apt
to argue as though Ḳoheleth could not possibly have allowed
himself a mixture of metaphors. But the boldest use of metaphors is found in the sublimest Hebrew poetry; e.g. Is. xxviii.
14–20, xxx. 27–33. Again, this treatment of the verses has been,
by more than one writer, severely styled as the "anatomical"
interpretation. And no doubt some of the writers who have
followed this method have deserved the criticism, both for the
absurd and unworthy explanations which they offer, and also
because they have run the theory to death in attempting to
apply it throughout the whole of the *vv.* 2–6. But the enumeration of parts of the body in order figuratively to describe
various weaknesses or excellencies is extremely common in the
Old Testament. Oriental notions of poetical fitness often differ
widely from our own. In the Song of Songs this feature
reaches a point far exceeding what is here claimed for Ḳoheleth. See also the narrative in *Shabb.* 152 a, quoted by Del.
(Engl. trans. p. 407 footnote).

v. 3. יָזֻעוּ "quake." Est. v. 9, Pilp. Hab. ii. 7. The "keepers
of the house" are the hands and arms.

הִתְעַוְּתוּ "make themselves crooked, or twisted," i. 15, vii. 13.
The "men of might" are the legs and knees, bowed and bent
in weakness. Contrast Song of Songs, v. 15.

בָּטְלוּ. Aram. בְּטִיל. As. *baṭâlu*, "cease."

הַטֹּחֲנוֹת, "The grinding maids," i.e. the teeth.

מִעֵטוּ. Piel here only; intrans. "be (or become) few," cf. חָתְּתָה
Jer. li. 56 (Ges. K. § 52 *k*). The rendering "when they have
wrought a little" would require the Hiphil, and a second verb.

חָשְׁכוּ of the eyes, Ps. lxix. 24, Lam. v. 17. No explanation
which refers הָרֹאוֹת literally to ladies looking out of windows
has satisfactorily accounted for this verb. It cannot mean 'be

in darkness,' or 'be gloomy, or sad'; it must have the same force as in *v.* 2.

It is unnecessary to press the metaphor of ארבות, either as windows latticed by lashes, or as sluices from which tears flow.

v. 4. דלתים. The connexion in which this stands with הטחנה ("the mill"—the place of grinding, i.e. the mouth) shews that its meaning is the "lips," cf. Ps. cxli. 3 דל שפתי. Del. understands it of the 'jaws,' comparing Job xli. 6 דלתי פניו, of the jaws of the leviathan; but in that case בשוק loses its force. The lips are the "doors on the street."

בשפל Ges. K. § 45 *c.*

ויקום [1] (Ges. K. § 72 *t*). The jussive, as in the case of ישׁב (*v.* 7), seems to be used for the imperfect, with no special force (*id.* § 109 *k*).

The meaning of the present text is very doubtful. Some of the proposed explanations are: "The bird (of evil omen) rises with a shriek." "He rises (i.e. is roused from sleep) at the sound of a bird," describing the wakefulness of an old man who is roused by the twittering of a sparrow; but the following words seem to describe his deafness. "He (i.e. his voice) rises into a sparrow's voice (a childish treble)." Σ καὶ παύσεται φωνὴ τοῦ στρουθίου leads Siegfr. to read וְיִקּוֹד קוֹל, "and the twittering of the sparrow sinks down—sounds faint." The same meaning is reached by Kraetzschmar with וקמל קול (following Cornill on Ez. vii. 11 החמס קם למטה רשע). Parallelism with וישחו would suggest ויקמל קול; it is true the imperf. is not found elsewhere, but that, in itself, would be no objection. It is questionable, however, if קמל can mean 'grow faint, or weak'; Is. xix. 6, xxxiii. 9 (the only passages in which it occurs) do not bear it out. But the suggestion is attractive.

בנות השיר is a general expression for 'songs,' or perhaps 'the individual notes' (Ges. K. § 128 *v*). For ישחו of the voice cf. Is. xxix. 4. השיר must be human song, as opposed to the song of birds.

The two expressions thus describe the old man's deafness: "and the sound of the sparrow fades, and all the notes of (human) song sink low."

---

[1] Printed ויקום in some editions.

v. 5 a. Four additional (נם) details of incapacity.

ייראו. The sudden introduction of the plural is awkward. Perhaps read יירא, the ו being a duplication of the following ו.

מנבה can hardly mean 'from above' as opposed to בדרך, which would require ממעל or ממרום. "They are (or he is) afraid of a high thing," i.e. he shrinks from mounting any high or steep place.

וחתחתים "dreadful terrors." The old man, blind and deaf, is frightened at every turn lest he may be injured on the road.

וְיָנֵאץ השקד is rendered by many "and the almond tree blossoms," treating the verb as Hiphil of נצץ; and since the almond blossom, which is usually pink, has sometimes been observed by travellers to bleach when about to fade, the expression is taken to refer to the white hair of the old man! The Hiphil is anomalous, whether from נצץ or נאץ, and it is natural to read וְיִנְאַץ, "and he rejects the almond," i.e. his appetite fails so that he can no longer enjoy luxuries.

ויסתבל החנב is the crux of the passage; lit. "and the locust carries itself as a burden—drags itself along." A fair sense could be made of it if יסתבל could mean 'is a burden'—is too heavy for him. The light, easily digested locust is food too solid for the old man. This would form a parallel to the preceding and following clauses, and is clearly the kind of meaning that the context suggests. It is possible that both words are corrupt[1]. The following are among the varied explanations suggested: "The τέττιξ is burdensome"—i.e. its lovely chirp fails to give pleasure (Taylor). "The locust creeps out"—in the dangerous cold days which usher in spring (Wright). חנב is a figure of the *coxa*, the hinder region of the *pelvis*, so that the rheumatic old man walks stiffly with failing joints! (Del.). 𝕲 Hier. "the locust becomes fat."

האביונה "The caper-berry," so called because it stimulated appetite[2]. 𝕲 Aq. ἡ κάππαρις[3]. Talm. אביונות. See Moore, in *Journ. Bibl. Lit.* x. (1891), 55–64.

[1] החנב may be the locust tree, the popular name given to the 'carob'— *ceratonia siliqua*; or החנב may be a corruption of הֶחָרוּב. Cf. Lk. xv. 16, Pesh. Syr.sin. cur. See art. 'Husks' in *Encycl. Bibl.*

[2] Whether it was used, as often supposed, for stimulating sexual desire is uncertain. The thought is quite unsuitable to the context.

[3] Σ is doubtful. S.H. suggests ἡ ἐπίγονος or -ονή, connecting it in some way with sexual passion. But codd. 248, 252 give ἐπίπονος, pointing to הָאֶבְיוֹנָה,

וְתָפֵר. Prob. read וְתֻפַּר with 𝔊 διασκεδασθῇ, Σ διαλυθῇ. Cf. Is. viii. 10. Aq. derives it from פרה—καρπεύσει. Some render "and the caper-berry bursts"; but even if this were true to natural history (see BDB s.v. פרר), it would be very difficult to assign a meaning to the expression.

Render "the caper-berry is made (becomes) ineffectual."

v. 5 b. The writer indicates the purport of the foregoing verses—"for man is on his way to his perpetual home, and the wailers go about in the street"; i.e. every man is on the way towards Sh°ol (הולך, cf. i. 4, iii. 20, vi. 6, ix. 10), and hired wailers are constantly going about for one funeral and then another.

The literal use of שוק in this verse need not cause any difficulty in the figurative use in *v.* 4.

v. 6. עד אשר לא marks a transition from pictures of old age to pictures of the moment of death, to the thought of which *v.* 5 b has just led.

ירחק *K°thib* "be removed" (Niphal ἅπ. λεγ.) . ירתק *K°ri* "be bound" (Nah. iii. 10 Pual only). Both are meaningless, and most commentators now read ינתק "be broken." See App. II. pp. 155 f.

חבל הכסף. This is evidently connected with the following גלת הזהב, and Nowack is probably right in referring it to the cord or chain which supports a lamp. The גלה of a golden lampstand occurs in Zech. iv. 2, 3 [1] (זהב being afterwards transferred to the oil in the bowl, *v.* 12). The fact that no other instance can be quoted of a lamp hanging by a silver cord, is not of the slightest weight. It is rich Oriental imagery, as e.g. Prov. xxv. 11. The snapping of the cord and the fall of the lamp, by which the bowl would crack and the oil be spilled, is a suitable metaphor for death [2]. This explanation is far more probable than those which refer the cord and lamp to parts of the body—e.g. the cord is the spinal cord (Del.) or the string of the tongue which is tied (ירתק) in death (Cheyne); the bowl is the head, and so on.

וְתָרוּץ. Either an irregular imperf. Ḳal from √רצץ with an intransitive force, or, more probably, to be read וְתֵרוֹץ. Thus

fem. of אביון "the poor soul" = "נשמתו ה". Field (Hex. *in loc.*) suggests that επιροNΟC was merely a corruption of επιποNOC.

[1] M.T. in *v.* 3 has גֻּלָּה, but גֻּלָּה should probably be read.

[2] Compare the metaphor of spilt water, 2 Sam. xiv. 14.

all four objects in *v.* 6 are 'broken,' the same verb being used of the two objects נלה and נלגל from the same root. The verbs are carefully chosen; the 'cord' and the 'pitcher' can be 'snapped' and 'shivered,' while the 'bowl' and the 'bucket' can only be 'crushed' or 'cracked.' See the same contrast between רצץ and שבר in Is. xlii. 3 (where יָרוּץ for יָרוֹץ follows in *v.* 4).

v. 6 *b.* A parallel illustration of collapse in death. "And the pitcher be shivered at the fountain, and the bucket be crushed [and fall] into the cistern." It seems likely that נלגל (which usually means a wheel) is here purposely used for a 'round bucket,' to produce assonance with נלה. But the force of the figure is substantially the same if the meaning 'wheel' be retained; it is then the wheel or pulley from which the bucket hangs, and this being cracked, the whole machinery, bucket and all, falls into the cistern.

v. 7. A literal statement of what has just been described figuratively. יָשֹׁב Jussive, with the force of an ordinary imperfect; see the following תָּשׁוּב (Ges. K. § 109 *k*), and cf. *v.* 4.

On the meaning of *v.* b see § 8, p. 48.

v. 8. The editor's closing formula, with the strengthened הבל הבלים, which occurs only in the editorial opening, i. 2.

vv. 9, 10. *First postscript.* The editor commends the teaching and writings of Ḳoheleth-Solomon. It is worthy of notice that in these two verses he has four words or constructions foreign to Ḳoheleth.

v. 9. יותר שׁ "Besides the fact that"—a meaning not found in Ḳoheleth's own writing.

עוד. He did more than live as a חכם; he taught the people besides.

לִמַּד. Cf. וּמִלַּט ix. 15 (Ges. K. § 52 *a*).

העם. If the true reading is האדם (App. II. p. 152), the editor praises the writer as though he were Solomon, ascribing world-wide effects to his teaching.

ואזן "and weighed"; here only in BH (der. מאזנים). On 𝕲 see App. II. p. 153.

וחקר "and searched out"; Piel here only.

תקן "arranged." Ḳoheleth uses the word only of straightening something that is crooked, i. 15 (see n.), vii. 13. The asyndeton perhaps shews that this verb alone governs משלים, the two former loosely governing דעת.

הרבה. G connects with the following verse. Pesh. has it in both verses.

v. 10. ישר is in apposition to כתוב with an adverbial force (Ges. K. § 118 *q*): "something written in uprightness." וּכְתוּב would be simpler (with G καὶ γεγραμμένον εὐθύτητος), forming a parallel with the preceding and following דברי. The emendation וְלִכְתּוֹב (Bick., Siegfr.) is unnecessary.

vv. 11, 12. *Second postscript.* The 'wise man' dwells on the value of short incisive *mᵉshalim*, such as are found in collections, and are ascribed in general to Solomon.

v. 11. כְדָרְבנות (Baer, *Qu. Vol.* p. 70) "like goads." Cf. הדרבן 1 S. xiii. 21 (where see Driver). There seems to be an intentional play on the words דברי and דרבנות; two other such plays, vii. 1, 6, have been noticed from the pen of the 'wise man.' The goad is an instrument for driving, and stimulating to action; and *mᵉshalim* have that effect on men's minds.

וכמשׂמרות "and like nails." Not שׂ (Baer, *Qu. Vol.* p. 70), the usual form being מסמרות (Jer. x. 4, 2 Chr. iii. 9) or ים- (Is. xli. 7, 1 Chr. xxii. 3). Cf. שׂכלות i. 17. On the masc. see Albrecht, *ZATW.* xvi. 90 f.

נטועים "planted" and so 'fixed'; ΣΘ πεπηγότες. Cf. Ps. xciv. 9, Dan. xi. 45.

בעלי אספות cannot refer to the "masters of assemblies," i.e. the members of the assemblies of the wise; to say that they are like firmly fixed nails is meaningless, especially when their words have just been described as goads. Siegfried's emendation בבעלי is unnecessary. בעל can be used of things, as in Is. xli. 15; and Del. explains it well, by reference to בעלי ברית (Gen. xiv. 13), בעלי שבאה (Neh. vi. 18), those who are bound together in a covenant or oath. The words of the wise are to a certain extent personified; they are bound together in collections.

מרעה אחד evidently refers to Solomon, who is regarded as the ultimate source of all proverbs. The metaphor of the shepherd (= teacher) has been led up to by the "goads." For מן after נתן cf. 2 K. xxv. 30. Cheyne accepts Klostermann's treatment of the clause: "the members of the assemblies have [in the case of Ecclesiastes] given them forth (נְתָנוּ) from another (אַחֵר) shepherd." But the Mas. text and punctuation yield a perfectly good sense.

v. 12. ויתר מהמה "and besides them," יותר having the same
force as in *v.* 9. The expression is somewhat loosely worded.
The writer means 'besides (attending to) those (words of the
wise), be warned,' and be not led away by the multitude of
books.

בני. The 'wise man' assumes the style of many of the
proverbs (Prov. i. 8, ii. 1, iii. 1, etc.).

להג "devotion to study"; unique in BH. See Nowack, *in loc.*

The words עשות...בשר are divided into two clauses (as in
Eng. Vv.), the second depending for its meaning on the first.
Hitzig makes יגעת בשר the predicate to all the rest: "making
many books without end, and much study, is a weariness of the
flesh"—which, as Del. says, is a truism.

Krochmal suggests that the "words of the wise" are the
Hagiographa, and the warning against books is a warning
against the reception of any others into the Canon (see Cheyne,
Job and Solomon, pp. 233 f.). But besides the fact that the
"words of the wise" is quite unsuitable as a description of the
Hagiographa as a whole, this explanation relegates *v.* 12 to a
very late date; whereas it is extremely probable that *vv.* 13, 14
were the latest addition to the book, and that they are alluded
to by B. Sira (see § 7, p. 35).

vv. 13, 14. *Third postscript.* The Ḥasid sums up his own
teaching.

סוף דבר stands grammatically unconnected with the following
words; cf. קץ דבר B. S. xliii. 27, and Engl. 'to conclude.'

הכל נשמע may be treated in three different ways:

(1) "All has been heard." The Ḥasid refers to the teaching about the fear of God, that he has already inserted in the
book.

(2) "Let us hear all," i.e. let us sum up the truth in a
word—נשמע being the pausal form of the 1st pers. plur. But
this colloquial use of the 1st person is unique in the book, and
improbable.

It should be noted, however, that B. S. xliii. 27 seems to
adopt this view with לא נוסף.

(3) Read שְׁמָע with 𝔊 MSS. (exc. V 253) Pesh. This is
adopted by Siegfr., and forms a parallel to ירא and שמר.

If the M.T. is to stand, (1) is the simplest explanation.
Two others may be noticed: Del. (following Mendelss.), "The

final result, all having been heard, (is this)—Fear God, etc."
But this is much more awkward than the analogous constructions which he quotes, Dt. xxi. 1, Ezra x. 6. Ewald explains
נשמע as *audiendum est,* and Hier., *auditu perfacilis est,* seems to
follow the same method.

כי זה כל האדם cannot mean "for this is the whole of man"
(Ew., al.), nor "the whole duty of man" (Engl. Vv.), nor "the
All of man" (Knobel); כל האדם must mean "every man," as
in iii. 13, v. 18, vii. 2. Del., Now. are undoubtedly right in
comparing Ps. cix. 4 "I am prayer," cx. 3 "thy people are
free-will offerings." And see vii. 26 אשר היא מצודים. The
expression "this is every man" means "every man is destined
for, and should be wholly absorbed in, this." To supply דְּבַר
(Siegfr.) or חובת (Bick.) is quite unnecessary.

v. 14. במ׳/על כל נעלם "into the judgment (which is passed)
upon every hidden thing" (Del., Now., Siegfr.). על cannot
mean 'together with' after the universal כל מעשה. And see
the *Ḥasid's* words in xi. 9 which he here echoes.

נֶעְלָֽם. The dagesh is to make distinct the pronunciation of
the quiescent guttural, as in 1 K. x. 3, cf. יחסר ix. 8.

אם טוב ואם רע refers to כל מעשה, not to כל נעלם. This was
indicated by the position of the Ethnach.

After *v.* 14 the Masoretes repeated *v.* 13, to avoid ending the
book with a severe thought. The same was done at the end of
Isaiah (ישעיה), the group of the Twelve minor prophets (תריסר),
and Lamentations (קינות); and the four books were noted by
the mnemonic letters יתׄקק.

3. A Translation[1].

Chapter I.

1. The words of Ḳoheleth son of David, king in Jerusalem.
2. Vapour of vapours, saith Ḳoheleth; vapour of vapours—all is a vapour.
3. What profit is there to a man in all his toil wherein he toileth under the sun?
4. A generation departeth and a generation cometh, and the earth perpetually abideth.
5. And the sun riseth and the sun setteth, and unto his place he panteth—he riseth there.
6. Going towards the south and circling towards the north, circling circling goeth the wind, and in its circlings returneth the wind.
7. All the streams go their way into the sea, but the sea—it is not full; unto the place whither the streams go, thither they go again.
8. All things are weary—a man cannot utter it; the eye is not satisfied at seeing, and the ear is not filled with hearing.
9. That which is is that which shall be, and that which hath been done is that which shall be done; and there is nothing new under the sun.
10. If there is a thing of which one saith See, this is new! it already existed in the ages which were before us.
11. There is no remembrance of earlier people [now]; and also of later people who shall exist—of them there shall be no remembrance with those who shall exist later [still].
12. I, Ḳoheleth, was king over Israel in Jerusalem.
13. And I gave my heart to investigate and to explore by wisdom concerning everything that is done under the heavens. It is a miserable task which God hath given to the sons of men to be occupied with.

[1] A variety of type is used for the purpose of exhibiting the results arrived at in §§ 4, 5. Expressions which involve an emendation of the M.T. are placed between asterisks. An obelus denotes that there is an omission of one or more words which occur in the M.T.

14. I saw all the actions which are done under the sun; and lo all is a vapour and a striving after wind.
15. A crooked thing cannot be corrected, and a deficit cannot be reckoned.
16. And I spake with my heart saying As for myself, lo I have greatly multiplied wisdom beyond any man who hath been before me over Jerusalem; and my heart hath seen to a great extent wisdom and knowledge.
17. And I have given my heart to know wisdom *and knowledge*, madness and folly. I know that this also is a striving after wind.

CHAPTER II.

1. I said in my heart Come, let me test thee with gladness, and enjoy thou good. And lo that also was a vapour.
2. Of laughter I said It is mad; and of gladness What doth this accomplish?
3. I explored in my heart to refresh my flesh with wine—my heart behaving as usual with wisdom—and to lay hold upon folly, until I might see what good there is for the sons of men that they may provide [for themselves] under the heavens during the [small] number of the days of their life.
4. I did great things; I built me houses, I planted me vineyards.
5. I made me gardens and parks; and I planted in them fruit trees of every kind.
6. I made me pools of water, to water from them a plantation springing up with trees.
7. I procured men-servants and maid-servants, and I had home-born slaves; I also had property in cattle and sheep in large quantities, more than all who were before me in Jerusalem.
8. I amassed me also silver and gold, and the treasure of kings and the provinces; I prepared me singing men and singing women, and the luxuries of the sons of men— a concubine, yea [many] concubines.
9. And I grew continually greater, beyond anyone who was before me in Jerusalem; yet my wisdom stood firm for my help.

10. And nothing that my eyes asked for did I keep from them: I withheld not my heart from any gladness; for my heart was glad as a result of all my toil; and this was my portion as a result of all my toil.

11. And I turned [to look] at all my works which my hands had wrought, and at the toil which I had toilsomely pursued; and lo all was a vapour and a striving after wind, and there was no profit under the sun.

12. And I turned to see wisdom and madness and folly; for what can the man do that cometh after the king? That which *he hath [? already] done*.

13. And I saw that wisdom hath advantage over folly, as the advantage of light over darkness.

14. As for the wise man his eyes are in his head, but the fool walketh in darkness. But I know, nevertheless, that one mischance will befal them all.

15. And I said in my heart, As the mischance of the fool, me also will it befal; and why was I then superlatively wise? And I said in my heart that this also was a vapour.

16. For there is no remembrance alike of the wise man and of the fool perpetually, because in the days to come all is already forgotten. And how doth the wise man die and the fool alike!

17. And I hated life, because the work was evil unto me which was done under the sun; because all is a vapour and a striving after wind.

18. And I hated all my toil wherein I was toiling under the sun; because I must leave it to the man who shall be after me.

19. And who knoweth whether he will be a wise man or a fool? And he must have control over all my toil wherein I have toiled and wisely wrought under the sun. This also is a vapour.

20. And I turned about to make my heart despair concerning all the toil wherein I had toiled under the sun.

21. For there is a man whose toil is in wisdom and knowledge and skill; and to a man who hath not toiled at it he must give it as his portion. This also is a vapour and a striving after wind.

M.   7

22. For what doth a man get by all his toil and his striving of heart in which he toileth under the sun?

23. For all his days his task is [full of] sorrows and trouble; even in the night his heart resteth not. This also is a vapour.

24. There is no good thing for man but that he should eat and drink and let himself experience pleasure in all his toil. This also I saw, that it is from the hand of God;

25. for who can eat or who can enjoy *apart from Him*?

26. **For to the man that is good before Him, He hath given wisdom and knowledge and gladness; but to the sinner He hath given the task of gathering and amassing to give to him that is good before God.**
    This also is a vapour and a striving after wind.

Chapter III.

1. For everything there is a fixed moment, and a time for every occupation under the heavens:

2. A time to be born, and a time to die;
   a time to plant, and a time to uproot what is planted.

3. A time to kill, and a time to heal;
   a time to break down, and a time to build.

4. A time to weep, and a time to laugh;
   a time to mourn, and a time to dance.

5. A time to cast abroad stones, and a time to gather stones;
   a time to embrace, and a time to abstain from embracing.

6. A time to seek, and a time to lose;
   a time to preserve, and a time to throw away.

7. A time to tear, and a time to sew;
   a time to be silent, and a time to speak.

8. A time to love, and a time to hate;
   a time of war, and a time of peace—

9. What profit hath a worker in that wherein he toileth?

10. I saw the task which God hath given to the sons of men to be occupied with.

11. Everything hath He made excellent in its time; also He
    hath placed eternity in their heart, but in such wise
    that man cannot discover the work that God doeth from
    beginning to end.
12. I know that there is no good thing for them, but that
    a man should be glad and provide well [for himself] in
    his life.
13. And, moreover, every man who eateth and drinketh and
    enjoyeth good in all his toil—it is a gift from God.
14. I know that everything which God doeth shall be per-
    petually; to it nothing can be added, and from it nothing
    can be subtracted.
    And God hath done it that men may fear before Him.
15. That which is, hath already been; and that which is
    [destined] to be, already is; and God seeketh out that
    which is driven away [into the past].
16. And further, I saw under the sun the place of judgment—
    there was wickedness: and the place of righteousness—
    there was wickedness.
17. **I said in my heart, The righteous and the wicked
    will God judge; for there is a time [of judgment]
    for every occupation and concerning every work†.**
18. I said in my heart [It is] for the sake of the sons of men,
    that God may shew them in their true light, and *make
    them see* that they are beasts †for their part.
19. For *as the mischance of the sons of men, so is the
    mischance of the beasts*, and one mischance [happeneth]
    unto them; as the one dieth, so dieth the other, and all
    have one spirit; and *what superiority* hath the man
    over the beast? None! for all is a vapour.
20. Everything goeth to one place; everything hath come
    into existence from the dust, and everything returneth
    to the dust.
21. Who knoweth [with regard to] the spirit of the sons of
    men *whether it goeth upwards*, and the spirit of the
    beasts *whether it goeth downwards* to the earth?
22. And I saw that there was nothing better than that a man
    should be glad in his works, for that is his portion; for
    who shall bring him to look upon that which shall be
    after him?

CHAPTER IV.

1. And I returned and saw all the oppressions which were wrought under the sun: and lo the tears of the oppressed, and they had no comforter; and from the hand of their oppressors [went forth] power; and they had no comforter.

2. And I congratulated the dead who were already dead, more than the living who were still alive.

3. And better than them both, him who hath not yet come into existence, who hath not seen the evil work that is done under the sun.

4. And I saw all the toil and all the skilful work, that it meant the jealousy felt for a man by his neighbour. This also is a vapour, and a striving after wind.

5. *The fool foldeth his hands and eateth his own flesh.*

6. Better is a handful of quiet than two handfuls of toil and striving after wind.

7. And I turned and saw an empty wretchedness[1] under the sun.

8. There is a solitary man, without a second; moreover he hath no son or brother; and there is no end to all his toil, yea his eye is not sated with wealth. And for whom do I toil, and deprive myself of good? This also is a vapour and an evil task.

9. *Two are better than one, because they have a good reward in their toil.*

10. *For if one fall, the other will raise up his friend; but alas for the solitary man that falleth, and there is not a second to raise him up.*

11. *Also if two lie [together], they have warmth; but the solitary man—how shall he be warm?*

12. *And if [someone] overpower the solitary man, [yet] two can withstand him; and a three-fold cord is not quickly snapped.*

---

[1] When הבל occurs outside the usual formula, it requires a variety of renderings according to the context.

13. Better is a youth poor and wise than a king old and a fool, who knoweth not how to be admonished any more.

14. For from the prison house he emerged to become king—for even in his kingdom he was born poor.

15. I saw all the living who were going about under the sun, [that they were] with the second youth who would stand up in place of him.

16. There was no end to all the people—to all at whose head he was. Moreover they who came afterwards would not delight in him. For this also is a vapour and a striving after wind.

17. Guard thy foot when thou goest unto the house of God; and if thou draw near to hearken, *better than the gift of fools is thy sacrifice*; for they know not *except how to do* evil.

Chapter V.

1. Be not rash with thy mouth, and let not thine heart be hasty to utter a word before God; for God is in the heavens, and thou art upon the earth; therefore let thy words be few.

2. For a dream cometh with a multitude of business; and the voice of a fool in a multitude of words.

3. When thou vowest a vow to God, delay not to pay it; for there is no pleasure in fools. That which thou vowest, pay.

4. It is better that thou shouldest not vow than that thou shouldest vow and not pay.

5. Let not thy mouth cause thy flesh to incur punishment; and say not before the angel It was an unintentional error. Why should God be angry at thy voice, and destroy the work of thy hands?

6. [[For with a multitude *of business* [come] dreams, and worthless follies *in* many words.]] But fear God.

7. If thou seest the oppression of a poor man, and the wresting of judgment and justice in a province, be not astonished at the matter, for one high official above another is watching, and there are higher ones above them.

8. But an advantage to a country in all respects is a king [devoted] to cultivated land.

9. A lover of money cannot be satisfied with money; and he who loveth wealth [shall have] no profit [from it]. This also is a vapour.

10. When good things increase, many are they that consume them; and what success hath their owner save the looking at them with his eyes?

11. Sweet is the sleep of the labourer, whether he eat little or much; but the satiety [which belongeth] to the rich man doth not let him sleep.

12. There is *an evil sickness* [which] I have seen under the sun—wealth kept for its owner to his hurt.

13. And that wealth hath perished with evil trouble; and [then] he hath begotten a son and there is nothing in his possession.

14. As he came forth from his mother's womb, naked shall he go again as he came; and he shall carry away nothing, by his toil, *which can go with him*.

15. This also is *an evil sickness*; just as he came so will he go; and what profit hath he that he should toil for the wind?

16. Moreover all his days [are spent] in darkness *and mourning and great vexation and sickness* and wrath.

17. Lo! what I have seen to be good and excellent is [for a man] to eat and drink and experience good in all his toil wherein he toileth under the sun, during the [small] number of the days of his life which God hath given him, for that is his portion.

18. Also every man to whom God hath given riches and possessions, and hath granted him the power of using[1] them and of taking his portion and of being glad in his toil—this is a gift from God.

19. For he will not much notice the days of his life, for God answereth by [giving him] the gladness of his heart.

[1] Lit. 'eat.'

CHAPTER VI.

1. There is an evil which I have seen under the sun, and it is great upon men.
2. A man to whom God giveth riches and possessions and splendid wealth, and he lacketh nothing for himself of all that he desireth, but God doth not grant him the power of using[1] it, but a stranger useth[1] it—this is an empty wretchedness[2] and an evil sickness.
3. If a man beget a hundred [children] and live many years, and many be the days of his years, and his soul be not satisfied with good things, and also if he have had no burial—I say, better than he is an untimely birth.
4. For in empty nothingness[2] it came, and in darkness it goeth, and in darkness shall its name be covered;
5. yea it hath not seen or known the sun. This hath rest more than the other.
6. And though [a man] have lived a thousand years twice told, and have not experienced good, do not all go to one place?
7. *All the toil of man is for his mouth, and yet the appetite is not filled.*
8. For what advantage hath the wise man over the fool? What [advantage] hath the poor man who knoweth how to walk before the living?
9. *Better is the sight of the eyes than the roaming of the appetite.*
    This also is a vapour and a striving after wind.
10. That which is, its name hath already been called, and it was foreknown what man was; and he cannot hold his own against Him that is stronger than he.
11. For there are many things that multiply empty wretchedness[2]! What profit hath man?
12. For who knoweth what is good for man in his life, during the [small] number of the days of his transient life[2]?— seeing that he maketh them like a shadow; for who can tell man what shall be after him under the sun?

---

[1] Lit. 'eat.'   [2] Lit. 'vapour.'

Chapter VII.

1. *Better is a name than ointment.*
   Better is the day of death than the day of *birth*.
2. It is better to go to a house of mourning than to go to a house of feasting, inasmuch as that is the end of all men; and let the living lay it to heart.
3. Better is sorrow than laughter, for in sadness of countenance it is well with the heart.
4. *The heart of the wise is in the house of mourning, but the heart of fools is in the house of gladness.*
5. *It is better to hear the rebuke of the wise than for a man to hear the song of fools.*
6. *For as the sound of thorns under a pot, so is the laughter of a fool.*
   And this also is a vapour.
7. *For oppression maketh a wise man mad, and a gift destroyeth the heart.*
8. *Better is the end of a matter than the beginning of it. Better is the patient in spirit than the proud in spirit.*
9. *Be not hasty in thy spirit to be vexed; for vexation resteth in the heart of fools.*
10. *Say not, Why is it that the former days were better than these?—for thou dost not ask in wisdom concerning this.*
11. *Wisdom is good with an inheritance, and a profit to them that see the sun.*
12. *For *as the defence of wisdom, so is the defence of money*; and the advantage of knowledge [is]—wisdom keepeth alive them that possess it.*
13. See the work of God; for who can correct that which He hath made crooked?
14. In a day of prosperity be in prosperity, and in a day of evil see—even the one over against the other hath God made, in order that man may discover nothing [which shall be] after him.
15. I saw everything in the days of my transient life[1]; there is a righteous man perishing in his righteousness, and there is a wicked man prolonging [his days] in his evil.

[1] Lit. 'my vapour.'

16. Be not very righteous, and make not thyself superlatively
    wise; why shouldest thou be desolated?

17. Be not very wicked, and be not foolish; why shouldest
    thou die before thy time?

18. It is good that thou shouldest take hold of the one, and
    also from the other slack not thine hand,
    **For he that feareth God shall be quit with regard
    to them all.**

19. *Wisdom strengtheneth the wise man more than ten rulers
    which are in the city.*

20. for as for man, there is not a righteous one on the earth
    who doeth good and sinneth not.

21. Also to all the words which men speak apply not thine
    heart, that thou hear not thy servant cursing thee.

22. For assuredly many times thy heart knoweth that thou
    also hast cursed others.

23. All this I tested by wisdom. I said I will make myself
    wise; but it was far from me.

24. Far off is that which exists, and deep deep; who can
    discover it?

25. I turned about *in* my heart to know and to explore and
    to search out wisdom and a reckoning; and to know the
    folly of wickedness and foolishness *and* madness.

26. And I find [a thing] more bitter than death—a woman
    who is nets, and her heart snares, and her hands fetters.
    **He that is good before God shall escape from her,
    but a sinner shall be captured by her.**

27. See what I have found, saith Ḳoheleth, [adding] one
    thing to another to find a reckoning,

28. which my soul hath sought again and again, and I have
    not found: one man out of a thousand I have found,
    but a woman among all these I have not found.

29. **Only see what I have found, that God made men
    upright, but they have sought out many contri-
    vances.**

Chapter VIII.

1. *Who is as the wise man, and who knoweth the interpre-*
    tation of a thing? The wisdom of a man lighteth up his
    countenance, and *he that is bold* in his countenance
    is changed.

2. †Observe the commands[1] of a king,
    But on account of [thine] oath to God, be not fright-
    ened.

3. Out of his presence shalt thou go; persist not in an
    evil thing.
    for he doeth whatever he pleaseth.

4. Forasmuch as the word of a king is authoritative; and
    who may say unto him, What doest thou?

5. He that observeth the commandment will counten-
    ance no evil thing; and the heart of a wise man
    knoweth a time and judgment.

6. Because for every occupation there is a time and
    judgment.
    [[For]] the misery of man is great upon him,

7. for he knoweth not what shall be; for how it shall be who
    can tell him?

8. There is no man that hath control over the wind[2] to restrain
    the wind[2], and there is no control over the day of death,
    and there is no leave of absence in the battle, and wicked-
    ness will not help its possessors to escape.

9. All this I saw, and applied my heart to all the work that
    is done under the sun. There is a time when man hath
    power over man to his hurt.

10. And then I saw wicked men buried, and they had
    come † from a holy place; [and] they used to go about
    and *congratulate themselves*[3] in the city because they
    had so done. This also is a vapour.

11. Because a sentence on the doing of evil is not
    executed speedily, therefore the heart of the sons
    of men within them is fully given up to doing evil,

---

[1] Lit. 'mouth.'
[2] Perhaps 'the spirit.'
[3] Or 'win to themselves flattery.'

12. because a sinner doeth evil a hundred times and prolongeth [his days].   Surely also I know that it shall be well with those that fear God, because they fear before Him.

13. And it shall not be well with the wicked man, and he shall shorten[1] his days like a shadow, because he feareth not before God.

14. There is an empty wretchedness[2] which is done upon the earth, that there are righteous men to whom it befalleth according to the work of the wicked, and there are wicked men to whom it befalleth according to the work of the righteous.   I said that this also was an empty wretchedness[2].

15. And I praised gladness, because there is nothing good for man under the sun except to eat and drink and be glad; and that should accompany him in his toil during the days of his life which God hath given him under the sun.

16. When I applied my heart to know wisdom, and to see the task which is done upon the earth—for both by day and by night He seeth no sleep with His eyes—

17. I saw all the work of God, that no man can discover the work which is done under the sun; forasmuch as man may toil in searching it, but he will not discover it; and even if the wise man think that he is about to know it, he is unable to discover it.

CHAPTER IX.

1. For I laid all this to heart, and *my heart saw all this*— that the righteous and the wise and their works are in the hand of God; men are ignorant of [His] love and hate alike; everything before them *is a vapour*,

2. forasmuch as one mischance [happeneth] to them all, to the righteous and to the wicked, to the good and to the pure and to the unclean, and to him that sacrificeth and to him that sacrificeth not; as with the good so with the sinner, he that sweareth as he that feareth an oath.

[1] Lit. 'not prolong.'
[2] Lit. 'vapour.'

3. This is an evil in all that is done under the sun, that one mischance [happeneth] to them all; and moreover the heart of man is full of evil, and madness is in their heart during their life, and after [a man's life]¹—to the dead!

4. For whosoever is joined unto all the living, there is hope [for him]; for a live dog is better than a dead lion.

5. For the living know that they shall die, but the dead know not anything, and they have no longer a reward, for their memory is forgotten.

6. Both their love and their hate and their jealousy alike hath already perished; and they have no longer any portion for ever in all that is done under the sun.

7. Go! eat thy bread in gladness, and drink thy wine with a cheerful heart, for already God hath consented to thy works.

8. At all times let thy garments be white, and let not oil on thy head be lacking.

9. Enjoy life with the wife whom thou lovest all the days of thy transient life² which He hath given thee under the sun †; for that is thy portion in life, and in thy toil wherein thou toilest under the sun.

10. All that thy hand findeth to do, do it with [all] thy might; for there is no work or reckoning or knowledge or wisdom in Shᵉol whither thou goest.

11. I returned and saw under the sun that the race was not to the swift, nor the battle to the mighty; and neither was bread to the wise, nor wealth to the clever, nor favour to the skilful; but time and accident befalleth them all.

12. For man knoweth not his time, as fish that are caught in an evil net, or as birds that are caught in a snare—like them are the sons of men entrapped at an evil time, when it falleth upon them suddenly.

13. This also I saw, [an instance of] wisdom under the sun; and it was great to my thinking:

14. A little city, and few men in it; and there came unto it a great king, and surrounded it, and built against it great *siege-works*.

15. And there was found in it a poor wise man; and he would have delivered the city by his wisdom: but men took no notice of that poor wise man.

¹ Lit. 'after him.'   ² Lit. 'vapour.'

16. And I said, Wisdom is better than might, but the wisdom of the poor man is despised, and his words are not heard.

17. *The words of the wise heard in quiet [are better] than the shouting of a chief among fools.*

18. *Better is wisdom than weapons of war; but one sinner destroyeth much good.*

CHAPTER X.

1. *Dead flies contaminate † a perfumer's ointment; a little folly is more highly esteemed¹ than wisdom *and* honour.*

2. *The heart of a wise man [tends] towards his right hand, but the heart of a fool towards his left.*

3. *And on the very road as the fool is going, his mind is lacking, and he saith concerning everyone, He is a fool.*

4. If the spirit of the ruler rise against thee, do not throw up² thy place; for soothing pacifieth great sins.

5. There is an evil that I have seen under the sun, like an unintentional error which proceedeth from the ruler.

6. Folly is set in high places, while the rich sit in a low place.

7. I have seen slaves on horses, and princes walking as slaves on the ground.

8. *He that diggeth a pit shall fall into it; and he that breaketh into a wall a serpent shall bite him.*

9. *He that taketh out stones [from a quarry] shall be hurt by them; he that cleaveth logs shall be endangered by them.*

10. *If the axe be blunt and he have not sharpened the edge, then he must strengthen his force; and an advantage to *the successful man* is wisdom.*

11. *If the serpent bite from lack of enchantment, there is [afterwards] no advantage in the charmer.*

12. *The words of the mouth of the wise man are [full of] grace; but the lips of a fool destroy himself.*

13. *The beginning of the words of his mouth is folly, and the end of his talk³ is evil madness.*

---

¹ Lit. ' is more valuable.'   ² Lit. ' let go.'
³ Lit. ' his mouth.' Perhaps the word should be omitted.

14. *...but the fool multiplieth words.*
    ⟦Man knoweth not what shall be; and what shall be after him who can tell him?⟧

15. *The toil of fools wearieth them, because [a fool] knoweth not how to go to town.*

16. Alas for thee O land whose king is a child, and thy princes feast in the morning.

17. Happy art thou O land whose king is of noble birth, and thy princes feast at the [right] time, with strength and not with drunkenness.

18. **By idleness* the roof falleth into decay, and by slackness of hands the house leaketh.*

19. *Men prepare a feast for laughter, and wine *to make life glad*; and money answereth all things.*

20. Even in thy thought curse not a king, and in thy bed-chamber curse not a rich man; for a bird of the heavens may carry the sound, and that which hath wings may declare a matter.

Chapter XI.

1. Cast thy bread upon the face of the waters; for in many days thou shalt find it.

2. Give a portion to seven, and also to eight; for thou knowest not what may prove to be an evil upon the earth.

3. If the clouds be filled with rain, they empty it out upon the earth; and if a stick fall northwards or southwards, the place where the stick falleth, there it is.

4. He that watcheth the wind shall not sow, and he that looketh at the clouds shall not reap.

5. As thou knowest not what is the way of the wind, as the bones in the womb of a woman with child, so thou knowest not the work of God Who doeth all things.

6. In the morning sow thy seed, and till evening slack not thine hand; for thou knowest not which shall succeed, whether this or that, or whether both of them may be alike good.

7. And the light is sweet, and it is good for the eyes to see the sun.

8. For if a man live many years, he may be glad throughout them all; but let him remember the days of darkness, for they shall be many. All that cometh is a vapour.

9. Be glad O young man in thy youth, and let thine heart cheer thee in the days of thy young manhood; and walk in the ways of thine heart and in the sight of thine eyes;

10. **But know that concerning all these things God will bring thee into judgment.**

11. and put away sorrow from thine heart, and remove evil from thy flesh—for youth and the prime of life are a vapour—

CHAPTER XII.

1. **But remember thy Creator in the days of thy young manhood.**

ere the days of evil come, and years draw nigh when thou shalt say I have no pleasure in them.

2. Ere the sun and the light and the moon and the stars be darkened, and the clouds return after the rain.

3. In the day when the keepers of the house quake, and the men of might are bent, and the grinding maids cease because they are few, and the ladies that look through the windows be darkened;

4. and the doors on the street be shut when the sound of the mill is low; and *the sound of the sparrow fade*, and all the notes of song sink low.

5. Moreover they are afraid of a high thing, and terrors are on the road; and *he rejecteth* the almond, and the locust-fruit is [too] heavy, and the caper-berry becomes ineffectual. For man is on his way to his perpetual home, and the wailers go about in the street.

6. Ere the silver cord be *snapped*, and the golden bowl be broken; and the pitcher be shivered over the spring, and the bucket[1] be broken into the cistern;

---

[1] Perhaps ' wheel.'

7. and the dust return to the earth as it was, and the spirit return unto God who gave it.

8. Vapour of vapours, saith Ḳoheleth; all is a vapour.

9. And Ḳoheleth, besides being wise, further taught the people knowledge; and he weighed and searched out, he arranged many proverbs.

10. Ḳoheleth sought to find words of pleasure, and *a writing of* uprightness, words of truth.

11. *The words of wise men are as goads, and as nails firmly planted, gathered in collections; they are given from one shepherd.*

12. *And besides those, my son, be warned; of making many books there is no end, and much devotion to study is a weariness of the flesh.*

13. In conclusion: all has been heard—fear God and keep His commandments; for this is [the duty of] every man.

14. For every work will God bring into the judgment [that is passed] upon every hidden thing, whether good or evil.

APPENDICES

APPENDIX I.

THE GREEK VERSION OF ĶOHELETH.

The close similarity which exists between the Greek version of Ķoheleth and the extant fragments of Aquila has often been noticed. Other portions of the LXX. exhibit some Aquilean traits, e.g. S. of Songs, and a few MSS. of Ezekiel. But in the case of Ķoheleth the relationship to Aquila in style and wording is so marked that Graetz[1] suggested an interesting explanation. Jerome twice mentions Aquila's "secundam editionem, quam Hebraei κατ᾽ ἀκρίβειαν nominant"[2]; and Graetz thought that the present Greek version might be in reality Aquila's first edition, and the fragments of Aquila which have survived by Origen's labours would represent the second[3]. Montfaucon in his *Preliminaria* to the Hexapla, p. 48, supposed that the 'Aquila' column was the *editio secunda*, but he did not make any suggestion with regard to the *editio prima*. Although several writers have inclined to the theory, no one has hitherto upheld it by a detailed examination of the text in conjunction with Aquila's fragments. On the other hand it has been strenuously opposed in a careful article by Dillmann[4]. But

[1] See also, earlier than Graetz, Frankel, *Vorstudien*, p. 238, note *w*.

[2] Hier. Opp. T. v. pp. 32, 624.

[3] The suggestion commends itself to König, *Einl. A. T.*, Klostermann, *St. Kr.* 1885, and Leimdorfer, *Kohelet im Lichte der Geschichte*, Hamburg, 1892. [Freudenthal, *Hellen. Stud.* p. 46.] Renan admits the probability, *l'Ecclésiaste*, pp. 54–57. On the other hand Salzberger, in Graetz's *Monatsschrift*, 1873, 168–174, holds that the present Greek version is by Aquila, and not the 'Aquila' column of the Hexapla !

[4] *Sitzungsberichte der königlich preussischen Akademie der Wissenschaften zu Berlin*, 1892, vol. i. pp. 3–16.

his arguments do not remove the strong impression produced
by fresh study. His conclusion is that an older Greek translation lay as the groundwork of the present text; and that this
older translation was corrected by means of a more accurate
one, for the most part that of Aquila. But on the one hand it
is scarcely conceivable that a reviser would, for purposes of
correction, alter an old translation so fundamentally as to
imbue it with the Aquilean style, both in the order of words
and in many of the smallest details of grammar and syntax.
On the other hand, if his object was to produce a new translation in *imitation* of Aquila, it is surprising that he was not
more thorough; for he has left a large number of words and
phrases which, judged by the standard of Aquila's fragments,
are not consonant with his style. But if Aquila himself made
an earlier translation, and then issued a revision of it, both these
features are to be expected. The early translation would be
imbued with his style, but would nevertheless contain many
words, phrases and grammatical points which would seem to
him to require revision. And there are not wanting facts which
tend to increase the probability that such a revision was made.
Aquila is known to have been a disciple of R. Akiba[1]. He
lived therefore at an epoch in the literary history of Judaism.
The Rabbinic authorities at Jamnia had but recently made a
final pronouncement on the Canon; and Ishmael ben Elisha
and Akiba each laid down rules which formed the basis of
future exegesis[2]. But the system of Akiba, by which every
particle and letter was made to give a special meaning,
necessitated a clear consensus as to the Hebrew text. And
it is in the highest degree probable that under his influence
an authoritative recension of the Hebrew Bible was issued.
Whether the standard adopted was guided by the agreement of
the majority of Rabbis, or of the majority of their extant manu-
scripts[3], cannot be determined. But the result was a text
which, being carefully preserved by tradition, remained nearly
intact till it was stereotyped centuries later by the Masoretes.

Now Akiba, although the chief exponent, was not the

---

[1] Hier. *in Isa.* viii. 14 " Scribae et Pharisaei quorum suscepit scholam
Akybas, quem magistrum Aquilae proselyti autumant."

[2] See Graetz, *History of the Jews* (Engl. transl.), vol. ii. pp. 358 f.

[3] Jer. *Taanith* iv. fol. 68 a.

first promoter of his exegetical method; tradition traces it to
Nachum of Gimso (Emmaus). And Aquila was a companion
and disciple of the Rabbis before he attached himself to Akiba.
If, then, Aquila issued two editions of his translation, it is
reasonable to suppose that the earlier edition was made under
the influence of the 'literal' school, but on the basis of an
unrevised Hebrew text; and the later edition on the basis of
the revised recension, under the direct influence of Akiba.

And this ceases to be a mere hypothesis when the present
Greek MSS. are carefully studied. In the second Appendix it is
shewn that B and 68 (Holmes and Parsons), which approach
the nearest to the original Greek of Koheleth, presuppose a
Hebrew text widely different from the MT. This, which was
one of Dillmann's main objections to the Aquila theory,
becomes, on the contrary, one of the main factors in the theory.

The following examination of the Greek text is based, to a
large extent, on the matter collected in Dillmann's article.

1. Apart from details, the closeness with which the translator adhered to his Hebrew text is remarkably shewn in the
extraordinary exactness with which he maintains the *order*
of the words; "this order is so strict that, with hardly an
exception, it would be possible to print the Greek text as it
stands as an interlinear translation[1]."

2. To come to details. First to be considered are striking
peculiarities of Aquila's style in the treatment of the Hebrew
syntax.

את (the sign of the accus.) rendered by σύν.

In M. את occurs 72 times (omitting ix. 14 (אתה)). In 𝕲[2] it is
rendered by σὺν 29 times[3] (or 32 times, including v. 3, 6, x. 20
where σὺ οὖν, σὺ and σου must be corruptions of σύν). These 32
include the cases where את is followed by כל, in many of which
σὺν πᾶς, σὺν πάντα etc. have been corrupted into συμπᾶς,
σύμπαντα etc. But of the 36 cases in which את is not rendered
by σύν, almost all are capable of explanation. Burkitt[4] remarks
as a peculiarity of Aquila: "when את is used without the

---

[1] Dale, *A Commentary on Ecclesiastes*, London and Cambridge, 1873.

[2] 𝕲 is used throughout the appendix for the Greek text of Koh., LXX. for
that of the rest of the O.T.

[3] vii. 15 ACS, x. 19 ACS[c.a.].

[4] *Fragments of the Books of Kings according to the translation of Aquila*,
p. 12.

article, i.e. before proper names or nouns with suffixes, or in the construct state, the Greek article is used instead of σύν, cf. 4 Kings xxiii. 27, 3 Kings xxi. (xx.) 15." This disposes of 31 cases: i. 13, ii. 3, 10, 14, 20, 24, iii. 15, iv. 5 *bis*, 8, 10, v. 5 *ter*, 18, 19, vii. 7 (8), 13 (14), 18 (19) *bis*, 21 (22), viii. 8 b, 9, 16, ix. 7, 12, xi. 5, 6, 8 [cf. Aq.], xii. 1, 13. In 5 cases there seems to be a development of this practice, when את is followed by אשר: ii. 12, iii. 11, iv. 3, vii. 13 (14), viii. 16. But if this is not allowed, there remain 9 instances in which no reason can be offered why את is not rendered by σύν: ii. 12¹, iii. 11, iv. 3, vii 13 (14), 14 (15), viii. 16, ix. 15, x. 19, xii. 13. But from the extant fragments of Aquila in other parts of the Old Testament it is clear that his use of σὺν is not invariable. See, for example, Gen. i. 28, ii. 6, vi. 6 (7), xxiv. 59, xxv. 34, xxxvii. 2, xliii. 24, l. 2.

Thus, though instances occur of Greek and Syriac MSS. being coloured by this Aquilean use (e.g. Cod. A 3 Kings xii. 24 g–n, Cod. 62 in Ezek., and in the Pesh. Gen. i. 1, 1 Chr. iv. 41 and 4 times in Cant.), there is no portion of the Greek O. T. in which it occurs with this almost complete regularity.

גם and וגם rendered by καί γε.

The former occurs 40, the latter 11 times. The only exceptions are καὶ = גם viii. 16, xii. 5 [ACS καί γε], καί γε = ו ix. 6, and καί γε = כי iii. 19. But Aq. himself does not invariably adhere to the usage; for in v. 18 he renders גם by ἀλλὰ καί. See Job vii. 11 τοιγαροῦν. 1 Sam. xxviii. 22, Job xxiv. 19, Jer. iv. 12, xxxi. (xxxviii.) 37, Mic. vi. 13 καί.

ל with infinitive rendered by τοῦ with infinitive.

This occurs not only when it expresses a purpose (as frequently throughout LXX.), but also when it forms simply the complement of a verbal expression:

e.g. after δύνασθαι i. 8, viii. 17 [i. 15 ASᶜ·ᵃ, vi. 10 AS, vii. 13 (14) ACSᶜ·ᵃ],

after γνῶναι iv. 13, x. 15 [vi. 8 C has που, either a corruption of τοῦ or an accidental repetition of the first syllable of πορευθῆναι],

after ἀφιέναι v. 11,

after ἀγαθὸν iii. 12, v. 17, viii. 15, xi. 7,

after καιρὸς iii. 2–8.

¹ In ii. 12 Sᶜ·ᵃV read σύν.

In i. 16 לֵאמֹר is rendered τῷ λέγειν. See Aq. 1 S. ix. 24.

Connected with this is another peculiarity, not mentioned by Dillmann. Burkitt[1] notes that "where a Hebrew noun is preceded by the preposition לְ, [Aquila] freely uses the Greek article to express it in all cases where εἰς would be inappropriate. His aim was consistency, regardless of the niceties of either language. As long as there was something to correspond to the Hebrew preposition in the Greek, it did not matter whether it was an article or a preposition. When Hebrew prepositions coalesce with their nouns, he usually avoids using both article and preposition."

ii. 16	τοῦ σοφοῦ.	לֶחָכָם.
ii. 26	τῷ ἀνθρώπῳ.	לְאָדָם.
iii. 1	παντὶ πράγματι τῷ ὑπὸ τ. οὐρανόν.	לְכָל חֵפֶץ תַּחַת הַשָּׁמִים.
iii. 17	τῷ παντὶ πράγματι.	לְכָל חֵפֶץ.
iv. 8	τῷ παντὶ μόχθῳ αὐτοῦ.	לְכָל עֲמָלוֹ.
iv. 11	καὶ ὁ εἷς.	וּלְאֶחָד.
iv. 16	τοῖς πᾶσιν οἱ ἐγένοντο.	לְכֹל אֲשֶׁר הָיָה.
vii. 27 (28)	μία τῇ μιᾷ.	אַחַת לְאַחַת.
ix. 4	ὁ κύων.	לְכָלֶב.
x. 3	τὰ πάντα.	לַכֹּל probably.
xi. 2	τοῖς ἑπτὰ καί γε τοῖς η´.	לְשִׁבְעָה וְגַם לִשְׁמוֹנָה.

מִן of comparison rendered by ὑπὲρ more than 20 times. παρὰ ii. 9, iii. 19 only; ἢ v. 4, vii. 2 (3) only; and the genitive never.

The particles δέ and γὰρ, elsewhere so common in LXX. (except Cant.), are foreign to the Greek of Ḳoheleth. δέ is read by Codd. V, 252, and Syr.-Hex. in vii. 4 (5) only; cf. Aq. Gen. vi. 2 (3). γὰρ occurs in v. 15 only. (See App. II. p. 160.)

Among other instances of disregard for the Greek idiom in favour of the Hebrew may be noticed:

The frequent use of the Greek future in gnomic or generalising statements to represent the Hebrew imperfect: i. 8, 15, 18, ii. 14, iii. 15, vii. 9 (10), 12 (13), 20 (21), viii. 1, 17, ix. 5 a, 18, xi. 5.

בְּ rendered by ἐν: ii. 1, iii. 22, vii. 14 (15) ἰδεῖν ἐν, רָאה ב"; v. 9 ἀγαπᾶν ἐν, אהב ב"; viii. 9 ἐξουσιάζειν ἐν, שׁלט ב"; xi. 9, xii. 14 ἄξει ἐν κρίσει, יָבֹא בַמִּשְׁפָּט.

[1] Aquila, p. 13.

The treatment of the Hebrew syntax of the relative:

ii. 21   ὅτι μόχθος αὐτοῦ.   יְשֶׁעֲמָלוֹ.

iv. 2   ὅσοι αὐτοί.   אֲשֶׁר המה.

iv. 9   οἷς ἐστιν αὐτοῖς.   יש להם. Similarly v. 18, vi. 2, x. 16.

viii. 14   ὅτι φθάνει ἐπ᾽ αὐτούς.   אֲשֶׁר מֵנִיעַ אֲלֵהם.

ix. 10   ὅπου σὺ πορεύῃ ἐκεῖ.   אֲשֶׁר אתה הלך שמה.

xi. 5   ὅσα ποιήσει τὰ σύμπαντα.   אֲשֶׁר יעשה את הכל.

Note also: iii. 18, vii. 15 περὶ λαλίας, and viii. 2 περὶ λόγου, to express על דברת (cf. Ps. cx. (cix.) 4 על דברתי, Aq. κατὰ λόγον, but LXX. κατὰ τὴν τάξιν); i. 10 ἀπὸ ἔμπροσθεν ἡμῶν for מלפנינו; ii. 9 ἀπὸ ἔμπροσθέν μου for מלפני; xii. 5 εἰς οἶκον αἰῶνος αὐτοῦ for אל בית עולמו.

3. Besides these syntactical peculiarities there are several words which exhibit Aquila's constant endeavour to express his Hebrew text as literally as possible:

vi. 6, vii. 22 (23)[1] καθόδους, פעמים. So Aq. frequently. Ex. xxxiv. 24, Dt. ix. 19, xvi. 16, 1 Sam. iii. 10 bis, 1 K. xxii. 16, Is. xli. 7.

v. 10, 12, vii. 12 (13), viii. 8, xii. 11 παρά with gen., בעל.

x. 12 καταποντίζειν, בלע. So Aq. Job ii. 3, x. 8, Prov. xxi. 20, Is. xxv. 7 [LXX. only in 2 Sam. xx. 19, Ps. liv. (lv.) 10, Lam. ii. 2, 5].

vii. 14 (15) συμφώνως, לעמת. So Aq. Ez. iii. 8, xi. 22, Ex. xxviii. 27 (see Field).

iv. 8, v. 10, 17, vi. 3, 6, vii. 14 (15), ix. 18 ἀγαθωσύνη, טובה. So Aq. v. 10, Ps. xxxvii. (xxxviii.) 21, and ἀγαθοσύνη Ps. xv. (xvi.) 2.

xii. 6 συντροχάσῃ, נרץ.

The above are the most striking in Dillmann's list of the words "which can with most probability be referred to an Aquilean source." His list also includes:

iv. 1, v. 7, vii. 7 (8) συκοφαντίζειν, עשק. So Aq. Ps. cxix. (cxviii.) 121, Prov. xxviii. 3. Words from the same stem occur 15 times in Aq. and only 6 times in LXX.

x. 5 ἀκούσιον, שגגה. So Aq. v. 5.

iv. 12 ἔντριτος, משלש, a ἅπαξ λεγ.

vii. 8 (9), x. 13 ἐσχάτη, אחרית (cf. i. 11 εἰς τὴν ἐσχάτην, לאחרונה). Aq. must have had ἐσχάτη in vii. 8 (9).

4. Another consideration, which Dillmann dismisses some-

---

[1] On the doublet in the latter passage see App. II. p. 163.

what lightly, is that there are several words or phrases in the fragments of Aquila in Koheleth which agree with ⅭⅣ :

Aq. alone. i. 7, ii. 11, 15, iii. 15, viii. 8, x. 15, perh. ii. 24, viii. 1 (see note).

Aq. and Θ. i. 13, ii. 13, 16, 19, iv. 3, 8, v. 13, 19, vi. 8, ix. 11, 12, x. 4, 5, xii. 11, 13, perh. vii. 7 (8), 24 (25).

Aq. and Σ. xi. 1, xii. 9, 12.

Aq. Σ Θ. i. 2, iv. 10, v. 1, vi. 2, vii. 18 (19), 26 (27), viii. 12, ix. 7, 8, x. 11, xi. 4, 9, xii. 7.

So far Dillmann's lists are in favour of the conclusion that the Greek text of Koheleth was due to the hand of Aquila. But he advances a series of objections which require examination.

1. After citing the above passages in which Aq. agrees with ⅭⅣ, he says "the passages are far more numerous where Aq. differs from ⅭⅣ." This, in the scattered fragments of Aq. which have survived, is true. But, on the one hand, it is just those passages in which differences occur‧which would be more likely to survive; commentators and scholiasts might occasionally mention instances of agreement, but only where they considered them interesting or striking. And, on the other hand, a second edition presupposes differences. The reasons for all the alterations are, of course, impossible to trace, though occasionally they seem to be discernible. But to disprove the Aquila theory it would be necessary to shew that the bulk of the words and phrases in ⅭⅣ are non-Aquilean. But the opposite is the case. Of the fifty or so which Dillmann collects as the "chief instances of difference," many occur elsewhere in fragments of Aquila, and some are frequent with him and rare in LXX.

(a) *Words which occur only, or frequently, in Aquila.*

ii. 8. ⅭⅣ περιουσιασμός. Aq. οὐσίαι. H. סגלה.

περιουσιασμός occurs in LXX. Ps. cxxxv. (cxxxiv.) 4. But cognate words are found in Aq. περιούσιον, סגלה Mal. iii. 17; περιουσία, רכוש Gen. xiv. 21 ; περιουσία, יתר Ps. xvii. (xvi.) 14.

x. 9.   Ǥ διαπονηθήσεται.   Aq. σπασθήσεται.   H. יעצב.

LXX. nowhere has διαπονηθῆναι or cognates for עצב; in
Aq., on the contrary, they are not infrequent:

διαπονηθῆναι, התעצב Gen. vi. 6, xxxiv. 7, 1 Sam. xx. 3, 34.

διαπόνημα, עֶצֶב 2 Sam. v. 21, Ps. xvi. (xv.) 4, cxxvii.
(cxxvi.) 2, Is. lviii. 3, Ps. cxv. 4 (cxiii. 12); see Field.

διαπόνησις מעצבה Is. l. 11.

i. 3.   Ǥ μόχθος and -θεῖν.   Aq. κόπος and -πιάζειν.   H. עמל.

μόχθος is the invariable rendering of עָמָל in Ḳoh., occurring
22 times; μοχθεῖν occurs 9 times, and κοπιῶ once, ii. 18. [But
AS μοχθῶ.]

Aq. has μόχθος, -θεῖν for עמל in Ps. lxxiii. (lxxii.) 16, Ḳoh.
ii. 11, 19, 21. But throughout the whole of the LXX. neither
the substantive nor the verb is found for עמל. Dt. xxvi. 7
μόχθον AF is probably a hexaplaric corruption.

(Aq. also has μοχθοῦν (a ἅπ. γεγρ.) in Is. vii. 13 bis for
הלאות. His use of κόπος finds a parallel in Ps. xciv. (xciii.) 20,
and probably lv. (liv.) 11, Job vii. 3.)

x. 20.   Ǥ ὁ ἔχων [τὰς] πτέρυγας¹.   Aq. ὁ κυριεύων πτέρυγος.
H. בעל [ה]כנפים.

The rendering ὁ ἔχων is foreign to LXX., except in
Dan. viii. 6, 20 (LXX. Θ).

But Aq. has it frequently:

Hos. ii. 18 (16) ἔχων με (LXX. Βααλείμ).

Is. xli. 15 ἔχοντα στόμα στομάτων (LXX. πριστηροειδεῖς).

Nah. i. 2 ἔχων θυμόν (LXX. μετὰ θυμοῦ).

Cant. viii. 11 ἔχοντι πλήθη (LXX. Βεελαμών).

Jer. xxxvii. (xliv.) 13 (acc. to S. H.) ὁ ἔχων τὰς ἐπισκέψεις
(LXX. ἄνθρωπος παρ' ᾧ κατέλυεν).

Job xxxi. 39 (id.) τῶν ἐχόντων αὐτήν (LXX. entirely astray).

Nah. iii. 4 (acc. to Hier.) ἐχούσης φάρμακα (LXX. ἡγουμένη
φαρμάκων).

See also Mal. ii. 11 καὶ ἔσχε, ובעל (LXX. ἐπετήδευσεν).

Is. lxii. 4 ἐσχημένη, בעולה (LXX. οἰκουμένη).

xii. 5.   Ǥ θάμβοι.   Aq. τρόμῳ τρομήσουσιν.   H. חתחתים.

Aq. is nowhere extant where the cognate words חַת, חָתַת,
חִתִּית, חִתָּה occur; but LXX. renders none of them by θάμβος.
As renderings of other Hebrew words θάμβος and cognates

---

¹ B ὁ τὰς πτέρυγας. ACS ὁ ἔχων πτέρυγας. See App. ii. p. 166.

are more frequent in Aq. than in LXX. (12 or 13 times in
Aq., 9 times in LXX.).

Field on Jud. ix. 4 (q. v.) says of a variant θαμβουμένους
"*versio Aquilam sapit.*"

xii. 4.   𝔊 αἱ θυγατέρες τοῦ ᾄσματος.   Aq. τὰ τῆς ᾠδῆς.   H. בנות השיר.

The construction τὰ τῆς ᾠδῆς is not found elsewhere in
Aq. But the use of θυγάτηρ is seen in Mal. ii. 11 τὴν θυγατέρα
θεοῦ ἀπηλλοτριωμένου, בת אל נכר (LXX. εἰς θεοὺς ἀλλοτρίους).
In Mic. iv. 14 תתנודדי בת נדוד, LXX. renders בת as a vocative,
while (acc. to Hier.) Aq., with ΣΘΕ´, preserves the construct
state of the Hebrew idiom. LXX. similarly in Lam. ii. 18
where Aq. *vacat.* (With regard to ᾆσμα and ᾠδή see below,
p. 127.)

To the above may be added the two following words, of
which Aquila's version has not been preserved:

ii. 14, 15, iii. 19 *ter*, ix. 2, 3.   𝔊 συνάντημα.   H מקרה.

LXX. nowhere renders thus; and it has the verb συναντάω
only in Num. xxiii. 16 וַיִּקָּר.

But Aq. has

συνάντημα (prob.) 1 Sam. vi. 9 (LXX. σύμπτωμα).
συνάντησις 1 Sam. xx. 26 (LXX. σύμπτωμα).
συνάντισμα Dt. xxiii. 11 (LXX. ῥύσις, MT מִקְרֵה).
συναντάω Is. li. 19, lx. 18, Jer. xxxii. (xxxix.) 23 (also
συνάντημα Is. lvii. 13, H. קבוץ).

x. 1.   𝔊 σαπριοῦσιν.   H יבאיש.

LXX. nowhere renders the verb thus; though it has
σαπρία αὐτοῦ for באשו in Joel ii. 20.

Aq. ἐσαπρίσατε Ex. v. 21 (LXX. ἐβδελύξατε); and the
substantive σαπρία Am. iv. 10 (LXX. ἐν πυρί), Is. v. 2 (LXX.
ἀκάνθας).

Under this heading may also be included some curious
instances in which 𝔊 has all the appearance of being Aquilean,
while the renderings ascribed to Aquila are foreign to his
usual methods:

viii. 11.   𝔊 ἐπληροφορήθη καρδία υἱῶν τοῦ ἀνθρώπου is a perfectly
literal rendering of מלא לב בני האדם, while Aquila's rendering ἐτόλμησαν οἱ υἱοὶ τῶν ἀνθρώπων is free and inaccurate.

xii. 10.   𝔊 καὶ γεγραμμένον εὐθύτητος as a rendering of וכתוב ישר
has a strong savour of Aquila, while his own καὶ συνέγραψεν
ὀρθῶς is paraphrastic. But in this case Aquila's phrase is
also ascribed to Σ, and may be a hexaplaric corruption.

i. 8.   𝔊 ἔγκοποι.   Aq. κοπιῶσιν.   H. יגעים.

iv. 17.   𝔊 τοῦ ἀκούειν.   Aq. ὥστε ἀκούειν.   H. לשמע.

v. 7.   𝔊 ἐπ᾽ αὐτούς.   Aq. μετ᾽ αὐτούς.   H. עליהם.

v. 18.   𝔊 καί γε.   Aq. ἀλλὰ καί.   H. גם.

vii. 10 (11).   𝔊 τί ἐγένετο.   Aq. διὰ τί.   H. מה היה.

vii. 17 (18).   𝔊 ἐν οὐ καιρῷ σου.   Aq. πρὸ τοῦ καιροῦ σου.   H. בלא עתך.

viii. 6.   𝔊 κρίσις.   Aq. τρόπος.   H. משפט.

ix. 13.   𝔊 πρός με.   Aq. παρ᾽ ἐμοί.   H. אלי.

ix. 18.   𝔊 σκεύη πολέμου.   Aq. σκεύη πολεμικά.   H. כלי קרב.

(b)   *Words which occur elsewhere in Aquila.*

i. 2 and *passim.*   𝔊 ματαιότης[1].   Aq. ἀτμὶς or ἀτμός.   H. הבל.

In LXX. ματαιότης is confined to the Psalter exc. Prov.
xxii. 8 (H. און); it is the rendering of הבל in Pss. xxxi. 7,
xxxix. 6, lxii. 10, lxxviii. 33, cxliv. 4. Elsewhere mostly
μάταιον, -α, εἴδωλον, κενός.

Aq. has ἀτμός only in Ps. lxxviii. (lxxvii.) 33 exc. in Ḳoh.
But he has ματαιότης in Is. lvii. 13, Jon. ii. 9, Job vii. 16, Prov.
xiii. 11 and possibly Jer. x. 8. (Also τὰ μάταια Jer. xiv. 22,
μάτην Ps. xxxix. (xxxviii.) 12, Job ix. 29.)

It seems, therefore, that ματαιότης was Aquila's usual
rendering of הבל, but in his 2nd edition of Ḳoh. he preferred
the more literal ἀτμός, which was afterwards adopted by
ΣΘ.

i. 5.   𝔊 ἕλκει.   Aq. εἰσπνεῖ.   H. שואף.

εἰσπνεῖ is a ἅπαξ λεγ. But Aq. has εἵλκυεν in Jer. ii. 24
(LXX. ἐπνευματοφορεῖτο), and ἀφειλκύσαντο Job v. 5 (LXX.
ἐκσιφωνισθείη).

i. 18, ii. 23.   𝔊 ἄλγημα.   Aq. βάσανος.   H. מכאוב.

LXX. nowhere renders מכאוב by ἄλγημα, though it occurs
once for כְּאֵב Ps. xxxix. 2. Aq. has it for מכאוב Ps. xxxii.
(xxxi.) 10 (LXX. μάστιγες). ἄλγος is found 6 times in Aq.,
and only thrice in LXX.

The only instance of βάσανος for מכאוב is cited by Field
from an unknown translator (perh. Aq.) in 2 Chr. vi. 29.

ii. 6.   𝔊 κολυμβήθρα.   Aq. λίμνη.   H. ברכה.

Aq. has κολυμβήθρα 2 Sam. ii. 13, iv. 12 (𝔊 in both κρήνη).

---

[1] G[B] ἀτμὸς ix. 9.

ii. 8. ᴳ ἐντρυφήματα. Aq. τρυφαί. H. תַעֲנֻגוֹת.

ἐντρυφήματα is a ἅπαξ λεγ. But Aq. has ἐντρυφᾶν for התענג Is. lviii. 14. So LXX. Is. lv. 2, lvii. 4.

LXX. and Aq. each use τρυφή in 4 passages; and Aq. also has τρυφήτης Dt. xxviii. 54, τρυφερία Gen. xviii. 12, 1 Sam. xv. 32.

iv. 10. ᴳ μέτοχος. Aq. φίλος. H. חֶבֶר.

φίλος for words from √חבר occurs nowhere else, except ᴼ. Dan. ii. 13, 17, 18. Aq. has μέτοχος Prov. xxviii. 24, Ps. cxix. (cxviii.) 63, and probably Hos. vi. 9 where Hier. translates his word *Participatio*.

v. 5. ᴳ ἄγνοια. Aq. ἀκούσιον (x. 5 ᴳ Aq. ἀκούσιον). H. שְׁגָגָה.

Aq. nowhere else uses ἀκούσιον, -ως, while it is the almost invariable rendering of LXX. in Lev., Num., Josh.

Aq. has ἄγνοια Lev. iv. 2, 22, v. 15[1]; also ἀγνοίαι for שְׁגִיאוֹת Ps. xix. (xviii.) 13.

v. 5. ᴳ διαφθείρειν. Aq. διαλύειν. H. חָבַל.

Aq. elsewhere uses διαλύειν once only, Ez. xix. 12, H. התפרקו. He renders חבל by διαφθείρειν Cant. viii. 5 (and by ἐκφθείρειν Is. liv. 16). LXX. Mic. ii. 10 only.

Aq., however, uses it 14 times for שחת.

v. 12. ᴳ κακία. Aq. πονηρόν. H. רעה (subst.) }
ix. 12. ᴳ κακός. Aq. πονηρός. H. רעה (adj.) }

The reason for Aq.'s alteration in these two passages cannot, of course, be known. But no stress can be laid on it, since throughout LXX. and Aq. רעה (subst. and adj.) are rendered by κακία, -κός, πονηρία, -ρός, quite indiscriminately.

vii. 3. ᴳ κακία. Aq. κάκωσις. H. רֹעַ.

No argument can be based on this, since Aq. is not extant in any other passage where רֹע occurs (LXX. has κακία for רֹע only in 1 Sam. xvii. 28, Hos. ix. 15). But κάκωσις is a word confined entirely to Σ, except Aq. ᴼ here, and ᴼ 1 Sam. xxviii. 10.

x. 6. ᴳ ὕψη. Aq. ὑψώματα. H. מְרוֹמִים.

Aq. nowhere else uses ὕψωμα for מרום, though it is his regular word for במה. But he frequently renders מרום by ὕψος, Ps. vii. 8, x. 5 (ix. 26) prob., lxxi. (lxx.) 19, xciii. (xcii.) 4, Prov. ix. 3, Is. xxxviii. 14, Jer. xlix. 16, Ez. xvii. 23. Of these LXX. has ὕψος only in Ps. vii. 8, Is. xxxviii. 14.

[1] In connexion with v. 15 see Field's note on iv. 27.

xi. 3.   𝔊 ἐκχέουσιν,   Aq. ἐκκενώσουσιν.   H. יריקו.

This cannot be considered an important variation.   Aq. has ἐκκενώσω Ps. xviii. (xvii.) 43, Jer. xlviii. (xxxi.) 12; but also ἐκχεόμενον Cant. i. 3 (LXX. ἐκκενωθέν).   And LXX. has the former 6 times, and the latter twice.

To these may be added some words which find parallels in Aquila, but of which Aquila's equivalents in Ķoheleth have not survived:

ii. 21, iv. 4, v. 10.   𝔊 ἀνδρεία.   H. כשרון ⎱
       x. 10.   𝔊 τοῦ ἀνδρείου.   H. הכשיר ⎰

See Prov. xxxi. 19, Aq. ἀνδρεία, H. כישור (distaff).

v. 2, 15.   𝔊 παραγίνεται.   H. בוא.

See Aq. Jud. ix. 37.

v. 12, 15, 16, vi. 2.   𝔊 ἀρρωστία.   H. חולה and חלי.

See Aq. Dt. xxviii. 16, Ps. xxxv. (xxxiv.) 13, lxxvii. (lxxvi.) 11, Prov. xviii. 14, Is. xxxviii. 9, liii. 3 [1 (3) K. xiv. 1, 5], in each of which (except 1 K.) LXX. has a different rendering.   Aq. is not extant in the five (canonical) passages in which LXX. has the word.

iv. 6, vi. 5, ix. 17.   𝔊 ἀνάπαυσις.   H. נחת.

Except in Ķoh. ἀνάπαυσις is used for נחת only in Σ Is. xxx. 15.   But in vi. 5 Field gives "'Α. Σ. Θ. ἀνάπαυσιν" from S.H. ܢܘܚ, and it is Aq.'s usual word for other derivatives of נוח, Ps. xcv. (xciv.) 11, Is. xi. 10, xxxiv. 14, lxvi. 1, Zech. ix. 1; and see Field on Lev. i. 9.

vii. 5 (6).   𝔊 ἐπιτίμησις.   H. גערה.

Aq. has it Ps. lxxvi. (lxxv.) 7, Prov. xiii. 8, xvii. 10, Is. xxx. 17, lxvi. 15, and for מִגְעֶרֶת Dt. xxviii. 20.   LXX. has it for גערה only 5 times, 4 of them being in the Pss.[1]

vii. 17 (16).   𝔊 ἐκπλαγῆς.   H. תשמם.

LXX. nowhere uses this as a rendering of a Hebrew word[2].   But it is Aq.'s usual equivalent for חרד, Gen. xxvii. 33, 1 Sam. iv. 13, xiii. 7, xvi. 4, xxi. 2 (1), xxviii. 5.

---

[1] Ps. xviii. (xvii.) 16 = 2 Sam. xxii. 16.
[2] It occurs in Wisdom and 2 and 4 Macc.

(c) *Instances in which a reason is discernible for*
Aquila's alterations.

(i) A rare or unique rendering of 𝕲 was replaced by a
commoner word.

iv. 8, 16, xii. 12. 𝕲 πειρασμός. Aq. τέλος (*vacat* in xii. 12). H. קץ.

πειρασμός occurs here only, πέρας being the usual LXX.
rendering of קץ (τέλος 5 times).

vii. 15 (16). 𝕲 μένων. Aq. μακρύνων. H. מאריך.

μένω for האריך is a ἅπαξ λεγ. 𝕲 has μακρύνω in viii. 13,
LXX. Ps. cxxix. (cxxviii.) 3, Is. liv. 2. Both LXX. and Aq.
have other renderings.

vii. 25 (26). 𝕲 ψῆφος. Aq. λογισμός. H. חשבון.

ψῆφος for חשבון is a ἅπαξ λεγ., but λογισμός is the regular
LXX. rendering of words from √חשב.

(LXX. has ψῆφος for חצץ Lam. iii. 16, and צר Ex. iv. 25,
only. Aq. for מספר Dt. xxxii. 8, Is. xl. 26, and see 2 (4) K.
xii. 5 (4) in Field.)

xii. 4. 𝕲 ᾆσμα. Aq. ᾠδή. H. שיר.

ᾆσμα is found in a few passages in LXX. for שיר and
שירה, whereas ᾠδή occurs *passim*. Aq. has ᾆσμα Ps. xxviii.
(xxvii.) 7, and ᾠδή only for הגיון Ps. ix. 17.

xii. 6. 𝕲 ἀνθέμιον. Aq. λύτρωσις. H. גֻּלָּה.

ἀνθέμιον is a ἅπαξ λεγ., while λύτρωσις (which should represent גְּאֻלָּה) is found for גֻּלּוֹת in LXX. Jud. i. 15, where Aq. in
despair transliterates Γολλάθ. In Ḳoh., Aq. was equally
puzzled, and took refuge in the meaningless guess of the
LXX., because it was clear that a proper name was here
impossible.

(ii) Changes for the sake of greater exactness.

i. 1, xii. 8 (i. 2, 12, xii. 10 Aq. *vacat*). 𝕲 ἐκκλησιαστής. Aq.
κωλέθ or κωελέθ.

The word ἐκκλησιαστής is a good instance of Aq.'s method
of rendering words 'ἐτυμολογικῶς.' But in his 2nd edition
he relapsed into a transliteration.

Other instances of such a relapse in his 2nd edition are
the following, quoted from Field's list:

Jer. xxi. 13	צור.	1. στερεά.	2. Τύρος.
xiii. 12	נבל.	1. ὑδρία.	2. νέβελ.

Jer. xlviii. (xxxi.) 12 ונבליהם. 1. καὶ τὰ κέρατα αὐτοῦ.
2. καὶ τὰ νέβελ αὐτοῦ.

Ez. viii. 16 האולם. 1. τῆς προστάδος. 2. τοῦ αἰλάμ.

xlii. 1 הגזרה. 1. (ap. Hier.) *separati.* 2. τοῦ γαζερά.

ii. 19, viii. 9. G ἐξουσιάζεσθαι. Aq. κυριεύειν. H. שלט.

(In viii. 8 G ἐξουσιάζων for שליט, ἐξουσία for שלטון. Aq. *vacat.*)

The following considerations suggest that Aq. made the change to distinguish the late word שלט from the classical משל:

(1) ἐξουσιάζειν in LXX. is almost unknown:—for שלט Ezr. vii. 24, Neh. v. 15 only; for משל Neh. ix. 37 only.

(2) It occurs in G ix. 17, x. 4 for משל, and is Aq.'s usual rendering, Gen. i. 16, 18, Jud. viii. 22, 1 K. v. 1 (iv. 21), Is. lii. 5, Ez. xix. 14, Job xxv. 2, Ps. viii. 7, lxvi. (lxv.) 7.

(3) κυριεύειν is Θ's rendering of שלט[1] 6 times in Dan. (LXX. Dan. ii. 38, 39 only).

vii. 25 (26). G ἐκύκλωσα. Aq. περιώδευσα. H. סבתי.

Aq. has κυκλόω for סבב Gen. xxxvii. 7, 1 Sam. xxii. 18. But he seems to have changed his rendering here to distinguish between gyrating (cf. i. 6) and travelling from one point to another.

vii. 29 (30). G πλήν. Aq. μόνον. H. לבד.

Aq. has πλήν 16 times, but always for אך (LXX. has it in none of these passages), while he uses μόνον only in this passage, presumably to adhere more closely to the meaning of the root בדד.

xii. 3. G διαστραφῶσιν. Aq. (acc. to Hier.) πλανηθήσονται. H. התעותי.

עות is rendered by πλανᾶν here only. The meaning of the word being quite different from that in i. 15, vii. 13, Aq. distinguished it by a different (though inadequate) rendering.

xii. 5. G θάμβοι. Aq. τρόμῳ τρομήσουσι. H. חתחתים.

It has been shewn above that Aq. frequently uses θάμβος. But he here wished to represent more closely the reduplicated form of the Heb. Cf. Is. xviii. 1 σκιὰ σκιά, H. צלצל; Jer. xlvi. (xxvi.) 20 καλὴ καὶ κεκαλλιωμένη, H. יפהפיה.

---

[1] κύριος for שליט occurs LXX. Θ. Dan. iv. 14 only.

(iii) Instances in which Aquila's variations from 𝔊 were probably the result of an altered opinion (derived from his Jewish teacher) as to the derivation or punctuation of Hebrew words. In Field's lists of words in his two editions a dozen or more of such variations occur.

i. 14, 17, ii. 11, vi. 9. 𝔊 προαίρεσις. Aq. νομή. H. רעות.

i. 18. 𝔊 γνώσεως. Aq. θυμοῦ. H. כעם. In his 1st edition Aq. read דעת.

ii. 8. 𝔊 οἰνοχόον καὶ οἰνοχόας. Aq. κυλίκιον καὶ κυλίκια. H. שדה ושדות.

In his 1st edition Aq. seems to have understood the words as 'cup-bearers'; in his 2nd, of 'cups.' (κυλίκιον occurs LXX. Est. i. 7.)

ii. 12. 𝔊 βουλῆς. Aq. βασίλεως. H. מלך.

If βουλῆς is not a mere scribal error for βασίλεως, Aq. read, in his 1st edition, מְלַךְ, an Aram. and NH word.

ii. 26. 𝔊 προσθεῖναι. Aq. συλλέγειν. H. לאסף.

In his 1st edition Aq. mistook אסף for יסף.

It is true that in LXX. προστιθέναι is used for אסף, but (except in one or two cases where Heb. is or should be read יסף) only in the special sense of being 'gathered' to one's fathers—people—grave.

(Aq. renders אסף by συλλέγειν Ps. xxxv. (xxxiv.) 15, xxxix. (xxxviii.) 7, and הָאָסִף by συλλογῆς Ex. xxiii. 16.)

xii. 5. 𝔊 διασκεδάσθη. Aq. καρπεύσει. H. תפר.

Aq. derived the word in his 1st edition from פרר, in his 2nd from פרה.

xii. 6. 𝔊 συντριβῇ. Aq. δράμῃ. H. תרוץ.

A change from √רצץ to √רוץ, if the text of 𝔊 is correct. But it is very unlikely that תשבר and תרוץ could have been rendered by the same word. συντριβῇ, v. 20, may be a corruption of συντρέχῃ (cf. συντροχάσῃ for the following נרוץ).

xii. 9. 𝔊 καὶ οὓς ἐξιχνιάσεται κόσμιον παραβολῶν.

Aq. καὶ ἠνωτίσατο καὶ ἠρεύνησε καὶ κατεσκεύασε παροιμίας.

H. ואזן וחקר תקן משלים.

In his 1st edition Aq. had a reading יחקר before him, and pointed the phrase וְאָזֵן יַחֲקֵר תִּקֵן מְשָׁלִים; in his 2nd he followed the authorised recension[1]. The bald literalness of 𝔊 is thoroughly Aquilean.

---

[1] Still, however, connecting אָזֵן with אֹזֶן.

There still remain 17 instances in Dillmann's list not yet examined.

ii. 25. 𝔊 πίεται, Aq. φείσεται are probably both corrupted from πείσεται. See App. II. p. 158.

xii. 11. The meaningless πεπυρώμενοι 𝔊^{ACS} is probably a corruption of πεφυτεύμενοι, which Aq. shares with 𝔊^{B}. The remaining words are:

i. 3. 𝔊 περισσεία. Aq. πλέον. H. יותר. (Neither occurs for יותר outside Koheleth.)

i. 9. 𝔊 πρόσφατον. Aq. καινόν. H. חדש. (𝔊 has καινόν in the foll. v.)

i. 13. 𝔊 κατασκέψασθαι. Aq. ἐξερευνᾶν. H. תור. (But since Aq. has the variety νοεῖσθαι in ii. 3, why should κατασκέψασθαι be denied him?)

i. 17, ii. 2, 12, vii. 7 (8), 25 (26), ix. 3. 𝔊 παραβολαί, περιφέρειν, -φέρεια, -φορά, παραφορά. Aq. πλάναι, -ησις, -ᾶν. H. הולל, הוללות.

iii. 8. 𝔊 φιλεῖν. Aq. ἀγαπᾶν. H. לאהב.

iv. 13. 𝔊 προσέχειν. Aq. φυλάσσεσθαι. H. הזהר. (𝔊 has φύλαξαι in xii. 12.)

vii. 20 (19). 𝔊 βοηθήσει. Aq. ἐνισχύσει. H. תעז.

vii. 27 (26). 𝔊 θήρευμα. Aq. παγίδες (or παγιδεύματα). H. מצודים. (Aq. also has ἀμψίβληστρον Ez. xii. 13, and ὀχύρωμα Ps. lxvi. (lxv.) 11, as renderings of מצודה. LXX. has θήρευμα only in Lev. xvii. 13 = 'game.')

viii. 10. 𝔊 καὶ ἐπῃνέθησαν. Aq. καὶ ἐκαυχήσαντο = וישתבחו.

viii. 15. 𝔊 συμπρόσεσται. Aq. συνεισέρχεται. H. ילונו. (Aq. also has προστίθεσθαι Jer. l. (xxvii.) 5.)

x. 9. 𝔊 ἐξαίρων. Aq. μετατιθῶν. H. מסיע.

xi. 6. 𝔊 στοιχήσει. Aq. εὐθετήσει. H. יכשר.

xii. 1 (v. 3, xii. 10, Aq. vacat). 𝔊 θέλημα. Aq. πρᾶγμα. H. חפץ. (There is no reason why Aq. should not have used θέλημα, since he has the varieties χρεία xii. 10, βουλὴ Prov. xxxi. 13, βουλήματα Ps. i. 2. 𝔊 has πρᾶγμα iii. 1, 17, v. 7, viii. 6, i.e. in 4 of the 7 passages in which חפץ occurs.)

xii. 4. 𝔊 ταπεινωθήσονται. Aq. κλιθήσονται. H. ישחו. (Aq. also has κατακύπτειν Ps. xlii. (xli.) 6, 12; and for שחה, Ps. xliv. (xliii.) 26.

xii. 11. 𝔊^{BC} συνθεμάτων. Aq. συνταγμάτων. H. אספות. (𝔊^{sc.a} has συνταγμάτων, and Aq.'s rendering is not quite certain.)

Of these few instances no clear explanations offer themselves. In some passages it is possible that Aquila translated directly from his Hebrew text, without troubling to take account of his 1st edition. But it is only natural that in a 2nd edition the writer should make several small changes of wording, the reasons for which cannot be traced. And this is illustrated by Field's list of Aquila's double renderings; in some cases the reason for a variation is discernible, but frequently it is not.

2. It can now be realised how little weight can be attached to a further series of words in 𝔊 which Dillmann states that "Aquila certainly expressed, or would have expressed, otherwise"! Four of them are repeated from his previous list—πρόσφατον i. 9, μένων vii. 15 (16), βοηθήσει vii. 19 (20), διασκεδασθῇ xii. 5.

i. 16. 𝔊 ἐν τῇ καρδίᾳ μου. H. עם לבי. This may have arisen from corruption in the Greek; or בלבי may have been a revised reading in the authorised Hebrew recension. But Aq. was not always accurate in his prepositions; see v. 7 μετ᾽ αὐτοὺς for עליהם, ix. 13 παρ᾽ ἐμοί for אלי.

In the case of σκληρὸς for סבל vii. 17 (18), and ὀχληρία for סבלות vii. 25 (26), it may be said of any other translator, quite as truly as of Aq., that he would "certainly have expressed them otherwise." No trace of such words for סבל or כסל is to be found in any passage in the LXX. or in the other translations. It is easier to believe that the Greek has been corrupted.

The same may be said of ἐκπέσῃ for קהה x. 10, unless Aq. misread the word as קרה, in which case the rendering would be characteristically literal.

On the other hand it is perfectly possible to imagine that Aq. wrote ἀργεία for שפלות x. 18, and ἐν ἀσθενείᾳ for בשפל xii. 4. The two words sufficiently represent the meaning of the root in the two passages. ταπείνωσις might have been more literal, but in each case ταπεινωθήσεται, -ονται, occurs in the verse.

In xi. 9, 10, xii. 1 νεότης is used twice to render ילדות and twice בחורות. This would be strange from the hand of any translator. But the use of νεανίσκε for בחור in v. 9 suggests that בחורות was rendered νεανιότης or νεανικότης, which could easily be corrupted to νεότης. See Ps. ix. 1, xlvi. (xlv.) 1, where Aq. has νεανιότητος and ἐπὶ νεανιοτήτων for על מות and על עלמות.

In xii. 3 Dillmann objects to ὀπὴ for ארבה, because Aq. has

καταρράκτης in Is. lx. 8, Hos. xiii. 3; but he does not note that he also has θυρίδες in Gen. vii. 11 (LXX. καταρράκται). Moreover this is the only passage in the O. T. where ארבה means 'an opening to look through'; and thus Aq. might think ὀπὴ suitable here and nowhere else.

Lastly, παχύνθη for הסתבל xii. 5 need present no difficulty. In Ps. cxliv. (cxliii.) 14 for מסבלים (LXX. παχεῖς) Aq. has σιτευτοί or σιτιστοί, shewing that he took the root סבל to imply 'fatness.'

3. Dillmann lays stress on the frequent free renderings of Hebrew expressions, and on many passages badly translated. It might be enough to reply that these would afford Aquila sufficient reason for issuing a new edition. But even in his acknowledged fragments, he is far from being invariably accurate or literal. See, for example:

ii. 5 πᾶν κάρπιμον, H. כל פרי. ii. 12 ἀφροσύνας, H. סכלות. iii. 11 ὡς οὐχ, H. מבלי אשר לא. iv. 3 τὸ πεποιημένον, H. נעשה. v. 12 εἰς πονηρὸν αὐτῷ, H. לרעתו. vii. 7 (8) εὐτονίας αὐτοῦ, H. מתנה. vii. 26 (27) πικρότερον, H. מר. x. 1 μύρον, H. שמן [רוקח]. x. 15 κακώσει αὐτούς, H. תיגענו. x. 20 πτέρυγος, H. [ה]כנפים. xii. 6 λύτρωσις, H. גלת.

To these may be added the eleven instances referred to on pp. 123 f. And a brief study in Field's *Hexapla* of any O.T. book of which Aquila's fragments survive will shew that it is possible to exaggerate his literal exactness. Montfaucon (*Prelim. Hexapl.*, p. 48) rightly says "potuit Aquila etiam in illa κατ' ἀκρίβειαν interpretatione non semper eadem religione in vertendo uti; nec insolitum est Interpretes quoslibet modo litterae haerere, modo elegantiore interpretandi genere procedere."

This examination shews that the Greek text is saturated with the style of Aquila; many of his unique characteristics are found in it; many words and phrases are used in it which can be amply paralleled from his fragments; on the other hand there is not a word or phrase in it that occurs frequently in the LXX. but is foreign to Aquila. No one, at that early date, who tried to revise an old Greek translation on the basis of Aquila, could have possessed the artistic skill and inventive subtlety necessary to do the work as it has been done; to go so far in adopting Aquila's methods, and yet not to go further and *Aquilise* where it would seem obvious to do so. While if

Aquila revised his own translation, the revision need not have resulted from more than Dillmann is willing to allow as possible—"correction or modification in many passages by marginal notes."

4. Dillmann, however, considers conclusive against Aquila the fact that Origen, Jerome and the Syro-Hexaplar all describe the present Greek text as that "according to the LXX." But in an uncritical age it was perfectly possible for a translation to disappear, and another to take its place as part of the LXX. It is probable that this happened in the case of Daniel. Professor Swete (*Introd. to the O. T. in Greek*, pp. 47—49) points out that "Theodotionic" renderings are quoted by writers earlier than Theodotion, even as early as the New Testament. And the inference seems to be inevitable that "there were two pre-Christian versions of Daniel, both passing as 'LXX.,' one of which is preserved in the Chigi MS.[1], while the other formed the basis of Theodotion's revision."

The reason for the disappearance of the latter of these may have been, as Prof. Swete suggests, that "Theodotion's revision of Daniel may have differed so little from 'the stricter Alexandrian version as to have taken its place without remark"; but the reason for the rejection of the Chigi LXX. is sufficiently explained by Jerome's words: "hoc unum affirmare possum quod multum a veritate discordet et ·recto judicio repudiata sit."

If, then, an old LXX. version of Koheleth was superseded by Aquila's first version, the reason was probably the same—the inaccuracy of the former. It was not till the end of the 1st century A.D. that Koheleth gained an undisputed position as inspired Scripture. Many of its expressions were doubtful and unorthodox, and it had seldom been used; and thus a pre-Christian translation of it might well have been careless and inadequate. And when an accurate translation appeared, which, by the nature of the book, could contain no anti-Christian renderings, Christians as well as Greek-speaking Jews would be glad to make use of it; and the older version, which, in any case, probably had a very limited circulation, speedily became obsolete.

But it is no less possible that a 'LXX.' version of Koheleth

---

[1] Cod. 87 (H. and P. 88).

never existed. The recent decision with regard to its canonicity[1] may have led Aquila to undertake its translation for the first time. If there were no other Greek version, a very few years would suffice to give it a place in the 'LXX.' And the very fact that Christians had adopted his first édition might have been one, among other, reasons which led Aquila to issue the second.

Further—Dillmann's objection, that Origen called the present Greek text 'LXX.,' applies with even greater force to his own suggestion that an old text was revised on the basis of Aquila. If, on the one hand, the Greek text was Aquila's first edition, there were about 100 years before Origen compiled his Hexapla in which it could be accepted as 'LXX.' But if, on the other hand, it was a revision of a LXX. text on the basis of Aquila, the LXX. text itself must have existed later than Aquila, and might have survived up to the time of Origen himself. In the latter case, the only remaining solution would be that the present Greek text is *Origen's* re-writing of the old text. This happened, as Burkitt points out, in the case of 3 Kings xii. 24 g–n as given in A and S.H. But the Greek text of Ḳoheleth is not on the same footing as that passage. Not only does the translation differ, in a large number of passages, from Aquila's fragments, but in about 40 per cent. of the readings in which B diverges from MT. it differs also from the Syro-Hexaplar.

---

[1] See p. 8.

APPENDIX II.

The study of the Greek text in this section is based upon the following authorities:

Hebrew text: Baer, *Quinque Volumina.*

Greek: For the uncials ABCS, Prof. Swete's Camb. manual.

For the uncial V, Holmes and Parsons. (By them it is numbered 23, as though a cursive.)

For the cursives, Holmes and Parsons, 68, 106, 147, 155 (*vac.* v. 8–viii. 12), 157 (*vac.* v. 6–16 and viii. 16–ix. 5), 159, 161, 248, 252, 253, 254, 261, 296, 298, 299 (*vac.* i. 1–6, viii.–xii.).

Syro-Hexaplar: H. Middeldorpf, *Prov., Job, Cant., Threni, Eccles., e Codice Mediolanensi,* Berlin, 1885.

Peshitta: Ed. Lee.

Jerome, *Comm. in Eccles.:* Migne. The text is also collected from the Commentary by Sabatier.

Targum: Walton's Polyglot.

E. Klostermann[1] gives a description of the cursives, and shews that they fall into groups. 68 is very closely related to B, but differs from it occasionally. 106, 261 are closely allied descendants from an uncial. 155 appears to be derived from an uncial. It stands by itself, but has some affinity with 296, which is also unconnected with other groups. 161, 248 are closely related, and abound in hexaplaric readings; 248 is for the most part followed by the Complutensian edition. 147, 157, 159, 298, 299 belong to one family; of these 147, 159 are twins, which with 157 are derived from an uncial; 298, 299 sometimes differ from the former three; 147, 157, 159 are nearly always followed by the Aldine edition, though there are cases in which

---

[1] *De Libri Coheleth versione Alexandrina*, Kiel, 1892.

that edition follows none of the present cursives; 298 is very closely allied with the commentary of Olympiodorus (Migne, XCIII.), so much so that Klostermann suggests (p. 19) that it is a collection from his comments, and not strictly a codex of the version. 253 is closely allied with V, and also with S$^{c.a}$; these have many hexaplaric readings, and in this they resemble 252, which is chiefly important from the fact that its margin is rich in citations from Aq. Σ and Θ; V, however, sometimes supports B 68. Similarly 254 has a somewhat composite text, frequently siding with B 68, but sometimes with S$^{c.a}$ V 253.

It is very unfortunate that so little Old Latin is available. The text of Jerome's commentary is eclectic, but is mainly a translation from the Hebrew, as his own words shew:

"...nullius auctoritatem secutus sum, sed de Hebraeo transferens magis me LXX. interpretum consuetudini coaptavi, in his dumtaxat, quae non multum ab Hebraicis discrepabant. Interdum Aquilae quoque et Symmachi et Theodotionis recordatus sum, ut nec novitate nimia lectoris studium deterrerem, nec rursum contra conscientiam meam fonte veritatis omisso opinionum rivulos consectarer."

A fragment of Old Latin of the 8th century is published by Berger in *Notices et extraits*. And a stray sentence can here and there be gleaned from Latin writers, such as Lucifer Calar., Priscillian, Cyprian, Optatus and Tyconius.

On the Peshitta see W. Wright, art. 'Syriac literature' in *Enc. Brit.* Originally a translation from the Hebrew, it has undergone numerous alterations to produce accordance with 𝕲; so that, as it stands, it has the appearance, in Ḳoheleth, of being almost as eclectic as Jerome.

It is not easy to assign values to the various groupings of the Greek MSS., but it is possible to point out some practical lines of working. (1) A very high place must be accorded to 68; it has the excellencies of B without some of its defects. It is specially valuable when it differs from B, and is perhaps the most important MS. of Ḳoheleth extant. (2) 147–157–159 are frequently in agreement with S, but sometimes with B 68 against S. In the former case they are mostly bad, and in the latter also they sometimes support a wrong reading; but they are usually good when combined with BS 68 or with BC 68.

(3) S^{c.a} V 253 abound both in hexaplaric readings and in deliberate scribal corrections to produce conformity with MT. They are therefore of value when they differ from S.H. and MT. (4) Similarly 161–248 and 252 deserve consideration when they differ from S.H. (5) There is no doubt that in some passages all extant Greek MSS. have been hexaplarised. And when the uncials are divided, S.H. is in most cases found on the side of MT., and the opposing variant is to be preferred. But in a large number of passages all Greek MSS. and S.H. are opposed to MT., Pesh., Hier. In these instances the presumption is that MSS. + S.H. point to a Hebrew variant at least older than Origen; but since comparatively few alterations or corruptions can have occurred in the Hebrew text after the time of the authorised 'Aḳiban' recension, the joint testimony of MSS. and S.H. against MT. must often go back to a pre-Aḳiban text. And this is also the case when all MSS. are opposed to Aq. or Σ, and to MT.; in these passages S.H. is of value, or not, according as it agrees with MSS. or with Aq. Σ. Lastly Θ, being based on 𝔊, cannot, for textual purposes, be classed with Aq. Σ. Its value is high when it sides with 𝔊 against Aq. Σ, or against S.H.

The readings in which B diverges from MT. fall into three classes :

A. Those which seem to imply a Hebrew variant before the 'Aḳiban' recension. The Hebrew text must have been in a very unsettled state, especially in a book like Ḳoheleth which was in many quarters an ἀντιλεγόμενον. It should therefore be carefully borne in mind that to say that 𝔊 points to an early Hebrew variant is not the same as to say that that variant was the true original reading. In many cases, for example, 𝔊 points to a reading which was evidently a mere corruption, and which was rightly corrected in the 'Aḳiban' recension. The adoption of emendations is in place only in a commentary ; and instances occur in the Notes on select passages. Here, with few exceptions, no preference is expressed for or against the M. reading.

B. There are a few cases in which the evidence seems to shew that changes have been made in the MT. after the time of Origen, and even of Jerome. Variants have occasionally been preserved along two lines of Hebrew descent, so that even the Tg. differs from M.

C. There remain the large number of instances in which divergencies in 𝔊 are probably the result of corruption in Greek MSS.—arising either from hexaplaric influence, or from mere scribal mistakes.

It remains to say that the results of this study of the text do not depend for their validity on the Aquila theory maintained in the previous section. The present writer believes that a pre-Aḳiban Hebrew text was used by Aquila for his first edition. But in any case the early Hebrew variants underlying 𝔊 must have been pre-Aḳiban.

A.

Pre-Aḳiban readings.

Ch. I. *v.* 1.   ὁ ἐκκλησιαστής MSS. | M. om. article.

vii. 27 (28), xii. 8 shew that the Mas. tradition did not decide uniformly with regard to the article; and it is probable that the early text had הקהלת.

Ἰσραήλ MSS. O.L. | om. M. Pesh. Tg. S.H. obelises the word. Hier. says "Superfluum quippe est hic *Israel*, quod male in Graecis et Latinis codicibus invenitur."

It had found its way into the pre-Aḳiban text, perhaps because 'king of Israel' was a common expression, while 'king in Jerusalem' was strange; perhaps it was due to *v.* 12. Pesh. 'king of Jerusalem.'

v. 8.   καὶ 1° MSS. S.H. Pesh. Some MSS. K. de R. | om. M. Hier.

v. 10.   ὃς λαλήσει καὶ ἐρεῖ = שידבר ויאמר. MSS. [V ὅ, 106–261 ὃς ἄν] S.H. Pesh. Hier. *quod loquatur* | M. Σ.

ἐν τοῖς αἰῶσιν MSS. (exc. A), S.H. | M. לעלמים A [Pesh. ܡܢ ܥܠܡ]. It is possible, however, that ἐν is only a repetition of the last syllable of γέγονεν.

v. 11.   τοῖς γενομένοις = שהיו MSS. (exc. foll.) S.H. Pesh. one MS. de R. | M. שיהיו V 147–159, Tg.

In the pre-Aḳiban text ראשנים and אחרנים together formed the subject to which להם referred.

v. 13. ὅτι MSS. S.H. | M. הוא. Hier. *hanc distantiam.* Σ (ap.
S.H.) ܗܘ ܚܣܝܪ ܗܘ ܚܣܝܪ. (Pesh. disregards both ὅτι and
הוא.)

v. 16. ἐν Ἰερουσαλήμ MSS. S.H. Pesh. Many MSS. K. de R. |
M. "עֹ יר.

v. 17. It is probable that the clause ואתנה…ודעת was absent
from the original Heb. text. See Sect. C.

v. 18. γνώσεως MSS. S.H. Hier. (*c. Pelag.*) | M. כעם Aq. ΣΘ
Pesh. Hier. C. But it may be a Greek corruption. See
Sect. C.

Ch. II. *v.* 3. εἰ ἡ καρδία μου ἑλκύσει MSS. S.H. | M. בלבי למשוך.
Aq. Θ ἐν τῇ καρδίᾳ μ. ἑλκύσαι. Pesh. Hier. Σ has ἐν τῇ κ. μου.

It is possible that 𝕲 is simply a corruption of the rendering
found in Aq. Θ, Σ. But it is strange that no MS. has been
corrected. The evidence is strongly in favour of the originality
of 𝕲. If the original Heb. was ותרתי אני בלבי משוך, it might
easily be misread, אני becoming אם, and משוך becoming ימשוך
by the doubling of the previous י[1].

ὡς οἶνον MSS. Θ, S.H. | M. ביין Pesh. Hier.

ביין may have arisen merely from a badly written ב; but if
it is original, the construction may be compared with Is. i. 25
ואצרף כבר סניך.

v. 8. καί γε χρύσιον = גם זהב BA curss. (exc. foll.) one MS.
Kenn. | M. וזהב. SV 106. 147–157–159 S.H. Pesh. [S.H. om.
καί γε before ἀργύριον.]

ἐντρυφήματα B 254. 298 [C *vac.*] | M. וסגלת. AS curss. rel.
S.H. Pesh. Hier.

v. 10. εὐφροσύνης μου B 155. 253. 254. 296 [C *vac.*] | M. שמחה.
AS curss. rel.[2] S.H. Hier. Pesh. Tg.

In this and the foregoing reading B is deserted by 68, and
the readings may be scribal corruptions. In the case of μου the
occurrence of the word with six other substantives in the verse
might lead to its insertion.

---

[1] It is worthy of remark that in Pesh. Lee's ed. adds ܟܠܗ ܒܝܬܗ
ܗܕܒܪ ܕܒܝܬ after ܚܘܡܣܐ, and some codd. give it before the beginning of
the verse. It is apparently due to *v.* 20 where the Urmi ed. has ܗܟܪܡܐ
for the ܒܝܬܟܘܢ of Lee's ed.

[2] 261 om. ἀπὸ πασ. εὐφρ. μου.

ἐν παντὶ MSS. S.H. Pesh. Hier. | M. מכל Σ.

v. 12. τίς ἄνθρωπος = מי אדם MSS. [V 147–157–159 τίς ὁ ἀνθ.] S.H. Pesh. Hier. *quis est hominum* | M. מה האדם Σ.

Om. כבר MSS. S.H. Θ Pesh. Hier. | ins. M. Tg.

v. 15. ἐγὼ πέρισσον BCS* 147–157–159. 155. 254. 298 [68. 161–248. 261 ἐγὼ τὸ περ.[1]] Pesh. | M. אני אז יתר. AS[c.a] V curss. rel. S.H. Hier.

The omission of אז in the early Heb. text may have been accidental, owing to its similarity to אנ, a scribe's eye passing from the first י to the second.

ἐλάλησα MSS. S.H. Hier. | M. ודברתי Pesh.

v. 19. καὶ εἰ ἐξουσιάζεται = והשלט.

Ins. εἰ MSS. (exc. 155) | om. M. 155. S.H. Aq. Θ Pesh. Hier.

ἐξουσιάζεται BASV curss. (exc. foll.) | M. ישלט (= -σεται) C 106–261. 155. 161–248. 252. Aq. Hier.

S.H. ܘܡܫܠܛ‍‍ probably points to ἐξουσιάζεται, and omits εἰ[2].

v. 20. ἐν BSV 68. 106. 253. 254. 298. 299 | M. על. MSS. rel. S.H. Pesh.

μόχθῳ μου BS 68. 253. 254. 261. 298. 299. S.H. Hier. | M. העמל. MSS. rel. μόχθῳ.[A 252. 296 τῷ μοχ.] Pesh.

v. 22. ἐν τῷ ἀνθρώπῳ B 68. 157. 253. 254. 261. 299 | M. לאדם. MSS. rel. S.H. Pesh. Hier.

v. 24. ἀνθρώπῳ BAC curss. [C seven curss. pr. τῷ] Pesh. Hier. 3 MSS. K. de R. | M. באדם. SV, S.H.

It is possible, however, that the omission of ἐν was accidental between -θον and ἀνθ-.

ὃ [A ὃς] φάγεται BAS* 68. 253. 298. S.H. Θ = M. שיאכל | משיאכל S.H.[mg] Pesh. Hier. Tg. So pr. πλὴν S[c.a] V 106. 254, pr. εἰ μὴ C curss. rel.

The evidence seems to shew that the pre-Aḳiban text had שיאכל, the מ having fallen out after the prec. ם. This was corrected in the 'Aḳiban' recension, resulting in two different corrections in 𝔊 MSS. But later even than the Tg. some Heb. MSS. omitted the מ; hence the present MT.

---

[1] This may be a corruption of τότε περ., but it may, on the other hand, have arisen by dittography from εγω.

[2] Field's note is misleading, in placing the statement of S.H. that Θ is "similar to the LXX." in connexion with 𝔊 καὶ εἰ ἐξουσιάζεται.

Ch. III. *v.* 1. ὁ χρόνος MSS. (exc. foll.) | om. art. M. S* 253. Σ.

v. 10. σύν + πάντα BV 68. 155. 253. 254 | om. M. ACS S.H. Pesh. Hier. Tg.

v. 11. σύμπαντα [σὺν πάντα] τὸν αἰῶνα BCV 68. 253. 254 | M. את העלם AS curss. rel. S.H. Pesh. Hier.

v. 16[1].

v. 17. καὶ εἶπα B 68. 248. 298 Pesh. | M. אמרתי SV curss. rel. (exc. 155). S.H. Hier.

AC 155 confuse καὶ with the ἐκεῖ in the prec. clause, thus indirectly favouring its insertion.

v. 18. καὶ εἶπα | M. שם: אמרתי.

The foll. five readings occur:

    (*a*) Om. שם and read καὶ εἶπα B 68.

    (*b*) Om. שם and read ἐκεῖ εἶπα ACS 106. 155. 159. 161.

    (*c*) ἐκεῖ· εἶπα (or εἶπον) V 147–157. 248. 253. 261. 296.
          298 S.H. Pesh.

    (*d*) ἐκεῖ· καὶ εἶπα 254.

    (*e*) ἐκεῖ· ἐκεῖ εἶπα 252. 299.

(*c*) is Masoretic; but (*b*) is not quite on the same footing. What was the cause which made three uncials and four cursives (106 being separated from 261 and 161 from 248) include ἐκεῖ in *v.* 18 instead of *v.* 17? Probably it was the fact that the scribes had before them the reading καὶ εἶπα. Thus (*b*) may be a witness for (*a*). Similarly in (*d*) the scribe of 254 must have had καὶ before him, and added ἐκεῖ owing to his knowledge of M. שם. (*e*) is a corruption either of (*d*) or (*c*).

The early text, therefore, probably omitted שם and began *v.* 18 with ואמרתי.

v. 19 [18]. καί γε αὐτοῖς = נם להם MSS. S.H. | om. נם M. Pesh. Hier. On המה see sect. B.

v. 19. συνάντημα 1°. The following readings occur:

    (*a*) συνάντημα AC curss. (exc. foll.) Hier.

    (*b*) οὐ συνάντημα B.

    (*c*) כי מקרה M. S.H. Greg. Agr. ὅτι. Pesh. ܡܝ,
          evidently corruption of ܗ ܡܝ.

    (*d*) ὡς συνάντημα SV 147–159. 253. 254. 299.

(*b*) is probably an orthodox gloss, and is included in sect. C. If it is, it favours (*a*). It is remarkable that no Greek MS. has

---

[1] 𝔊 τοῦ δικαίου probably does not represent הצדיק. vii. 15 (16) shews that the translator used the word as neuter.

received ὅτι from S.H. (d) may either have arisen from a misreading of M. as במקרה, or be a corruption of (a) by dittography from the preceding -οις.

All are explicable if the early Heb. text omitted כי.

v. 20. εἰς τόπον BS*V 68. 147–157–159. 254 | pr. הולך M. ACS^{c.a} curss. rel. S.H. Aq. Θ (ap. S.H.) Pesh. Hier.

The pre-Aķiban text evidently omitted הולך. Its subsequent insertion may have been due to its presence in vi. 6.

ἐπιστρέψει = ישב B 68. 159. 254. 261. 296 S.H. Hier. | M. שב ACS curss. rel. Pesh. It may, however, be a Greek corruption, since a confusion between φ and ψ would be easy.

v. 21. καὶ τίς MSS. S.H. Pesh. Many MSS. K. de R. | מי M. Hier.

Ch. IV. *v.* 2. σύμπαντας [σὺν πάντας] BC^{vid} 68. 106. 253. 254. 299. Hier. in Ep. Eph. Ambr. *de fide Resurr.* | את המתים M. ASV curss. rel. S.H. Pesh. Hier. C. Ambr. in Ps. cxviii.

v. 4. ὅτι τὸ ζῆλος ἀνδρί. Although B is the only MS. which has both τὸ ζῆλος and ἀνδρί, it has good support for each. And this is probably the true reading, pointing to כי קנאת איש. The authorities are as follows:

(1) τὸ ζῆλος B*CS 147–157–159 (ὁ ζῆλ. 253. 261). Pesh. Hier. om. pronoun | M. היא קנאת B^{ab} V curss. rel. S.H.

(2) ἀνδρὶ B 106. 155. 254. 296 [C *hiat*] | ἀνδρὸς ASV curss. rel. S.H. Pesh. Hier. ἀνδρὶ need not imply a Heb. variant. It denotes 'the envy felt *by* a man'; it is slightly more difficult than the objective gen. ἀνδρὸς, hence the latter was a natural alteration.

v. 8. καί γε ἀδελφὸς = גם אח MSS. (exc. S*[1] 296) S.H. | M. ואח 296. Hier. Pesh. ܘܐܚܘܗܝ.

v. 17. ἐν ᾧ ἐὰν (or ἄν) = באשר MSS. (exc. foll.). Several MSS. K. de R. Θ S^{c.a} V 253 ἐν τῷ πορεύεσθαι | M כאשר.

ὑπὲρ δόμα [-ματων 106, -ματα 296. 299] = ממתת. MSS. (exc. foll.) S.H. Pesh. | M. מתת S^{c.a} V 253 ὑ. τὸ δοῦναι. Aq. Θ δόμα = מַתַּת.

θυσία [S -ίας, 253 -ίαν] σου = זבחך. MSS. (exc. V) S.H. | M. זבח V Aq. Θ. Pesh. ܗܕܒ̈ܚܐ ܕܡܣܒ.

V has θυσίαν, and the omission of the pronoun may have been accidental, for 253 has θυσίαν σου.

---

[1] S* om. υἱὸς καὶ γε, supplied by S^{c.a}.

Ch. V. *v.* 5.   τοῦ θεοῦ MSS. S.H. Pesh. | M. המלאך.   Aq. ΣΘ Hier. Tg.

An interesting example of rabbinic revision. To avoid irreverence the excuse is represented as being offered, not in the presence of God, but of the priest, His "angel." Cf. Mal. ii. 7[1].

v. 9. αὐτῶν [or αὐτοῦ] MSS. See sect. C.

The evidence seems to shew that an original לוא had been corrupted in the pre-Akiban text to לו, and this was corrected in MT.

v. 10. ἐν πλήθει = ברב MSS. (exc. 253) S.H. Pesh. Hier. | M. ברבות 253.

ἀγαθωσύνης = טובה MSS. (exc. foll.) | M. pr. art. 161–248. 253.

ὅτι ἀρχὴ τοῦ ὁρᾶν BACS* curss. (exc. foll.) S.H. | M. כי אם (Kᵉri ראות) ראית. ὅτι ἀλλ᾽ ἤ τ. ὁρ. Sᶜ·ᵃ V 253. 254. Pesh. ⟨⟨⟨. Θ εἰ μή. 252. Σ εἰ μὴ μόνον. Hier. *nisi ut.*

Thus all Greek MSS. (exc. 252) preserve ὅτι, which must have been part of an expression equivalent to כי אם, perhaps ὅτι ἄν. If, then, ἀλλ᾽ ἤ was a later correction = כי אם, the reading of Sᶜ·ᵃ etc. is a conflation, in which AN was ousted by the following ΑΛ. This portion of the evidence, therefore, belongs to sect. C.

With regard to ἀρχή, Euringer suggests that it may be a corruption of ἀλλ᾽ ἤ. But this is very doubtful. It is easier to suppose that in a pre-Akiban MS. the Kᵉri ראות had found its way into the text side by side with the Kᵉthib ראית, and that the translator misread the latter as ראשית. Σ θεωρία points to the Kᵉthib.

The orig. 𝔊 would thus be ὅτι ἄν ἀρχὴ τοῦ ὁρᾶν = כי אם ראשית ראות.

v. 12. ἀρρωστία MSS. S.H. | M. רעה חולה.   Tg. בישותא מרעיתא. Σ Pesh. Hier. all attest the presence of רעה, but they render 'an evil sickness.' And in *v.* 15, 𝔊 S.H. Pesh. Hier. render 'an evil sickness' [Σ *vac.*].

But it is in the highest degree improbable that, were רעה חולה original, πονηρὰ ἀρρωστία could have been the rendering of it. Such an ignorance of the construction of the Heb. participle is

---

[1] No argument, therefore, can be drawn (as has sometimes been done) with regard to the date of Koheleth, from this reminiscence of Malachi.

beyond anything of which the translator is elsewhere guilty; and he can render רעה רבה (ii. 21) correctly—πονηρία μεγάλη.

In v. 12 the early Heb. text may have run יש רעה חלי (read רָעָה חֹלִי)—"there is an evil, a sickness" (cf. vi. 1, x. 5); and similarly in v. 15—"moreover this is an evil, a sickness" (cf. זה רע ix. 3). In the former verse רעה had accidentally disappeared before the time of 𝔊; hence 𝔊 ἔστιν ἀρρωστία. In the latter verse 𝔊 probably ran καί γε τοῦτο πονηρία ἀρρωστία, which a scribe, perhaps influenced by vi. 2, would easily corrupt into πονηρὰ ἀρρωστία.

v. 15. περισσεία αὐτοῦ = יתרונו BV curss. S.H. Ambr. de Nativit. c. 6 abundantia ejus | M. יתרון לו ACS Σ Pesh.

v. 18. πᾶς ἄνθρωπος = כל אדם MSS. (exc. V) | M. כל האדם V.
In the 'Aḳiban' recension the article was added to אדם almost uniformly throughout the book, cf. vi. 7, vii. 2 (3), viii. 17 bis, x. 14.

v. 19. περισπᾷ αὐτὸν MSS. S.H. Pesh. | M. מענה Hier.[1]
𝔊 seems to point to ענהו [אלהים].

Ch. VI. v. 4. πορεύεται = הֹלֵךְ MSS. (exc. foll.) Hier. | M. ילך. 147-157-159. 253. 299. S.H. Pesh.

v. 6. (a) εἰς τόπον ἕνα πορεύεται B (299 πορεύσεται).
(b) ἐ. τ. ἕ. τὰ πάντα πορ. M. 248. 252. 254. 296. 298 (106 -ονται, 161 -σεται) S.H. Hier.
(c) ἐ. τ. ἕ. πορ. τὰ πάντα ACSV 68. 253. 261 (147-157-159 -σεται) Pesh.

The isolation of B, and intrinsic evidence, both condemn (a); and of the other readings (c) has far the stronger support, and points to a pre-Aḳiban הולך הכל.

v. 7. ἀνθρώπου B 68. 296. 298 | M. pr. art. ACS curss. rel. See on v. 18.

v. 8. ὅτι περισσεία BS* 68. 147-157-159. 254. 299 [V 253 περισσεύει] Pesh. S.H. * 'ΑΘ τίς ⟋ | M. מה יותר. ACS^{c.a} curss. rel. Aq. Θ Hier.

It is probable that מה יותר (perh. written מיתר) had been corrupted in a pre-Aḳiban text to מותר; cf. iii. 19. And this corruption may have been either accidental or polemical.

[1] Hier. C. quia Deus occupat in laetitia cor ejus would require כי א "מ בשמחה לבו. But his rendering is probably an attempt to make the best of the MT. as it stands. Vg. eo quod Deus occupet deliciis cor ejus may mean that he afterwards adopted the pronunciation שִׂמְחַת.

But it is possible, of course, that the omission of τίς was an error of a Greek scribe.

διότι ὁ πένης οἶδεν MSS. (157 διατί, 299 om. ὁ) S.H. Pesh. | M. מה לעני. Hier. *quid pauperi nisi ut vadat.*

There seems to have been an early corrupt reading למההעני, probably due in part to the preceding ל in הכסיל. In Ed. Saphetana 1578 there is an interesting emendation מה לעני יותר.

v. 12 [G vii. 1]. ἀγαθὸν BV 68. 106–261. 296. 299 [C *vac.*] | M. מה טוב. pr. τί AS^{c.a} [S* τις] curss. rel. S.H. Σ Pesh. Hier.

καὶ ἐποίησεν αὐτὰ = ועשם MSS. [C *vac.*] S.H. Pesh. ܘܥܒܕ (ܥܒܕ being a corruption of ܥܒܕ) favours G | M. ויעשם Hier.

ἐν σκιᾷ = בצל MSS. (exc. foll.) S.H. | M. כצל V 253. 106–261 Pesh. Hier.

Ch. VII. v. 1 (2). γεννήσεως[1] BS* 68. 147–157–159. 161. 299 Pesh. S.H. * Ἀ αὐτοῦ ⟋ | M. הולדו ACS^{c.a} V curss. rel. Aq. Hier. This points to an early reading הַיָּלֶד [Bickell הֻלֶּדֶת].

v. 2 (3). καθότι = כאשר MSS. | M. באשר Hier. [S.H. and Pesh. ܒ ܐܟܡܐ.]

ἀνθρώπου BA curss. (exc. foll.) | M. pr. art. CSV 157. 161–248. 252. 299. See on v. 18.

v. 6 (7). ὡς φωνὴ BS 68. 147–157–159. 296. 299. S.H. * ὅτι ⟋ | M. pr. כי AC curss. rel. Pesh. Hier. Tg.

ἀκανθῶν B 68. 248. 254. 296 | M. pr. art. ACSV curss. rel.

The art. is more likely to have been inserted in the 'Akiban' recension to complete the parallelism with הסיר, than omitted if it was already present[2].

v. 8 (9). λόγων MSS. (exc. foll.) | M. דבר V 253. 298 S.H. Σ Pesh. Hier.

The foll. מ may have been accidentally doubled, forming דברם.

v. 10 (11). ἐν σοφίᾳ = בחכמה MSS. S.H. Pesh. | M. מחכמה. [Tg. "על ח.]

v. 12 (13). αὐτῆς 1° MSS. S.H. | om. pron. M. Σ Pesh. Hier.

In the pre-Akiban text the ה of החכ" had been accidentally doubled.

ἐν σκιᾷ, κ.τ.λ.

   (a) ἐν σκιᾷ...ὡς σκία MSS. S.H.
   (b) בצל...כצל app. Σ Pesh. Hier.
   (c) בצל...בצל M.

---

[1] ACSV 252. 296 γενέσεως.

[2] Σ (ap. S.H.) διὰ γὰρ φωνῶν ἀπαιδεύτων cannot be used as evidence.

The corrupt reading בצל...בצל evidently stood in the pre-Akiban text. This was corrected to (b), which is idiomatic, and makes good sense; but afterwards corrupted again to בצל...בצל.

ἀργυρίου BV 68. 254. 298 | pr. art. M. ACS curss. rel. Σ.

v. 13 (14). ὁ θεὸς MSS. S.H. Hier. | om. M. Σ Pesh. (pass. ptcp. "him that is made crooked")[1].

v. 24 (25). ὑπὲρ ὃ ἦν = משהיה MSS. S.H. Hier. Pesh. (in the order משהיה רחוק) | M. מה שהיה. In the early Heb. text the word was probably understood as מָשְׁהיה, cf. vi. 8 מיתר.

v. 25 (26). ἀσεβοῦς ἀφροσύνην MSS. | M. כסל רשע. Pesh. ܪ̈ܫܝܥܐ ܘܣܟܠܐ. Hier. *impietatem stulti.* It is impossible not to think that the translator would have rendered MT. by ἀσεβείαν ἀφροσύνης. S.H. transposes the words—ܘܣܟܠܐ ܕܪ̈ܫܝܥܐ = כסל רָשָׁע. It is, therefore, probable that the pre-Akiban text had כסל רשע, and that when the words were transposed, ᴳ was similarly treated to produce correspondence.

ὀχληρίαν MSS. | M. pr. art.

καὶ περιφοράν MSS. S.H. | M. הוללות. Aq. Σ Hier.

The similar passages, i. 17, ii. 12, are in favour of the coordination with סכלות by "and."

v. 26 (27). θήρευμα = מצוד BC curss. (exc. foll.) Θ Hier. | M. מצודים ASV 106. 161–248. 252. 253. 296 Aq.

δεσμὸς εἰς χεῖρας αὐτῆς MSS. (253 δεσμοὶ) | M. אסורים ידיה Pesh. Hier. Aq. (ap. Hier.) *Vinctae sunt manus ejus.*

It is difficult to suppose ᴳ to be a corruption of δεσμοὶ αἱ [or εἰσι Ed. Alex.] χεῖρες αὐτῆς. Aq. suggests another solution. If אסורים were spelt אסורם in an early text, the expression might easily be corrupted into אסור בידיה 'a chain is on her hands.' And with the revised Heb. text Aq. still expressed the same thought.

v. 27 (28). ὁ Ἐκκλησιαστής MSS. (exc. 252) | om. art. M. 252 Tg.

v. 28 (29). καὶ ἄνθρωπον MSS. S.H. O.L. (Berger) | M. אדם Pesh. Hier.

---

[1] By means of the masc. ὅν and αὐτόν the translator expresses a thought afterwards found in Σ and in Tg.—that עותו refers to man being made crooked (Σ "punished") by God. This was evidently the Rabbinic view of the passage, and the rendering favours the Aquilean authorship.

Ch. VIII. *v.* 4. καθὼς = כאשר MSS. Pesh. Some MSS. K. de R. |
M. באשר.

Om. דבר BS*V 68. 147–157–159. 248 S.H.ᵐᵍ | ins. M. ACSᶜ·ᵃ
curss. rel. S.H. Aq. Σ Θ Pesh. Hier.

Of the cursives which read λαλεῖ, 253, 254 with S.H. Hier.
have it before βασιλεὺς; the rest, with ACSᶜ·ᵃ, after ἐξουσιάζων.

Aq. Θ Pesh. Hier. all render as a verb; Σ only λόγον.

S.H.ᵐᵍ notes that Origen τοῦ λαλεῖ οὐκ ἐμνήσθη ἐν τοῖς εἰς τὸν
Ἐκκλησιαστήν (Field).

v. 5. ὁ φυλάσσων MSS. (exc. 253) | M. om. art. 253. The ה
prob. arose from the doubling of ה in the prec. word.

κρίσεως MSS. S.H. Some MSS. K. de R. | M. ומשפט Pesh.
Hier. The reading in the 'Aḳiban' recension must have been
due to the foll. verse.

v. 6. γνῶσις = דעת MSS. S.H. Θ. Six MSS. K. de R. | M. רעת
Σ Pesh. Hier.

v. 8. ἐν ἡμέρᾳ πολέμου MSS. [A θανάτου] S.H. Pesh. | M. במלחמה
Σ Hier.

It is possible that ביום in an early text was the result of a
doubling of במ in במלחמה.

v. 9. καὶ 1° MSS. S.H. Pesh. | om. M. Hier. Tg.

τὰ ὅσα = את אשר one MS. Kenn. MSS. [πάντα ὅσα 147–157–159
S.H. ὅσα Sᶜ·ᵃ] | M. את אשר Aq. Σ Pesh. Tg.

It is more probable that את was an early variant, than that
(as Euring. suggests) a Greek scribe, who knew just enough
Hebrew to understand את, stumbled at עת and deliberately
changed his text.

v. 10. εἰς τάφους εἰσαχθέντας = קברים מובאים MSS. S.H. | M.
קברים ובאו Aq. Σ (vid.) Pesh. Hier.

καὶ ἐκ τ. ἁγ. MSS. S.H. Pesh. Hier. with M. | om. καὶ Aq.Σ (vid.).

καὶ ἐπορεύθησαν MSS. (exc. foll.) S.H. Aq. Θ | M. יהלכו Sᶜ·ᵃ
V 253. Σ Pesh. Hier. (254 confl. ἐπορ. καὶ ἐπορ.).

The first of the above readings is clear. The doubling of
the מ from קברים led to the corruption of ובאו into מוּבָאִם.

In the two latter readings the evidence is divided, so that it
is difficult to say whether M. originally stood as at present, or
whether it was corrupted after its first publication. But the
balance seems to favour pre-Aḳiban readings ממקום and ויהלכו.
(On τοῦ ἁγίου see sect. C.)

v. 11. ἀπὸ τῶν ποιούντων = מֵעֲשֵׂי MSS. S.H. Pesh. Hier. | M.
מעשי Tg., cf. v. 5.

v. 12. τὸ πονηρόν MSS. | M. om. art. A corruption due to
the prec. ה; either it was doubled in the early text, or the
second ה was omitted in the MT. by homoeoteleuton.

ἀπὸ τότε = מאז MSS. S.H. | Aq. Σ ℗ ἀπέθανεν = מת | M. מאת
Pesh. Hier. strives to find a suitable meaning both in *ex tunc*
and in *mortuus est.* None of these three readings is satis-
factory[1]. The ellipse of פעם after מאת is very harsh, and מאה is
nowhere else used as an indefinite expression for a large number.
A solution is required which will account both for the ו and for
the ה at the end of the word. And two are possible:

1. A scribe began to write ומאריך, but having accidentally
omitted the ו discovered his mistake when he had written מאר,
and wrote the word again. Then מארומאריך was written "ומ אז,
and, later, "ומ מאת.

2. The original text had מאר, which would similarly give
rise to the two variants.

ἀπὸ μακρότητος = מֵאֹרֶךְ MSS. S.H. (misreading 𝕲 as ἀπὸ ματαιό-
τητος) | M. מאריך Pesh. Hier.

v. 13. ἐν σκιᾷ MSS. (exc. S*) S.H. | M. בצל Pesh. Hier. S*
has confl. ὡς ἐν σκιᾷ (Sᶜ·ᵃ om. ὡς). Σ (ap. Hier.) om. בצל altogether.

v. 14. ἐπ᾿ αὐτοὺς = עלהם B 68. 147–157–159. 298 | M. אלהם.
πρὸς αὐτοὺς ACVS curss. rel. S.H. Pesh. Hier. The alteration
was made to conform to אלהם below.

v. 16. ἐν οἷς = באשר MSS. (exc. 252) S.H. two MSS. K. de R. |
M. כאשר.

(Σ 252 διό. Pesh. ܟܡܐ ܕ. Hier. *quapropter.*)

τὴν σοφίαν MSS. (exc. foll.) | om. art. M. 147–159.

v. 17. ἄνθρωπος 1° MSS. | M. pr. art. See v. 18.

ἄνθρωπος 2° BACV curss. (exc. foll.) | pr. art. M. S. 161–248.
252. 254. 296.

σοφὸς BV 68. 157. 252. 253. 254. 296 | pr. art. M. ACS curss. rel.

Ch. IX. *v.* 1 [𝕲 viii. 17]. καὶ καρδία μου σύμπαν εἶδεν τοῦτο MSS.
(with small variations[2]). S.H. = κ. κ. μ. τοῦτο σύμπαν εἶδεν. Pesh. =
κ. κ. μ. εἶδεν σύμπαν τοῦτο | M. ולבור את כל זה Σ (ap. Hier.). Hier.
Tg.

The early text ran ולבי ראה את כל זה. The transposition
σύμπαν εἶδεν seems to have been hexaplaric.

---

[1] מאז is adopted by Bickell and Siegfried.

[2] B* καρδία…ἴδον.

vv. 1, 2 [𝕲 *v.* 1]. τὰ πάντα πρὸ προσώπου αὐτῶν ματαιότης ἐν τοῖς πᾶσιν. MSS. S.H. This points to a pre-Akiban reading הכל לפניהם הבל : באשר לכל וג׳—"all that is before them is vanity; inasmuch as to all there is one mischance...etc." In this case ἐν τοῖς πᾶσιν must be an early Greek corruption of ἐν οἷς τοῖς π. (cf. viii. 16, xi. 5; and in viii. 4 MT. has באשר).

In the 'Akiban' recension the only change made was to read כאשר for באשר. So Σ τὰ πάντα ἔμπροσθεν αὐτοῦ ἄδηλα, *propterea quod omnibus eveniunt similia* (see Field). And the Vg., though free, is evidence for this: *omnia in futurum servantur incerta, eo quod universa aeque eveniant...* etc.

But in a line of Heb. MSS. which did not affect the Vg., but which produced the present MT., הבל was corrupted to הכל, necessitating its inclusion in the second, instead of the first, clause.

Lastly Pesh. has a conflation, reading הבל at the end of the first clause, and הכל כאשר לכל at the beginning of the second.

v. 2. καὶ τῷ κακῷ MSS. S.H. Pesh. Hier. | om. M. Tg.

This is placed here because Pesh. Hier. may have adopted the words from 𝕲. But if they knew a Heb. reading ולרע, the omission was a corruption at a later stage in the MT.

τὸν ὅρκον MSS. | M. om. art.

v. 3. καὶ ὀπίσω αὐτῶν = ואחריהם MSS. S.H. Pesh. ´Σ (vid.) | M. ואחריו Hier. Tg. (vid.).

(Hier. *et post haec.* Σ τὰ δὲ τελευταῖα αὐτῶν.)

v. 4. ὁ ζῶν = החי MSS. Did. *de Trin.* κύων ὁ ζῶν | M. החי. Σ κυνὶ ζῶντι.

It is possible, however, that this does not point to a Heb. variant, but that the article was instinctively inserted by a scribe, making the expression parallel to τὸν λέοντα τὸν νεκρόν. On the Aquilean ὁ κύων for לכלב see App. I. p. 119.

v. 5. γνώσονται = ידעו MSS. (exc. foll.) | M. יודעים. V. 253 γινώσκουσιν. Pesh. Hier.

The alteration in MT. was probably due to the foll. יודעים.

αὐτοῖς ἔτι MSS. S.H. Pesh. Hier. | M. transp.

The agreement of MSS. and versions points to an early reading להם עוד. But it is possible that the transposition occurred in a Greek MS. owing to αὐτοῖς ἔτι in the foll. verse.

v. 6. καί γε μερὶς = גם חלק BS* curss. (exc. foll.). Hier. *sed et* | M. וחלק ACS^(c.a) 161–248. 252. 253. 296 S.H. Pesh.

v. 9. καὶ ἴδε MSS. S.H. Pesh. | M. ראה Σ Hier.

τὰς δοθείσας...ἀτμοῦ σου. It is probable that the two clauses (*a*) אשר נ" ל" ת" ל/" השמש, and (*b*) כל ימי הבלך, were absent from the pre-Akiban text used by the translator. In the case of (*b*) this amounts to a certainty. For

(i) B (alone) has πᾶσαι ἡμέραι ἡμέραι (*sic*) ἀτμοῦ σου, which is clearly a corruption of Aq. πᾶσαι αἱ ἡμέραι ἀ. σ.

(ii) In CSV 147–157–159. 161–248. 296 S.H. a literal rendering has been supplied from the earlier similar clause in the verse—πάσας [τὰς] ἡμέρας [τῆς] ματαιότητός σου.

(iii) The clause is omitted in A curss. rel. Pesh. Hier. Tg. and in some Heb. MSS. K. and de R.

Clause (*a*) is found in all Greek MSS. (exc. 106–261) and in S.H. But Pesh. om. The rendering τὰς δοθείσας is foreign to the style of the translation, and may have been supplied from Σ or ⊕, as clause (*b*) was from Aq. It is omitted, together with the first clause, in ten MSS. K. de R.

ἐν τῇ ζωῇ σου MSS. S.H. | om. pron. M. Pesh. Hier. (om. pron. with μόχθῳ also).

This may, however, be a mistake of a Greek scribe, owing to the occurrence of σου with nine other words in *vv*. 7–9.

v. 10. ὡς ἡ δύναμίς σου = ככוחך MSS.[1] S.H. | M. בכוחך Pesh. Hier. Tg.

v. 14. ἐπ' αὐτὴν 1° = עליה MSS. S.H. Pesh. Hier. | M. אליה Hier.

v. 17. ἐξουσιαζόντων = מושלם MSS. S.H. | M. מושל Σ Pesh. Hier. The ם may have arisen from a doubling of the foll. ב, cf. vii. 8 (9).

ἐν ἀφροσύναις = בכסלים MSS. (157. 298 S.H. -νη. 147. 159 ἐν εὐφρ.). Pesh. "a foolish ruler." | M. בכסילים Σ Hier.

The plural of כסל is elsewhere used only for 'loins.' It is probable that the word was written without the י in the early text, but was intended to be read בכסלים.

Ch. X. *v*. 1. τίμιον ὀλίγον [B* ὁ λόγος[2]. 252 λόγος] σοφίας [106–261 ὀλίγη σοφία] ὑπὲρ δόξαν ἀφροσύνης μεγάλης [-ην] MSS. ⊕ (ap. S.H.) ended the clause with μεγάλην, if he did not follow 𝔊 throughout. This points to a pre-Akiban reading

יקר מעט חכמה מכבוד סכלות רב

---

[1] 106. 253. 254 ὅση δύν.
[2] The *lapsus calami* is corrected in B*.

This makes good sense, forming the converse to the thought of *v.* a.

On the other hand the Rabbinic revisers produced a thought synthetically parallel to *v.* a. Three forms of their reading have survived:

   (i)   Pesh. = יקר מחכמה ומכבוד רב סכלות מעט,

   (ii)   Hier. the same, but omitting רב, and

   (iii)   MT. the same, omitting רב, and ו (before מכבוד). But ומכבוד in many MSS. K. de R.

   v. 3.   ὑστερήσει = יחסר MSS. S.H. | M. חסר Pesh. Hier.

The early reading probably arose from a doubling of the prec. ו.

   πάντα. If τὰ πάντα is the true reading (see sect. C) it points to הכל. So Hier. *et dicit omnis insipiens est.*

   v. 5.   ἐξῆλθε = יצא MSS. | M. שיצא S.H. Pesh. (Σ ἐξελθὸν, Hier. *egrediens* are uncertain[1]).

   ἐξουσιάζοντος BS 68. 161–248. 253 | M. pr. art. ACV curss. rel. S.H. Σ.

   v. 10.   καὶ αὐτὸς πρόσωπον = והוא פנים MSS. (exc. V 253) S.H. Pesh. | V κ. αὐ. ἑαυτῷ πρόσ. 253 κ. αὐ. αὐτοῦ πρόσ. = לו פ" | M. לא Tg. (vid.).

It seems probable that לוא had fallen out of the pre-Akiban text, and was restored in the revised text. This was corrupted in Eastern copies to לו. Hier. reflects the uncertainty as to לוא and לו. He first has *et faciem* ejus *turbaverit*, and then *et hoc non ut prius* (so Vg.).

Euringer's suggestion that αυτος is a corruption of αυτος αυτο [= αὐτῷ] is unlikely.

   v. 11.   ὄφις BAS curss. (exc. foll.) | M. pr. art. CV 161–248. 252. 296.

It is very rare to find C supporting M. against BAS; and the addition of ο in C may have been due, not to M., but to the accidental doubling of the following ο.

But of course it is possible that the omission in the former group may have been accidental.

   v. 13.   ἐσχάτη αὐτοῦ = אחריתו B 68. 106–261 | M. אחרית פיהו MSS. rel. S.H. Pesh. Hier.

---

[1] Euringer cites Aq. Θ as omitting the relative. But Hier. only states that Aq. Θ and 𝔊 *interpretati sunt Quasi non spontaneum, id est* ὡς ἀκούσιον, *a facie principis*—thus passing over the question of שיצא.

Internal evidence favours the reading of B, since a scribe would be more likely to add στόματος owing to the prec. clause, than to omit it. It was the desire for parallelism which probably caused the insertion of פיהו in the 'Akiban' recension. But if פיהו was the original reading it may have been omitted in an early text owing to its similarity to ‑ריתו.

v. 14. ἄνθρωπος BV 68. 106–261. 253. 296. 298 | pr. art. M. ACS curss. rel. See on v. 18.

v. 17. πρὸς καιρὸν = לעת MSS. (exc. 253)[1] S.H. | M. בעת 253. Pesh. ܒܙܒܢܐ.

αἰσχυνθήσονται probably points to a corrupt בשת in the pre-Akiban text. See sect. C.

v. 19. οἶνον τοῦ εὐφρανθῆναι = לשמח B 68. 147–157–159. 254[2]. Pesh. Hier. *ut epulentur viventes* | M. ישמח ACVS curss. rel. οἶνος εὐφραίνει (or εὐφρανεῖ) S.H.

τὰ πάντα = הכל BS* 68. 147–157–159. 254 S.H. | M. pr. את. ACV curss. rel. σὺν τὰ πάντα[3].

v. 20. κοιτώνων = משכביך MSS. (exc. foll.) | M. משכבך. 155. 248. 252. 298 S.H. Pesh. Hier.

λόγον σου MSS. S.Ḥ. Pesh. ܡܠܬܟ | M. om. pron. Hier.[4]

Ch. XI. *v.* 1. ἡμερῶν B. 68. 254. 298 | M. pr. art. ACS curss. rel. (exc. foll.).... τῶν ἡμ. σου V 106–261. 252.

v. 5. κυοφορούσης BV 68. 155 | M. pr. art. MSS. rel.

v. 6. καὶ ἐν ἑσπέρᾳ perhaps points to an early ובערב. So Ed. Saphetana. But see sect. C.

ἐπὶ τὸ αὐτὸ = יחדו MSS. S.H. | M. כאחד Pesh. Hier.

Ch. XII. *v.* 5. καὶ 1°. B 68. 147. 155. 252[mg] | M נם ACS curss. rel.[5] S.H. Pesh. Hier.

καὶ may point to a reading ומנבה, which became נם מ" through the doubling of the מ. But ϝε might easily fall out from καιϝεειϲ.

v. 6. καὶ συντροχάσῃ = ויריץ MSS. (exc. 253) S.H. Pesh. | M. ונרץ. 253 καὶ συντριβῇ. Hier. *et confringatur.*

---

[1] 155 πρὸς καιρῷ.

[2] 261 οἶνος εὐφρανθῆναι.

[3] Sᶜ·ᵃ τὰ σύμπαντα.

[4] Hier. also omits pron. with *vocem* in prec. clause.

[5] 248 καὶ τι, which must be a corruption of καί γε.

v. 9. τὸν ἄνθρωπον = הָאָדָם MSS. (exc. foll.) S.H. | M. הָעָם
V 253 Pesh. Hier. Copt.

ἐξιχνιάσεται = יַחְקֹר MSS. (exc. Sᶜ·ᵃ) S.H. | M. וְחֵקֶר [Sᶜ·ᵃ¹] Aq.
Pesh. Hier.

This is the only variation in the consonants as read by the
translator: but he followed a different pronunciation to that
adopted afterwards; 𝔊 = "מִ תָּקֵן יַחְקֵר וְאָזֵן. Aq. has καὶ ἠνωτίσατο
καὶ ἡρμήνευσε καὶ² κατεσκεύασε παροιμίας. 106–261 have a complete
conflation of Aq. and 𝔊.

v. 11. τῶν συνθεμάτων [συναγμάτων, συνταγμάτων] MSS. | M.
om. art.

v. 13. ἄκουε = שְׁמַע MSS. (exc. foll.) Pesh. | M. נִשְׁמַע V 253.
S.H. reads ἀκούετε which is probably a corruption of ἀκούεται,
and in marg. "'ΑΘ similar to Ο'." Hier., *auditu perfacilis est,*
seems to follow M.

v. 14. ἐν παντὶ MSS. (exc. 252) S.H. | M. עַל. 252 Σ περί.
Pesh. Hier.

(In xi. 9 𝔊 has ἐπὶ with M.)

B.

'Akiban' readings which suffered later alteration in the Hebrew text.

Ch. I. *v.* 13. τὸν οὐρανὸν = הַשָּׁמַיִם BACS* 68. 106–261. 155.
161–248. 254 S.H. and M. | τὸν ἥλιον = הַשֶּׁמֶשׁ Sᶜ·ᵃ V. curss. rel.
Pesh. Hier. Tg. The former reading is found in a cod. of Pesh.,
and the latter in several Heb. MSS. (Kenn. and de R.). The
variant is thus found preserved till a late date.

Ch. II. *v.* 3. καὶ κατεσκεψάμην MSS. S.H. Aq. Σ Θ | M. תַּרְתִּי
Pesh. Hier.

v. 24. καὶ ὃ πίεται BCS 68. 161–248. 254. 298 Pesh. | M. וְשָׁתָה
AV curss. rel. S.H.

καὶ ὃ δείξει BACS curss. (exc. foll.) Aq. Pesh. | M. וְהֶרְאָה
V 147–157–159. 253. 299. S.H.

The evidence is strong for an early reading וְשָׁתָה וְשֶׁהֶרְאָה.

v. 25. παρὲξ αὐτοῦ = חוּץ מִמֶּנּוּ MSS. S.H. Pesh. Hier. Copt.
eight MSS. K. de R. | M. מִמֶּנִּי "ח Vg. Tg.

---

[1] Sᶜ·ᵃ καὶ οὓς αὐτοῦ ἐξιχνίασατο = וְאָזְנוּ חֵקֶר.

[2] Ten MSS. K. de R. have וְתֻקַּן.

Ch. III. *vv.* 4, 5. τοῦ κόψασθαι. τοῦ ὀρχήσασθαι. τοῦ συναγαγεῖν MSS. Pesh. | M. om. ל.

v. 18. om. המה MSS. | ins. M. S.H. Pesh. Evidently a repetition of the last syllables in בהמה.

v. 19. συνάντημα 3°. MSS. S.H. Pesh. Hier. Tg. Several MSS. K. de R. | M. pr. י.

καὶ τί ἐπερίσσευσεν = ומה יותר (? written ומיתר) MSS. (exc. foll.) S.H. Σ τί πλέον. Sᶜ·ᵃ V 253 ⊙ τίς περισσεία | M. ומותר Pesh. Hier.

Ch. IV. *v.* 3. σὺν πᾶν = את כל BC vid. [S* *vac.*] 68. 254. Aq. ⊙¹ Hier. *in Ep. Eph.* | M. את ASᶜ·ᵃ curss. rel.² S.H. Pesh. Hier. C.

v. 12. ἐπικραταιώθη = יְתָקֵף MSS. (exc. 253) S.H. The same consonants are attested by 253 ὑπερισχύσει, Σ -χύσῃ, Pesh. = יְתַקּף | M. יתקפו Hier.

Ch. V. *v.* 2. ἐνύπνιον MSS. Σ | M. pr. art. It is possible, however, that 𝔊 represents באה חלום; but the word is nowhere distinctly feminine, though the plural is always חלומות.

v. 5. τὰ ποιήματα = מעשי MSS. Hier. Vg. eight MSS. K. de R. | M. מעשה³. Cf. vii. 13 (14), viii. 17, xi. 5.

v. 16. καὶ ἐν πένθει = ואבל MSS. [V om. ἐν] S.H. Copt. | M. יאכל Pesh. Hier.

The extreme difficulty of יאכל makes it improbable that it was adopted instead of ואבל in the 'Aḳiban' revision. (Seven MSS. K. de R. have ילך.)

καὶ ἀρρωστία MSS. S.H. Pesh. | M. וחליו Hier. Tg.

As in the preceding instance, it is the difficulty of the Mas. reading which makes it probable that it is a later corruption. It could easily arise from the doubling of the following ו in וקצף.

Ch. VII. *v.* 12 (13). ὡς σκιὰ = כצל MSS. S.H. Σ (vid.⁴) Pesh. | M. בצל. See sect. A.

v. 13 (14). τὰ ποιήματα MSS. Σ Hier. Vg. | M. מעשה. See v. 5.

v. 14 (15). ζῆθι = חיה MSS. S.H. Aq. ⊙ Copt. | M. היה Σ Pesh. Hier. Tg.

---

¹ Σ τὰ κακὰ ἔργα τὰ γινόμενα. The plural may imply the presence of כל.

² 253 ουπω (*sic*).

³ S.H. and Pesh. are uncertain, since their reading depends on the presence or absence of the *ribbui*.

⁴ ὡς (252ᵐᵍ) or ὁμοίως (S.H.) σκέπει τὸ ἀργύριον.

Ch. VIII. *v.* 2. στόμα om. אני MSS. (exc. 253[1]) S.H. O.L. (Berger), Pesh. Tg. | M. 253 pr. אני.

אני is evidently corrupt, but it is not easy to account for its insertion. Possibly פי was written twice, and then by some confusion with the foregoing א in ישנא the corrupt פיפי became אניפי.

v. 10. καὶ ἐπῃνέθησαν = וישתבחו MSS. S.H. Aq. Σ ☉ (see Field) Hier. some MSS. K. de R. | M. וישתכחו Tg. Pesh. ܐܬܛܥܝܘ = ἔλαθον.

v. 17. τὰ ποιήματα MSS. Σ Hier. Vg. | M. מעשה. See v. 5.

Ch. IX. *v.* 2 (1). ματαιότης = הבל | M. הכל. See sect. A.

v. 2. ὡς ὁ ὀμνύων = כנשבע MSS. S.H. Pesh.[2] Hier. Vg. | M. הנשבע.

v. 4. κοινωνεῖ = Ḳᵉri יחבר MSS. [106–261. 296 Hier. -νησει] S.H. Σ Pesh. Hier. Tg. | Kᵉth. יבחר.

Ch. X. *v.* 1. σαπριοῦσιν MSS. (exc. 253). Σ 253 σήψει. 𝔊 S.H. Σ Pesh. Hier. Tg. have one verb only | M. יבאיש יביע.

[On σκευασίαν see sect. C.]

v. 10. τοῦ ἀνδρ[ε]ίου = הכשר ACS 248. 252. 253. 254. 296. 298. S.H. Pesh. Hier. *fortitudinis* | M. הכשיר.

This reading yields good sense: "and an advantage to *the successful man* is wisdom," and it explains the following corruptions:

τωανδριου B, interpreted as τῷ ἀνδρὶ οὐ 68, τῷ ἀνδρὶ (om. οὐ) 248, τοῦ ἀνδρὸς 147–157–159. 161, τῷ ἀνδρείῳ 106–261.

v. 14. τί τὸ γενόμενον = מה שהיה MSS. (exc. foll.) S.H. Σ Pesh. Hier. four MSS. K. de R. | M. מה שיהיה. S 147–157–159. 298 τί τὸ γενησόμενον.

The former reading yields good sense, and the contrast between היה and יהיה is in accord with i. 9. The latter reading was probably due to viii. 7.

Ch. XI. *v.* 5. ἐν οἷς = באשר MSS. S.H. Aq. ἐν ᾧ three MSS. K. de R. | M. כאשר Hier.

Cf. viii. 16 and for M. באשר viii. 4.

τὰ ποιήματα = מעשי MSS. Hier. Vg. | M. מעשה. See v. 5.

---

[1] 253 ἐγὼ παραίνω ῥῆσιν βασιλέως φυλάσσειν.

[2] Pesh., however, has ܐܝܟ both for καθὼς and ὡς [ὁ ἁμαρτάνων].

Ch. XII. *v.* 6. ἀνατραπῇ MSS. If the suggestion made in sect. C is right, that this is a corruption of ἀναρραγῇ or, perhaps, of ἀπορραγῇ, the commonly adopted reading ינתק (for ירתק K^ethib or ירתק K^eri) gains additional force. Σ Hier. both render "be broken," Pesh. ܢܬܦܣܩ "be cut off"; and ינתק is used in iv. 12 (᳔ ἀπορραγήσεται) of a thread or cord, where Pesh. has the same word as here.

v. 12. τοῦ ποιῆσαι = לעשות BACS^c.a curss. (exc. foll.) S.H. Aq. Σ | M. עשות S* ποιῆσαι βιβ.   147–157–159 βιβ. ποιῆσαι.

C.

Greek Corruptions.

Ch. I. *v.* 5. αὐτὸς ἀνατέλλων B 68. 147–157–159. 261 | M. tr. MSS. rel. S.H. Hier.

It is scarcely possible that a reading הוא זורח could have existed.

v. 7. οἱ χείμαρροι 2° B | M. pr. שׁ. pr. οὗ MSS. rel. S.H. Hier.

v. 11. αὐτῶν BAS 155. 254. 296 | M. להם. αὐτοῖς CV curss. rel. S.H. Hier.

αὐτῶν cannot represent a Heb. variant, and is foreign to the style of the translation.

v. 17. καὶ ἔδωκα...γνῶσιν.

Om. 68. 106. 161–248. 253. 261. 296. 298. S.H. has it with ✳. Clem. Al. Olymp. Copt.

Add after γνῶσιν M. ABSV 252. 254. Pesh. Hier. [C *vac.*].

Add after Ἰερουσαλὴμ 147–157–159 ed. Rom.

The evidence is strongly in favour of the omission of the clause. If the pre-Origenian Greek text omitted it, two solutions are possible: 1. At an early stage in the Greek transmission a scribe's eye passed accidentally from γνῶσιν to γνῶσιν. But, being included in the other hexaplar translations, it found its way back into the Greek text. 2. The original Heb. text omitted, and it arose as a doublet. The latter is the more probable, and the insertion is on that account placed here as a Greek corruption.

v. 18. γνώσεως | M. בעם. The words σοφία and γνῶσις occur twice (or once) in the prec. verse, which might lead to the mistake. See sect. A.

Ch. II. *v.* 3. ἐπ᾽ εὐφροσύνῃ (-ην) MSS.[1] Pesh. | M. בסכלות Hier.

The use of שכלות ('folly') in i. 17 for סכלות, where all
𝔊 MSS. have ἐπιστήμην (foll. by Pesh.), shews that in the early
Heb. text the two words were sometimes confused, and it is
possible that some MSS. of that text read שכלות here. But the
present reading is more probably a corruption of ἐπ᾽ ἀφροσύνῃ.
εὐφρ. is usually the rendering of שמחה (cf. *vv.* 1, 2, 10 al.), and
ἀφρ. stands for εὐφρ. in other passages where there can be little
doubt that it is a scribal error[2].

v. 6. Om. ξύλα B. Evidently a slip, followed by no other
MS.[3] [C *vac.*]

v. 15. διότι [ὁ] ἄφρων ἐκ περισσεύματος λαλεῖ. Inserted after
ματαιότης in BC 155. 254. 298 Pesh. Copt., and after ἐν καρδίᾳ μου
in ASV curss. rel. (exc. 253) S.H. Hier. | om. M. 253[4].

It is evidently a gloss, possibly from a Christian source;
cf. Mat. xii. 34 ‖ Lk. vi. 45.

The alteration of the clauses by which περισσὸν (or ἐγὼ περ.)
was connected with ἐλάλησα seems to have been due to polemical
reasons, and is perhaps from the same source.

v. 16. αἱ ἡμέραι ἐρχόμεναι. The article before the participle
is omitted in BCS* 155. 252. 254. 299 | ins. M. AS^{c.a} curss. rel.
S.H. Hier.

The reading ταῖς ἡμ. ταῖς ἐρχ. is found in AS^{c.a} and several
cursives, and seems clearly a grammatical correction. 147–
157–159 have αἱ ἡμ. διερχ. which must be derived from an uncial
in which ΑΙ was mistaken for ΔΙ, and they are therefore
reckoned among the MSS. which preserve the article. The
omission of αἱ in B and C was easy after ἡμέραι, and cannot
point to a Heb. variant.

v. 19. καὶ ἐσοφισάμην B*S* 106–261. 147–157–159. 155. 299 |
M. ושחכמתי. B^{ab} ACS^{c.a} curss. rel. καὶ ᾧ ἐσοφ. S.H. Pesh. Hier.

v. 21. ἄνθρωπος ᾧ BS. S.H. ⊙ | M. אדם "ש. C curss. (exc.
106) -πῳ ὅς Aq. Pesh. Hier.[5]

---

[1] Except 253 ἐπιστήμη.

[2] εὐφρ. for ἀφρ. ii. 12 cod. V, vii. 25 (26) codd. 147–159. ἀφρ. for εὐφρ. ii. 2
cod. 253, vii. 5 cod. 106.

[3] Pesh. ܐܝܠܢܐ.

[4] The confusion arising from its variation in position is shewn in S.H.,
which adds after the interpolation ܆ καὶ ἴδε καί γε τοῦτο ματαιότης ܇ .

[5] -πος ὅς S^{c.a} V 106. 161^{mg}. A om. ὅς.

v. 22.   ὅτι γίνεται MSS. (exc. 157) S.H. | M. כי מה הוה 157.
Σ Pesh. Hier.

A Heb. variant is impossible.   τι was accidentally omitted
between οτι and ϝι-.

v. 25.   πίεται MSS. ℗ Pesh.   ܢܣܒ | φείσεται S.H. Aq. Σ. Hier.
parcet | M. יחוש Tg. חששא.

Ewald defends πίεται, referring to the Arab. *ḥasa* 'drink';
but there is no corresponding Heb. root.   Both Greek readings
appear to be corruptions of πείσεται.   On the one hand the
occurrence of φάγεται and πίεται in the prec. verse caused the
slip in a primitive MS.; hence πίεται is found in all 𝔊 MSS.
and ℗.   On the other hand יחוש would easily be read יחוש = יחום,
as was done by Aq. Σ (ap. S.H.), and hence ܢܣܘܣ = φείσεται
found its way into S.H. text.

Both readings are explained by πείσεται.   In NH. and Aram.
חוש, שו = feel pain.   So Tg. here.   Hence it may be used for
any kind of strong feeling—here one of enjoyment.

Ch. III. *v.* 11.   σύμπαντα + ἃ MSS.[1] (exc. 155) S.H. Pesh. | M.
om. rel. 155 Hier.   The reading שעשה would yield good sense;
but the α would so easily be doubled that it is safer to regard it
as a Greek corruption.

v. 16.   εὐσεβής MSS. S.H. | M. הרשע Pesh. Hier.   It is im-
probable that this was a slip for ἀσεβής.   It must have been a
deliberate alteration in the cause of orthodoxy.

v. 18.   ὅτι διακρινεῖ [6 curss. κρινεῖ] MSS.[2] S.H. | M. לברם
Pesh.

Hier. has both *quia separat* and *ut eligeret*.   No explanation
can be offered of this difficult reading, except that it may have
been a primitive corruption of τοῦ διακρῖναι.   It seems to have
been due to a scribe who did not understand the ellipse before
על דברת.

v. 19.   οὐ συνάντημα B.   Probably an orthodox gloss.   See
sect. A.

Ch. IV. *v.* 1.   ἰδοὺ B | M. והנה, pr. καὶ AC[vid.] SV curss. S.H.
Pesh. Hier.

v. 9.   δύο B 252. 254 S.H. Pesh.[3] | M. pr. art.   ACSV curss.
rel. ℗.   The omission of οἱ was easy after ἀγαθοί.

---

[1] 261 ὅσα.
[2] 252[ms] has τοῦ ἐλέγξαι αὐτοὺς ὁ θεός, καὶ τοῦ δεῖξαι αὐτούς, which may be a
more or less accurate citation of Aq.
[3] Pesh. om. art. also with ἕνα.

Ch. V. *v.* 1. ἄνω BC 68. 147–159. 253. 254. 298 | om. M. ASV curss. rel. S.H. Pesh. Hier. Clearly a repetition of the same syllables in οὐρανῷ[1].

v. 3. οὐκ ἔστιν B | M. pr. כי ACSV curss. S.H. Pesh. Hier. Σ οὐ γάρ ἐστι.

σὺ οὖν ὅσα MSS. Pesh.　σὺ ὅσα S.H. Aq. | M. את אשר. Θ ὅσα. Hier. *quaecunque.*

The particle οὖν is foreign to the translation. Both σὺ οὖν and σὺ are corruptions of σύν.

v. 5. ἵνα μὴ MSS. S.H. Hier. | M. למה. Pesh. ܕܠܡܐ.

𝔊 is a loose rendering which cannot point to a Heb. variant. The corruption is probably hexaplaric, perh. from Σ, for ἵνα τί.

v. 6. σὺ BS curss. (exc. foll.) S.H. Pesh. | M. את. σὺν AC 147–155–159. 299. Om. σὺ 298 Σ. Om. ὅτι σὺ 68.

v. 7. ὑψηλὸς B 68 | M. pr. כי ACSV curss. rel. S.H. Pesh. Hier. oτι would easily fall out after the prec. ᴀᴛι.

v. 8. ἐπὶ παντὶ MSS. (exc. V) Σ | M. בכל V S.H. Θ Pesh. Athan. Hier. A scribe was apparently influenced by the foregoing ἐπάνω and ἐπί, and thought of the king as the climax in the series of officials.

v. 9. αὐτῶν BS* 68. 147–159. 298. 299. [261]. S.H. | αὐτοῦ ACS^{c.a} curss. rel. [V 106]. (V has αὐτοῦ corrected to αυτω. 261, 106 have conflations, the former αὐτῶν...οὐκ, the latter αὐτοῦ...οὐκ.) | M. לא Pesh. Hier. Both the Greek readings appear to be corruptions of αὐτῷ = לו. See sect. A.

v. 10. ὅτι probably a corruption of ὅτι ἄν. See sect. A.

ὀφθαλμόν B* | M. עיני. The plural is read by B^{ab} and all other MSS. and the versions.

-μοις B^{ab}ACSV curss. (exc. foll.) S.H. Θ Hier.

-μοι 161–248.

-μων Σ Pesh.

It is scarcely possible that -μον could be a corruption of -μοις. It is far more likely to be corrupted from -μων[2], and -μοις would be a natural correction adopted from Θ.

v. 15. πονηρὰ ἀρρωστία. It is suggested in sect. A that this is a corruption of πονηρία ἀρρωστία.

---

[1] In consequence of the insertion of ἄνω, the word κάτω is found after ἐπὶ τῆς γῆς in S, 6 curss., Orig., Ath., Greg. Nyss. Both insertions may have been due to Exod. xx. 4.

[2] See Montef. *Pal. Graec.* pp. 131 f.

ὥσπερ γὰρ παρεγένετο οὕτως καὶ ἀπελεύσεται MSS.[1] S.H. Hier.

The whole clause savours of Σ, though παραγίνεται = בא occurs in 𝔊 v. 2; the use of γὰρ is foreign to the translation; οὕτως καὶ is loose; ἀπέρχεσθαι occurs nowhere in this book in 𝔊 for הלך (which is normally rendered πορεύεσθαι), while Σ has it in x. 15, and συναπελεύσεται in v. 14; and lastly in vii. 14 (15) 𝔊 renders לעמת by the Aquilean συμφώνως.

καὶ ἡ περισσεία B 68 | M. ומה יתרון. καὶ τίς ἡ π. MSS. rel. S.H. Σ Pesh. Hier.

v. 17. εἶδον ἐγώ BS^{c.a} 68. 253. 261. 296. 298 [S.H.²] | M. אשר ראיתי, pr. ὅ ACS* Pesh. Hier. ὅ would easily drop out in 𝔊, while a Heb. variant is improbable.

v. 18. ἐξουσίασεν αὐτῶν B | M. השליטו. ἔξουσ. αὐτῷ C 68. 161–248. 254. 261. 296 [106. 252. 298³]. Hier. concessitque ei... ἔξουσ. αὐτὸν ASV curss. rel. vi. 2 shews that αὐτῷ is right. αὐτὸν is a correction.

v. 19. οὐκ ἄλλα B | M. לא הרבה. οὐ πολλὰ B^{ab} V 68 [147–159 om. οὐ] 253. 261. S.H. Aq. Θ Pesh. Hier. ... οὐ πολλὰς ACS curss. rel.

πολλὰς is an attempted improvement, to make the word agree with ἡμέρας.

Ch. VI. v. 1. ὑπὸ τὸν ἄνθρ. BS* 253 | M. על האדם. ἐπὶ τ. ἀ. S^{c.a} MSS. rel. S.H. Pesh. Hier. ὑπὸ is a slip, probably due to the foregoing ὑπὸ τὸν ἥλιον.

v. 5. ἀναπαύσεις BASV 68. 161–248. 253. 254 | M. נחת. -σις C 106. 252. 261. 298 Pesh. Hier. ... -σιν curss. rel. Aq. Θ [Σ⁴], from the idea that the word was governed by ἔγνω. -σεις was a case of itacism in an early MS.

v. 6. πορεύεται B. Accidental omission of τὰ πάντα. See sect. A.

---

[1] 106 om. γὰρ. 299 καὶ πορεύσεται.

[2] ܐܢܐ ܚܙܝܬ ܚܙܘܐ = ἰδὼν εἶδον ἐγώ. Σ ἐμοὶ οὖν ἐφάνη is too loose to be used as evidence.

[3] Those in brackets read ἐν αὐτῷ, repeating the last syllable of the verb.

[4] S.H. cites Σ not only as ἀνάπαυσιν, but also καὶ οὐκ ἐπειράθη διαφορᾶς ἑτέρου πράγματος πρὸς ἕτερον. So 254 after ἀναπαύσεις, and V 253 after ὑπὲρ τοῦτον. In this, and in S.H. text and Tg., נחת is given the meaning of the NH נוח ל׳ 'better than.' And from this arose the punctuation by which ἔγνω gov. ἀνάπαυσιν. The stichometrical arrangement in B has the same effect. But there is no reason to depart from the meaning which נחת bears in iv. 6, ix. 17.

Ch. VII. *v.* 2 (3).   ἢ ὅτι πορευθῆναι BACS* 68. 161–248. 252. 254 | M. מלכת.   παρὰ πορευθ. S^{c.a} V 253 (clearly a correction). ... ἢ πορευθ. curss. rel. S.H. Pesh. ܡܢ ܒܠܕܒ܀ܐ Chrys. Thdt.

ὅτι is a primitive corruption somewhat difficult to account for. The only explanation that suggests itself is that either н or the π of πορευθ. was accidentally doubled, and read as τι, which a later scribe wrote as ὅτι[1].

δώσει + ἀγαθὸν MSS. Pesh. | om. M. S.H. Σ Hier.

A striking instance of the freedom with which early scribes treated the Greek text. The insertion was probably caused by the influence of the six-fold recurrence of ἀγαθὸν in *vv.* 1–8.

v. 3 (4).   ἀγαθυνθήσεται om. καρδία B S.H. * ᾽ΑΘ καρδία ⟨ | M. ACSV curss. Aq. Σ Θ Pesh. Hier.

The Heb. sentence would be awkwardly abrupt if it closed with ייטב. The omission must have been due to the foll. καρδία.

v. 7 (8).   εὐγενείας αὐτοῦ BC 68. 147–157–159 | M. מתנה. εὐτονίας [-αν S*] αὐτοῦ AS^{c.a} curss. rel. (exc. foll.) S.H. Aq. Θ Hier. ... τὴν εὐτονίαν τῆς καρδίας αὐτοῦ V 106–261. 253. The last reading is a deliberate alteration of the second, to produce some sense.

εὐγενείας is clearly a corruption of εὐτονίας, the latter being probably the true reading. The translator derived the word מתנה from √ מתן 'be strong' (whence מתנים 'loins'), perhaps assuming a sing. מֹתֶן and reading מָתְנה. The care with which (acc. to Hier.) Σ transliterates ΜΑΤΘΑΝΑ, and adds the explanation τοῦτ᾽ ἔστι δῶρον, would suggest that he was the first translator to give the true Masoretic meaning.

v. 8 (9).   πνεῦμα τιμῆς BS* 68, the мнс of μὴ σπεύσῃς being doubled. | M. רוח. πνεύματι MSS. rel. versions.

v. 13 (14).   ὁ θεὸς MSS. S.H. Hier. | om. M. Σ Pesh.

It is very unlikely that האלהים would have been omitted had it stood in the pre-Aḳiban text[2].

---

[1] Isid. Pel. ὅτι πορευθ. Cyr. Al. ἢ τὸ πορευθ. Hier. om. the verb: *quam ad domum convivii.*

[2] By means of the masc. ὃν and αὐτὸν the translator expresses a thought afterwards found in Σ and Tg., i.e. that עותו refers to man being made crooked (Σ "punished") by God. This was evidently the view taken of the passage in the Rabbinic schools; and the rendering is so far in favour of the Aquilean authorship.

v. 14 (15). καὶ ἴδε ἐν ἡμ. κακ. ἴδε MSS. (exc. foll.) | M. וביום רעה ראה. Om. ἴδε 1° S. H. Pesh. Hier. Om. ἴδε 2° S^{c.a} V 106–261.

The original 𝔊 was evidently in accordance with M., κ. ἐν ἡμ. κ. ἴδε. But when a stichometrical arrangement was adopted by which ἴδε was connected with καί γε σὺν...κ.τ.λ., a scribe supplied ἴδε as a verb for ἐν ἡμ. κακ. The omission of the second ἴδε in S^{c.a} etc. was a supposed improvement on this.

καί γε σὺν τούτῳ B 68.

καί γε τούτῳ 159.

καί γε τοῦτο ACS curss. rel. Hier.

συμφώνως τοῦτο B 68.

-ον τοῦτο AV 253.

-ον τούτῳ S curss. rel. Hier.

-ει τούτῳ C.

Σ καὶ γὰρ τοῦτο ἀνάλογον τούτου.

These varieties can best be explained if 𝔊 originally ran καί γε σὺν τοῦτο συμφώνως [or -ον] τούτῳ, in strict accordance with M.

vv. 16 (17), 17 (18). These verses seem to have suffered some corruptions which cannot now be traced. μηδὲ is foreign to the style of the translation, and savours rather of Σ: and no less strange are μή ποτε and ἵνα μὴ for M. למה...למה. For the former Σ has ἵνα μὴ, but for the latter he is not extant.

Pesh. ܐܠܐ and ܕܠܡܐ. S.H. ܕܕܠܡܐ and ܕܠܐ. Hier. *ne* and *ne*. And for the second למה 147–157–159. 299 have μή ποτε.

It seems probable that the early Heb. text had two different words, and that 𝔊 has been corrupted.

v. 18 (19). μὴ μιάνῃς MSS. (exc. 253). The result of dittography—ΜΗΜΗΑΝΗC. μὴ ἀνῇς ⊙ 161^{mg}. μὴ ἀφῇς Aq Σ 253.

φοβουμένοις BS 68. 106. 157. 161–248. 252 [254 τοῖς φοβ.] | M. ירא. -νος CV 147–159. 261. 296. ὁ φοβ. A 253. 298. 299. Aq. Σ ⊙.

The reading of B etc. was probably a corruption of -νος by a scribe who did not understand the construction ἐξελεύσεται τὰ πάντα[1].

v. 21 (22). ἀσεβεῖς BS* curss. (exc. foll.) Pesh. Tg. | om. M. ACS^{c.a} V 248. 252. 253. 296. S.H. Σ Hier.

It is improbable that רשעים would have been omitted, had it stood in the pre-Aḳiban text. ἀσεβεῖς must have been added

---

[1] Was he influenced by Rom. viii. 28?

by an early scribe, partly from a wish to supply λαλήσουσιν with
a subject, and partly, perhaps, influenced by the thought of
the prec. verse. This same cause must have affected the Tg.
independently.

v. 22 (23). On this verse Field quotes a note of Montef. to
the effect that two versions are here combined—the former that
of 𝔊 : ὅτι πλειστάκις πονηρεύσεται σε καρδία σου, the latter that of
Aq.: ὅτι καθόδους πολλὰς κακώσει καρδίαν σου. But the evidence
suggests another explanation:

πονηρεύσεται MSS. Σ.

σε MSS. | om. M. S.H.

καρδία B Σ | καρδίαν MSS. rel.

ὡς καί γε MSS. (exc. foll.) S.H. | ὡς καί γε ὡς S*.   καί γε Sᶜ·ᵃ.
καί γε ὡς 254.

It is probable that 𝔊 originally ran ὅτι καί γε καθόδ. πολλ. κακ.
καρδίαν σου, which is certainly Aquilean; while the first clause
seems to be made up from other sources. πονηρεύσεται and
καρδία are from Σ (see Field). πλειστάκις[1] may be from Θ (see
Field on Ps. cxix. (cxviii.) 64); and if he also had κακώσει, σε
would easily arise from the doubling of the σει.

The foll. words ὅτι ὡς are a doublet. ὅτι καί γε was apparently
ousted from the prec. line by the καὶ which was placed before
καθόδους to combine the two renderings.

Pesh. alone follows M. ידע.

v. 25 (26). ἀσεβοῦς ἀφροσύνην. It is probable that the words
have been transposed. See sect. A.

v. 26 (27). αὐτὴν MSS. S.H. ÷ | om. M. Pesh.[2] Hier.

A primitive corruption by a scribe who thought that εὑρίσκω
referred to Koheleth's search after the five things mentioned in
the prec. verse, and felt it necessary to supply an object to
the verb.

καὶ ἐρῶ BS* 68 [καὶ εἶπα Sᶜ·ᵃ, καὶ εἶπον V 253. 254] | om. M.
AC curss. rel. Pesh. Hier.

This may have been a gloss added to supply a verb to
govern σὺν τὴν γυναῖκα, since εὑρίσκω was already occupied by
αὐτήν. But the readings of Sᶜ·ᵃ etc. rather suggest that there
was some confusion in a Heb. MS., which caused אנימר— to be
read אני]ואמר[מר.

---

[1] After πλειστάκις V 253. 254 add καιροῦ from Σ.
[2] Pesh. reads ומצאתי for ומוצא אני.

v. 28 (29). ἐπεζήτησεν MSS. (exc. 147–159 ἐζήτ., 157 ἐξεζήτ.). S.H. "sought," om. עוד | M. עוד בקשה Pesh. Hier. επ was a mistake for ετι.

Ch. VIII. *v.* 1 [𝕲 vii. 30]. τίς οἶδε(ν) σοφοὺς MSS. [147–157. 161 σοφίαν. 248 -φον] S.H. | M. מי כהחכם Pesh. Hier. But Aq. τίς ὧδε σοφὸς = מי כה חכם, which helps to explain 𝕲. If ὧδε σοφὸς was written οΔεσοφοϲ, it would easily be corrupted to οἶδε σοφοὺς[1], owing to the foll. τίς οἶδεν λύσιν.

v. 10. ἐκ τοῦ ἁγίου MSS. [V 253 ἀπὸ τ. ἁγ.] | M. ממקום קדוש Aq. Σ Pesh. Hier. τόπου was perhaps abbreviated τοῦ. On the rest of the verse see sect. A.

v. 12. αὐτῶν MSS. S.H. | M. לו Σ Pesh. Hier. A corruption of αγτωι[2].

ἐστι(ν) BV 68. 161–248. 252. 253. 254 | M. יהיה AC[S εστε] curss. rel. Σ Pesh. Hier. A case of itacism. ἔσται is preserved in the contrasted clause 13 a.

v. 15. ὡς δ' B* | ὅτι B^ab MSS. rel. (exc. foll.) ... 161 ὥστε, 254 ὡς are attempted improvements.

v. 16. μου γνῶναι B | μου τοῦ γνῶναι MSS. rel.

v. 17. ὅσα ἂν 2° MSS. S.H.[3] Pesh. ܡܐ ܕ | M. אם, Hier. *siquidem et si.* Evidently due to the prec. ὅσα ἂν μοχθήσῃ.

Ch. IX. *v.* 1 [𝕲 viii. 17]. σύμπαν ἴδον [εἶδεν]. A transposition, found in all MSS., of εἶδεν σύμπαν. See sect. A.

v. 1. ὁ ἄνθρωπος MSS. (exc. foll.) Aq. Σ Hier. M. S 147–159 ἄνθρωπος before εἰδώς. Ed. Ald. ὁ ἄνθρ. before εἰδώς.

But S.H. ascribes ὁ ἄνθρωπος with * to Aq. It is thus a reading in which all extant MSS. have received a hexaplaric corruption, although Origen's critical mark has survived.

ἐν τοῖς πᾶσιν. Probably a corruption of ἐν οἷς τ. πασ. See sect. A.

v. 9. ἐν τῇ ζωῇ + σου. Perhaps a scribe's slip owing to the occurrence of σου with nine other words in *vv.* 7–9. See sect. A.

v. 11. δρόμος, πόλεμος B | M. pr. art. MSS. rel. The scribe was led astray by the instinct to preserve symmetry with ἄρτος, πλοῦτος, χάρις[4].

---

[1] Montef. *Pal. Graec.* pp. 131 f.

[2] 252^mg has the same slip in citing Σ.

[3] 106–261 ὅσα ἐάν. 253 S.H. ὃ ἐάν.

[4] The art. is suitable with מרוץ and מלחמה, but not with the other three

τῷ σοφῷ B 68. 147–157–159 | M. לחכמים MSS. rel. Pesh. Hier.

Internal evidence favours M. τοισσοφοις might easily be misread τοισοφοι. See viii. 1 in this section.

καὶ 4°. B 254. S.H. | M. נם. MSS. rel. καί γε.

v. 12. καί γε καὶ B 68. 254. 296. 298 | om. καὶ 2° M. MSS. rel. S.H. Hier.

It is probable that καὶ was written without γε in an ancestor of B, and καί γε was a marginal correction which found its way into the text, forming a doublet.

καλῷ B | M. רעה. κακῷ MSS. rel. [C om.] S.H. Aq. Θ Pesh. Hier.

S has the same slip in iv. 17. The omission in C was probably due to the similarity of κακω to the foll. και ω[s].

v. 16. οὐκ εἰσακουόμενοι BV 68. 155. 261 | M. אינם נשמעים. οὐκ εἰσι(ν) ἀκουόμενοι MSS. rel.

Ch. X. v. 1. μυῖαι θανατοῦσαι MSS. (exc. foll.) S.H. 161–248 μ. θανοῦσαι, so Optat. *muscae moriturae.* 253. Σ μυίων θάνατος | M. זבובי מות Pesh. Hier.

It is difficult to think that the translator rendered זבובי מות "flies that cause death." 𝕲 is probably a corruption of μυῖαι θανάτου, the σαι arising from the doubling of the foll. σαπ.

σκευασίαν MSS. (exc. 253) S.H. | om. M. 253 = Σ Pesh. Hier.

In Ez. xxiv. 10 σκευασία is Θ's word for מרקחה, and is probably his rendering of רוקח here, which has found its way into 𝕲 through the Hexapla.

v. 3. καὶ ἃ λογιεῖται πάντα MSS. S.H. Pesh. | M. ואמר לכל.

The true reading was probably καὶ λέγει τὰ πάντα, corrupted first to καὶ ἃ λ. τ. π., and then to the present text.

v. 8. ὁ ὀρύσσων MSS. S.H. | M. om. art.

All MSS. render the parallel פרץ without an art., and the ο of ὀρύσσων would easily be doubled. Perhaps due to the same cause as the foll. εἰς αὐτόν.

εἰς αὐτὸν B 68. 106–261. 147–157–159. 254 | M. בו. ἐν αὐτῷ MSS. rel. S.H.

A Heb. variant is impossible. εἰς αὐτὸν may have been due to the Greek of Prov. xxvi. 27, B.S. xxvii. 26.

words. But the same desire for symmetry led scribes to insert it throughout : before ἄρτος MSS. (exc. B 68. 253. 254. 298) ; before πλοῦτος MSS. (exc. BV 68. 155. 161. 253. 254. 298) ; before χάρις ACS 147–157–159.

v. 11. τῷ ἐπᾴδοντι MSS. [V 253 + γλώσσῃ] Pesh. | M. לבעל הלשון.

It is inconceivable that this could have been the work of a translator who renders בלא לחש ἐν οὐ ψιθυρισμῷ. S.H. gives ܠܫܘܐ for לחש, and ܠܒܡ ܗܠܢܐ for לבעל הלשון. Since, then, Σ has ἐπῳδῆς for לחש it is probable that τῷ ἐπᾴδοντι was also his, and entered 𝔊 through the Hexapla. On the other hand Hier. *habenti linguam* suggests that 𝔊 had τῷ ἔχοντι τὴν γλῶσσαν. Cf. *v.* 20 ὁ ἔχων πτερύγας.

v. 14. τί ὀπίσω αὐτοῦ B 147-157-159. ... ὅτι ὀπ. αὐτ. MSS. rel. (exc. 254) S.H. ... διότι ὀπ. αὐτ. 254 | M. מאחריו Aq. Σ ℮ Pesh. Hier.

B is in bad company; and מה אחריו with relative omitted is not in Ḳoheleth's style. ὅτι must be a doubling of the foll. ὀπ., and τί is an attempted improvement: while διότι is probably the result of the conflation τι οτι.

v. 16. πόλις MSS. S.H. Pesh. | M. ארץ Σ Hier.

The parallelism of *v.* 17 makes it probable that γῆ was the original reading. Either there were special contemporary circumstances which induced a scribe to alter the word, or it was the result of pure carelessness owing to πόλιν in the prec. clause.

v. 17. αἰσχυνθήσονται MSS. S.H. | M. בשתי Pesh.

If Hier. *in confusione* was based on 𝔊, the present reading must be a corruption of αἰσχύνη—either hexaplaric, or due to the foregoing φάγονται. This points to an early corrupt reading בשת.

v. 19. καὶ ἔλαιον BSV curss. (exc. foll.) Pesh. | om. M. AC 155. 252. 296. 298. S.H. ℮ Hier.

Perhaps a reminiscence of Ps. civ. (ciii.) 15, or of the similar interpolation in Ps. iv. 8 (7).

ταπεινώσει ἐπακούσεται BS* 68. 254. Pesh. ܟܬܒܡ¹ ܗܒܒܡ | om. ταπεινώσει M. ACVSᶜ·ᵃ V curss. rel. S.H. Σ εὐχρηστήσει. Hier. *obediunt.*

A doublet formed from a marginal gloss.

v. 20. σου τὴν φωνήν BSᶜ·ᵃ 254 | M. את הקול Hier.

τὴν φ. S* 68. τ. φ. σου AC curss. rel. S.H. Σ ℮ Pesh.

An unusual distribution of MSS. The reading of B etc. explains the others, and is itself a corruption of σὺν τ. φ.

¹ ? corruption of ܟܬܒܡ.

ὁ τὰς πτέρυγας B 68. 296. S.H.   ...ὁ ἔχων πτέρυγας MSS. rel. [exc. V 253 ὁ τὰς πτέρυγας ἔχων]. Hier. *habens pennas.* M. בעל הכנפים.

The presence of the article is attested by the Kᵉthib. But it is difficult to believe that any translator could render by such an expression as ὁ τὰς πτέρυγας. Field refers to Chrys. *in Pauli Ep.* T. I. p. 553 as an instance in point. I cannot find the passage; but even if Chrysostom allowed himself such a construction, the frequent use of ἔχων by Aq. in similar phrases (see App. I. p. 122) renders it certain that it should be retained here.

Ch. XI. *v.* 5.   οὐκ ἔστιν MSS. S.H. | M. אינך.   ἔσῃ Aq. Σ Pesh. Hier.

A scribe mistook ϵϲΗ for ϵϲτι.

v. 6.   ἐν ἑσπέρᾳ MSS. (exc. foll.) S.H. Pesh. Ed. Saphet. | M. לערב.   εἰς ἑσ. S. 147–157–159 Hier.

Intrinsic evidence favours M., since the tendency would be to assimilate the prep. to the foregoing. The Hexapla may have been the source of the corruption; but the reading is doubtful.

v. 9.   ἄμωμος MSS. S.H. with ÷ | om. M. Pesh. Hier.

An orthodox gloss, inserted on account of the prejudice with which the verse was regarded[1].

In B 68 the insertion ousted καρδίας σου, which is preserved in all other MSS. and the versions.

μὴ BS* 68. 147–157–159. 254 | om. M. ACSᶜ·ᵃ V curss. rel. S.H. Pesh. Hier.

Another orthodox gloss.

Ch. XII. *v.* 5.   καὶ εἰς τὸ ὕψος B 68. 147. 155. 252ᵐᵍ | M. גם מגבה. καὶ γε ἀπὸ ὕψους MSS. rel.[2] S.H. Σ Pesh. Hier.

εἰς τ. ὕψ. was evidently an intentional alteration to produce some sort of meaning with ὄψονται. And since 252ᵐᵍ is so rich in hexapl. readings, it may well be from Θ.

The ϝϵ might easily fall out from καιϝϵϵιϲ, or on the other hand καὶ may point to an original ומנבה.

---

[1] See Midr. Ḳoh. quoted by C. H. H. Wright, p. 12.

[2] 252. 254 καὶ γε ἀπὸ τοῦ ὕψ.   248 καὶ τί ἀπὸ ὕψ.

v. 6.   ἀνατραπῇ mss. | M. K^ethib ירחק, ...K^eri ירתק.

Σ has κοπῆναι. Pesh. ܢܣܬܕܩ. Hier. *rumpatur*. It is probable therefore that 𝕲 is a corruption of either ἀναρραγῇ or
ἀπορραγῇ. In iv. 12 ἀπορραγήσεται stands for ינתק, where Pesh.
has the same word as here. See sect. B.

v. 9.   ὅτι 2° mss. [296 ὅτε, 298 ὅτι ὅτε] S.H. Pesh. | M. עוד
Hier.

A slip for ἔτι[1].

---

[1] All mss. (exc. B 68. 155. 254 and S.H., Pesh.) have suffered from a scribal
'correction,' καί being inserted before ὅτι, probably to make the clause a parallel
statement to ὅτι ἐγέν. Ἐκκ. σοφ. [V 253 καί, om. ὅτι].

INDEX TO THE INTRODUCTION

INDEX OF PASSAGES REFERRED TO IN THE INTRODUCTION

For EU product safety concerns, contact us at Calle de José Abascal, 56–1°,
28003 Madrid, Spain or eugpsr@cambridge.org.

www.ingramcontent.com/pod-product-compliance
Ingram Content Group UK Ltd.
Pitfield, Milton Keynes, MK11 3LW, UK
UKHW012342130625
459647UK00009B/464